Children and Young People's Mental Health

Early intervention, ongoing support and flexible evidence-based care

Dr Louise Theodosiou, Dr Pooky Knightsmith,
Paula Lavis and Professor Dame Sue Bailey

Children & Young People's
Mental Health Coalition

Pavilion

Children and Young People's Mental Health: Early intervention, ongoing support and flexible evidence-based care

Published by:

Pavilion Publishing and Media Ltd

Blue Sky Offices, Cecil Pashley Way, Shoreham by Sea, West Sussex, BN43 5FF

Tel: 01273 434 943   Email: info@pavpub.com   Web: www.pavpub.com

Published 2020

A catalogue record for this book is available from the British Library.

ISBN: 978-1-912755-40-0

Pavilion Publishing and Media is a leading publisher of books, training materials and digital content in mental health, social care and allied fields. Pavilion and its imprints offer must-have knowledge and innovative learning solutions underpinned by sound research and professional values.

Authors: Dr Louise Theodosiou, Dr Pooky Knightsmith, Paula Lavis, Professor Dame Sue Bailey

Production editor: Ruth Chalmers, Pavilion Publishing and Media Ltd

Cover design: Phil Morash, Pavilion Publishing and Media Ltd

Page layout and typesetting: Phil Morash, Pavilion Publishing and Media Ltd

Printing: CMP Digital Print Solutions

Contents

About the authors

Dr Paul Abeles (Chapter 17) is a Consultant Clinical Psychologist based at Royal Manchester Children's Hospital (RMCH), Manchester UK. He was awarded Honours and Doctor of Philosophy degrees in Psychology at University College London in 1995 and 1999 respectively. He gained a Doctor of Clinical Psychology degree from Kings College London in 2001 where he trained at the Maudsley Hospital. Since then, he has worked in both specialist and district CAMHS in Manchester's CMFT NHS Trust. One of Paul's main areas of work has been at Galaxy House, an inpatient CAMHS unit specialising in child neurodevelopmental problems, eating disorders and pervasive arousal withdrawal syndrome. He also works in the regional Social Communication service seeing many children and adolescents with autistic spectrum disorder. He also works in the RMCH Paediatric Clinical Psychology service (lead for Cleft Lip and Palate) and is the clinical lead for RMCH's CFS/ME service. Paul's research experience has covered diverse areas of child and adolescent psychology, including CBT, anxiety, depression, effective MDT working, visuospatial working memory, inpatient CAMHS dependency measurement and E-health interventions.

Professor Alka Ahuja (Chapter 2) is a Consultant Child and Adolescent Psychiatrist and Lead for the Tertiary Neurodevelopmental service at Aneurin Bevan University Health Board. She is a Visiting Professor at the Welsh Institute for Health and Social Care, University of South Wales. She is the Public Engagement lead for Royal College of Psychiatrists (RCPsych) in Wales and Finance Officer, Child and Adolescent Faculty RCPsych in London. She has expertise in qualitative research methodology and her areas of special interest include neurodevelopmental conditions including autism and ADHD, user and carer involvement in healthcare services and employment of innovative digital technology in healthcare.

Dr Sangeeta Ambegaokar (Chapter 20) is a Consultant Child and Adolescent Psychiatrist who has worked in the CAMHS Substance Misuse Team in Birmingham since 2006. For the last eight years she has also provided psychiatric input into the Birmingham Youth Offending Service and in addition has been doing regular sessions with the 18-25 ADHD service within Birmingham since 2018. She is an active member of the Child and Adolescent Substance Misuse group within the Royal College of Psychiatrists.

Yvonne Ayo's (Chapter 4) career began in the cultural industries in the 1970s and 1980s and worked in the Department of Ethnography in the British Museum and the then Commonwealth Institute before a change in her career in the 1990s. Since qualifying as a family therapist Yvonne has worked in the voluntary sector with families whose children were excluded from school and in child and adolescent mental health services in London in a community-based team. As a therapist Yvonne has developed interests in issues of race and culture in systemic practice and of mixed heritage families. She has undertaken a research project which explored the extent to which therapists consider the mixed ethnicities of clients and has completed her doctorate on cultural heritages of mixed heritage individuals in step families of mixed ethnicities.

Dr Eunice Ayodeji (Chapter 15) is a CAMHS Nurse who has worked in wide variety of CAMHS settings. She has extensive therapeutic experience working with children, young people and families with complex mental health and social needs. She is committed and passionate about the provision of a comprehensive evidenced based mental health care for children and young people. Eunice currently teaches at Salford University's undergraduate and postgraduate nursing programme and is also a practising clinician in a community CAMHS team. Eunice's research interests include depression and self-harm. She is also a member of the Guideline Committee, NICE, depression in children and young people: Identification and management (2019).

Liz Bailey (Chapter 9) qualified as a Clinical Psychologist from the University of Manchester in 2004 and has worked in Child and Adolescent Mental health Services (CAMHS) for Looked After Children since then. She is a former committee member of the British Psychological Society Faculty for Children and Young People and past chair of the National Network for Clinical Psychologists working with Looked After and Adopted Children (CPLAAC). She is currently Principal Clinical Psychologist in the Manchester Looked After Children CAMHS team and is currently developing and leading a virtual mental health team for Looked After Children with disabilities placed outside of Manchester. Liz is interested in the engagement of young people in service design and delivery.

Professor Dame Sue Bailey (editor) lives and works in Manchester. After studying medicine and psychiatry at the University of Manchester, Sue worked as a Child and Adolescent psychiatrist for over thirty years. Through subsequent roles as President of the Royal College of Psychiatrists and past Chair of the Academy of Medical Royal Colleges, Sue's national health policy and research work has focused on how to improve health care delivery through education and training of practitioners to help them understand the unique circumstances of every patient. She was formerly the Chair of The Children and Young People's Mental Health Coalition and is now Chair of the Centre for Mental Health.

Dr Jane Barlow (Chapter 5 and Chapter 6) is Professor of Evidence-Based Intervention and Policy Evaluation in the Department of Public Health, and a Professorial Fellow of St Hilda's College. Prior to moving to Oxford she was Professor of Public Health at Warwick Medical School, University of Warwick, and Director of Warwick Infant and Family Wellbeing Unit. In 2007 she was awarded an honorary fellowship of the Faculty of Public Health. She is President of the Association of Infant Mental Health, Associate Editor of the Infant Mental Health Journal, and Affiliates Council Representative on the WAIMH Board of Directors. She has contributed to a number of NICE guidelines and co-chaired the development of the CYP IAPT curriculum 0-5 years. Her research focuses on the evaluation of innovative methods of working in pregnancy and the postnatal period, and she is currently the Primary Investigator for the national evaluation of the A Better Start Programme. She also evaluates the effectiveness of interventions in reducing child abuse and neglect.

Adrian Bethune (Chapter 8) is a Teacher and Healthy Body and Mind Leader at a primary school in Hertfordshire. He also delivers wellbeing-focused training in schools across the UK and Europe through his organisation: www.teachappy. co.uk. In 2012, he was awarded a 'Happy Hero' medal by Lord Richard Layard at the House of Lords for his work on developing wellbeing in schools. In 2015, he was invited to speak at the Action For Happiness event, Creating A Happier World, on stage with the Dalai Lama. Adrian is author of *Wellbeing In The Primary Classroom – A Practical Guide To Teaching Happiness* (Bloomsbury, 2018). He writes regularly for the Times Education Supplement and has contributed to several other books including *Global Perspectives in Positive Education* (John Catt, 2018) and *Just Great Teaching* (Bloomsbury, 2019).

Simon Blake (Chapter 24) is Chief Executive of Mental Health First Aid England, a social enterprise that aims to improve the mental health of the nation, and deputy chair of Stonewall, the LGBT charity. Simon is a writer, trainer and campaigner and has a long history of campaigning on social justice issues. He was awarded an OBE for services to the voluntary sector and young people. Simon keeps well and happy by running, swimming and spending as much time as possible with his horse (Boris) and dog (Dolly).

Kate Bonser (Chapter 9) is a Consultant Clinical Psychologist and Head of CAMHS for Looked After and Adopted Children in Manchester. Kate has an interest in multi-agency working and setting up and developing services that target vulnerable populations. She is particularly interested in developing consultation models with professionals working with Looked After and Adopted Children and developing services that support the system around the children. Kate has been involved in developing post adoption support services within a regional adoption agency and developing models of support for this group of children.

Rachel Bostwick (Chapter 13) is Senior Partnerships and Enterprise Consultant for the Carnegie School of Education at Leeds Beckett University. The role includes developing strategic partnerships with schools and other organisations. Rachel leads the Carnegie Centre of Excellence for Mental Health in Schools which exists to strengthen the mental health of the next generation by supporting schools to make a positive change at all levels and the School Mental Health Award which support schools in developing a whole school approach to mental health.

Layne Boyden (Chapter 12) is a member of the Youth Advisory Group (YAG) at the University of Birmingham Institute for Mental Health (IMH). The IMH YAG was established to create, shape and challenge research into youth mental health.

Rick Bradley (Chapter 18) is Head of Organisation Design and Development at Addaction, a mental health and substance use charity with services across England and Scotland. He wrote and developed Mind and Body, a multi-award winning intervention designed to support young people involved in or deemed vulnerable to a range of self-harming behaviours.
Rick is a regular conference speaker on the subjects of substance use, self-harm and early intervention, also writing and providing media content on these topics. You can follow Rick on Twitter: @RickBradley.

Christine-Koulla Burke (Chapter 10) Christine heads up the Mental Health Foundation's work on prevention and combating inequalities, as well as the Foundation for People with Learning Disabilities. She joined the Mental Health Foundation from the Institute of Applied Health and Social Policy at King's College London. Previously she worked as Deputy Chief Executive of Circles Network and as a senior manager in various organisations for over 35 years. She has developed and managed many service improvement programmes in both health and social care and supported them to change to inclusive, person-centred services for people with learning disabilities, nationally and internationally. Christine has promoted co-production and the involvement of self-advocates and families in all programmes. She holds a BA Hons in Psychology, MSc in Child Psychology and a Diploma in Psychotherapy.

Dr Marc Bush (Chapter 7) is the Director of Evidence and Policy at YoungMinds, a Visiting Professor in Public Health at the University of Northampton, and a member of the Disability Advisory Committee of the

Equality & Human Rights Commission. He has a background in research, policy, and practice in the fields of disability, the NHS, mental health and psychotraumatology.

Niyah Campbell (Chapter 12) is the Youth Participation Lead at the Institute for Mental Health, University of Birmingham. He is particularly interested in conducting and supporting research that aims to address inequalities in physical and mental health.

Dr Sarah Carr (Chapter 12) is a Senior Fellow in Mental Health Policy at the Institute for Mental Health at the University of Birmingham. She has a particular interest in service user and survivor knowledge and research and mental health social care. She has personal experience of mental distress and mental health service use and uses this to inform all her work.

Professor Prathiba Chitsabesan (Chapter 2 and Chapter 14) is a Consultant in Child and Adolescent Psychiatry working in a large mental health trust (Pennine Care NHS Foundation Trust). Lead Consultant since 2005, she became Clinical Director in 2015 before working with the national policy team on children's mental health. She has an interest in the mental health and neurodevelopmental needs of children and young people in contact with the criminal justice system. Over the last 13 years she has published in peer reviewed journals and books and contributed to national reports and guidance. She continues to be research active as a Visiting Chair (Manchester Metropolitan University) and has been involved in a number of regional and national transformation programmes.

Fiona Donnelly (Chapter 16) initially trained as a General Adult Psychiatrist, completing an endorsement in addiction and liaison psychiatry. After working for six years as both a Community Adult Psychiatry and Home Treatment Team Consultant she moved to working with the transition age group and is currently a Child and Adolescent Psychiatrist in both Salford Community CAMHS and the Emerge transition service. She is a member of the Apex working group which developed the APEx liaison psychiatry training course. In addition to developing the course, her involvement included writing course manuals and materials, acting as a course tutor and training new course tutors. She is a keen to reduce the stigma of mental illness and for seven years was Chair of the Doctors Support Network, a national charity supporting doctors with mental illness.

Richard J Drake (Chapter 16) is a key figure in the treatment of psychosis. He started his research career working on the SOCRATES trial of cognitive-behavioural therapy in early psychosis. He is the Health Innovation Manchester

Clinical Co-lead for Mental Health, Senior Lecturer at the University of Manchester (https://www.research.manchester.ac.uk/portal/en/researchers/richard-drake(3b77691c-f889-493d-affb-7a158b37cb04)/contact.html) and Honorary Consultant Psychiatrist at Greater Manchester Mental Health NHS Foundation Trust Early Intervention Service.

Dr Bernadka Dubicka (Chapter 2 and Chapter 15) qualified in medicine and psychology at University College London, completing child psychiatry training in Manchester, together with a doctorate (MD) in adolescent depression at the University of Manchester, where she is an honorary reader. She was an Adolescent Unit Consultant for over a decade, working with young people with complex mental health problems, and in 2018 moved to Pennine Care Foundation Trust, Greater Manchester where she is helping develop crisis services for young people and is a Research Lead. In 2017 she was elected Chair of the Royal College of Psychiatrists Child and Adolescent faculty. She has a research interest in mood disorders, has been involved with several large depression trials (IMPACT, ADAPT), and is currently an investigator in the STADIA study which aims to improve the detection of emotional disorders. She has been a member of the National Institute of Health Research, is the Deputy Editor on *Child and Adolescent Mental Health*, publishes and speaks regularly in the media and at national and international conferences.

Dr Rachel Elvins (Chapter 17 and Chapter 19) is a Consultant Child and Adolescent Psychiatrist at Royal Manchester Children's Hospital and an Honorary Senior Lecturer in the School of Biological Sciences at the University Of Manchester. She has worked with young people in a variety of settings, including hospital, community and outreach services, and has recently been elected to the executive committee of the Faculty of Eating Disorders for the Royal College of Psychiatrists. Rachel is a clinical research lead for Manchester and Salford Child and Adolescent Mental Health Services (CAMHs), and has special interests in anorexia nervosa, neurodevelopmental conditions and therapeutic relationships in mental health treatment.

Dr Sarah-Jane Fenton (Chapter 12) is a Lecturer in Mental Health Policy at the Institute for Mental Health at the University of Birmingham. Sarah-Jane's research focuses on the architecture of mental health services. She has research expertise in youth mental health (16-25) policy and service delivery.

Jonathan Glazzard (Chapter 13) is Professor of Teacher Education at the Carnegie School of Education at Leeds Beckett University. He leads on research for the Carnegie Centre of Excellence for Mental Health in Schools and the

Centre for LGBTQ+ Inclusion in Education. He teaches across a range of QTS and non-QTS programmes and is an experienced teacher educator. He is a qualified teacher and taught in primary schools before moving into higher education.

Professor Jonathan Green (Chapter 17) is Professor of Child and Adolescent Psychiatry at University of Manchester and Consultant Child Psychiatrist at Royal Manchester Children's Hospital. He is a Clinical Scientist who runs the specialist Social Development Clinic at the Royal Manchester Children's Hospital and leads the Social Development Research Group at the University of Manchester, investigating disorders in child social development and their consequences. As well as clinical work, he has led a number of clinical trials in autism, was part of a NIHR/MRC methodology research group developing better methods of process and causal analysis in trials and sat on the NICE committee on treatments for autism in 2013. He was Practitioner Reviews Editor of JCPP 2011-2018 and in 2018 was made a NIHR Senior Investigator.

Dr Lee Hudson (Chapter 23) is an Associate Clinical Professor at the UCL Great Ormond Street Institute of Child Health, Consultant Paediatrician at Great Ormond Street Hospital, and Chief Officer for Mental Health at Great Ormond Street Hospital. He co-leads the UK paediatric eating disorder network. He works clinically, researches and teaches on the crossover of physical and mental health – especially feeding and eating disorders. He specialises in adolescent health, serving on the executive group of the RCPCH's Young Peoples Special Interest group, and on the board of Association of Child and Adolescent Mental Health (ACAMH).

Ellen Jones (Chapter 24) is a Campaigner, Speaker and Writer with a focus on LGBTQ+ rights, mental health and disability.

Pookie Knightsmith (editor) is an internationally respected face of child and adolescent mental health, and works tirelessly to 'be the change she wants to see'. A prolific keynote speaker, lecturer, trainer and author, she develops and shares practical, evidence-informed approaches to promoting mental health – arming health, social care and education staff with the skills, understanding and knowledge they need to support the children in their care.
Pooky has a PhD in child mental health from the Institute of Psychiatry, is the author of many books and is the current chair of the Children and Young People's Mental Health Coalition. She lives in South London with her two daughters, husband, mother-in-law and four (yes four) dogs. She's a keen climber and a tenor in her local choir. She lives with PTSD and autism. You can follow Pooky on Twitter: @Pookyh, Instagram: @PookyH or her website: www.pookyknightsmith.com

Dr Leo Kroll (Chapter 3) trained as a Paediatrician and then switched career to Psychiatry, working as a Consultant for 20 years in Stockport and Salford, Manchester. He has a strong interest in child development, adolescent psychiatry and therapies for adolescents and has developed a number of Needs Assessment Instruments together with colleagues from Forensic Adolescent Services and the University of Manchester. Leo retired on 2015 and worked for a while as an associate specialist with a private multi-disciplinary team and in a specialist NHS Community Eating Disorder Team. He currently works as a research psychiatrist and represent values-based practice development within CYPMHS at the Royal College of Psychiatrists. He is interested in Mindfulness Therapies, Compassionate Focused and Acceptance and Commitment therapy and their application within CYPMHS.

Paula Lavis (editor) (Chapter 10) has a background in psychology and has considerable experience of working in children and young people's mental health policy. She worked at YoungMinds for about 14 years, and more recently for the Children and Young People's Mental Health Coalition in policy development and stakeholder engagement roles. During that time, she was seconded to work for various government departments and national programmes. More recently she was seconded to the Department of Health to support the CAMHS Taskforce, which produced the policy document *Future in Mind*. She now works for NHS Clinical Commissioners as Member Network and Policy Manager and supports their Mental Health Commissioners Network.

Elaine Lockhart (Chapter 2) has worked as a consultant in paediatric liaison psychiatry in the Royal Hospital for Children in Glasgow since 2001, developing close working relationships with paediatric colleagues, particularly in the neurosciences, chronic pain and PICU teams. Since January 2017 she has also worked as a Lead Consultant for CAMHS in Greater Glasgow and Clyde's Specialist Children's services. She has been Chair of the RCPsych in Scotland Child and Adolescent Faculty since 2016 and has recently joined the Scottish Government Children and Young People's Mental Health taskforce. Having been a member of the RCPsych Paediatric Liaison network since its inception, she became Joint Chair along with Dr. Birgit Westphal in 2016.

Ruth Marshall (Chapter 19) is a Consultant Child and Adolescent Psychiatrist at Galaxy House, Children's Inpatient Service at Manchester University NHS Foundation Trust. During her career she has worked as a consultant in both outpatient and inpatient settings and is Clinical Lead for CAMHS. In her role as inpatient consultant she has worked extensively with young people with eating disorders and is a member of the Eating Disorder Faculty for the Royal College of Psychiatrists. She is also a clinical advisor to the CAMHS Strategic Clinical Network for Greater Manchester.

James Molloy's (Chapter 12) drive to support projects that shape mental health services led to him being awarded The Star Award by The Children's Society in 2018. As well as contributing to the Institute for Mental Health's activities, James is Assistant Chair and Communications Lead for the Think4Brum YAG. Currently studying media, James hopes to build a skillset to allow him to spread awareness of mental health-related matters through his work.

Dinah Morley (Chapter 4) has a background in health, social care and education, as well as experience in the voluntary sector as deputy at YoungMinds. Her PhD thesis was on the mental health of mixed race young people, which formed the basis of her book with Cathy Street – *Mixed Experiences*. She is an honorary senior lecturer at City University of London, a trustee of People in Harmony and a nursing charity in Suffolk. Until recently she was an honorary researcher at the Unit of Social and Community Psychiatry in East London. She is also a fellow of the Dartington Social Policy Unit.

Holly Moyse (Chapter 12) is studying a Masters in Drama Therapy at Derby University. Holly's particular research interests are research projects that utilise arts-based methodologies to address issues in mental health. In her spare time, Holly challenges herself by taking on half-marathons and triathlons, all fuelled by a huge appetite for caffeine.

Dr Josephine Neale (Chapter 23) is a Consultant Child and Adolescent Psychiatrist at Priory Hospital Ticehurst House. She has experience across a range of subspecialties in both inpatient and outpatient settings and now works on a general adolescent inpatient unit. She is actively involved in research, particularly in the field of medical education, feeding and eating disorders, and inpatient care. She also has a role in teaching medical students and MSc students at UCL.

Dr Roshelle Ramkisson (Chapter 22) is a Consultant Child and Adolescent Psychiatrist, Clinical Lead at the Royal Oldham Hospital Healthy Young Minds (aka CAMHS) and Associate Director of Medical Education in Pennine Care NHS Foundation Trust, with a keen interest in adolescent emotional disorders. She is a Psychiatry Training Programme Director with Health Education North West. She is a Research Consultant in Global Mental Health and a Honorary Senior Lecturer (teaching) at the University of Manchester. Her various roles are tasked with delivering high quality services, driving quality improvement, furthering research and education, to shaping the workforce to address the various challenges and needs in children and young people's mental health.

Imaan Rathore (Chapter 12) has recently completed her A-levels and hopes to study Law at University of Birmingham. Imaan joined the IMH Youth Advisory

Group in the hope that her contributions would have a positive impact on research being conducted into youth mental health.

Barbara Rayment (Chapter 3) spent her professional life working primarily in voluntary sector services for young people. She was Chief Executive of Youth Access, the Youth Information, Advice and Counselling Services (YIACS) network and more recently worked for the Children and Young People's Mental Health Coalition. Her experience includes national policy and service development. This includes involvement in NHSE's CYP IAPT programme; the Taskforce leading to Future in Mind and chairing groups developing NHS waiting time standards for crisis care and wider CYP mental health services. She also developed various resources to support the delivery of YIACS.

Bethany Skinner (Chapter 12) is a PhD student at the University of Birmingham who hopes to turn personal experiences with poor mental health into positive change. She can often be found in the outdoors running or hiking, or searching for coffee and cake.

Mike Shooter (Chapter 1) has helped to look after children, young people, their families and carers for over thirty years. At first in the capital city and then in the poverty-stricken valleys of South Wales. He was the first Child and Adolescent Psychiatrist to be elected as President of The Royal College of Psychiatrists, is an Honorary Fellow of six Royal Colleges and has been president, chair or trustee of many national organisations in the third sector. He has written books, chapters and articles on many aspects of childhood and has advised governments and services in the UK and abroad. He is married to a former Head Teacher and has four grown-up children and eight grandchildren of his own. He still lives in the midst of his clinical patch

Briony Spedding (Chapter 18) is a Mental Health Social Worker and Approved Mental Health Professional (AMHP) currently working in a Community Mental Health Team. She has been a Social Worker since 2003 and has worked in adult mental health services as well as working in a Child & Adolescent Mental Health Service and a young person's voluntary sector mental health service.
Briony works with people in community and hospital settings and also carries out statutory assessments under the Mental Health Act 1983. She is also involved with the learning and development of student social workers.

Dr Sarah Stansfeld (Chapter 21) is a Consultant Child and Adolescent Psychiatrist working for Manchester University NHS Foundation Trust, specialising in seeing young people in the community aged 16-18 with moderate to severe mental health problems.

Cathy Street (Chapter 11) has held senior research, consultant and management roles at a number of national UK mental health charities over the last twenty years, including YoungMinds and Rethink Mental Illness where she actively promoted co-production with children and young people. Cathy is currently the Patient and Public Involvement (PPI) research lead at Warwick Medical School on the MILESTONE Project, a five-year pan-European study looking at young people's health transitions funded by the EU's 7th Framework Programme for research, technological development and demonstration.

Dr Peter Sweeney (Chapter 16) is a Consultant Child and Adolescent Psychiatrist, who works in North Manchester. He also has a role in Early Intervention Services in Manchester, providing consultation for young people presenting with a first episode of psychosis. Peter trained in Belfast, and completed his specialist training in the North West of England. In addition to psychosis, his specialist interests include ADHD and adolescent psychiatry.

Dr Louise Theodosiou (editor) (Chapters 1, 11, 16, 17, 20, 21, 22 and 24) is a Consultant Psychiatrist in Manchester University NHS Foundation Trust. She is a Clinical Advisor for the Greater Manchester & Eastern Cheshire Strategic Clinical Network. Louise is a member of the Royal College of Psychiatry Child and Adolescent Faculty Executive and the Royal College of Psychiatrists Rainbow Special Interest Group.

Charlie Tresadern (Chapter 12) is a keen advocate for positive community engagement and provision of safe spaces for young people experiencing poor mental health. Previously, Charlie has volunteered for the CAT Café Autism Club, a volunteer-led youth club for 16-25 year olds with Asperger's syndrome.

Dr Angela Underdown (Chapters 5 and Chapter 6) has a background in children's public health and was an Associate Professor at Warwick University Medical School and Deputy Director of Warwick Infant and Family Wellbeing Unit. Angela led the writing and production of the 'Getting to Know your Baby' videos: http://www.your-baby.org.uk. She authored the NSPCC's Baby Steps Perinatal Programme which has been developed and evaluated by the NSPCC. Angela is a Video Interaction Guidance (VIG) Supervisor and Infant Mental Health (IMH) Advisor to the Institute of Health Visiting.

Hope Virgo (Chapter 12) is the author of *Stand Tall Little Girl*, and an international award winning leading Advocate for people with eating disorders. Hope helps young people and employers (including schools, hospitals and businesses) to deal with the rising tide of mental health issues.

Steven Walker (Chapter 4) has an MPhil in Child and Adolescent Mental Health, 30 years' experience in the field and was Head of CAMHS at Anglia Ruskin University as Principal Lecturer. He has published fourteen books and over 50 peer-reviewed papers in International Journals while presenting his research at ten International conferences. He is a volunteer for a Youth Charity in North Essex and a sessional lecturer at the University of Essex post graduate psychology course.

Jane Whittaker (Chapter 19) is a Consultant Child and Adolescent Psychiatrist at the Cheshire Eating Disorder Service, Cheshire and Wirral NHS Foundation Trust. She has been a clinician in inpatient and outpatient eating disorder services, worked with the Royal College of Psychiatrists College Centre for Quality Improvement (QNIC, QNICC & QED) and been a member of the Royal College Eating Disorders Faculty. With other Psychiatrists and Paediatricians she has contributed to both versions of the Junior Marsipan (Management of Really Sick Patients with Anorexia Nervosa, children and Young Peoples version) guidelines.

Beckye Williams (Chapter 12) is currently studying Social Policy and Sociology at University of Birmingham. She is particularly invested in supporting research that aims to address issues with and raise awareness of all things relating to mental and physical health.

Richard Wilson (Chapter 2) is a Consultant Child and Adolescent Psychiatrist working in Northern Health & Social Care Trust, Northern Ireland.

Foreword

Anne Longfield OBE, Children's Commissioner for England

The aim of this book, on children and young people's mental health, is to help raise awareness about all the important issues affecting our next generation of young adults. Written by subject experts, it provides key information for workers who are not currently mental health specialists.

It is my desire to get things right for children and young people at this key stage of development. As Children's Commissioner I hear time and again from children who are unable to access the help they need. Three quarters of mental health conditions are likely to develop before the age of 18. If children do not get the right support, they can face a lifetime of consequences for their relationships, their education, and throughout their lives.

We know that many children and young people with unmet mental health difficulties go ten years between first becoming unwell and getting the help they require. Despite the recent increase in spending on children's mental health services, some early intervention support is still being cut back. This year my office published a report which found that nearly 60% of local authorities saw a real-terms fall in spending on low-level preventative mental health services between 2016/17 and 2018/19, despite an increase in funding across all areas in England. There is no justification for this kind of postcode lottery for children and young people suffering with conditions such as anxiety, depression and eating disorders. This book provides valuable guidance on how to enhance existing services.

As Children's Commissioner, I am calling for a wholesale reconfiguration of our approach to children's mental health. I want to see a further increase in spending on children's mental health, in order to redress the current disparity between these services and the support for adults. The NHS Long Term plan has committed extra funding for children and young people's mental health, but it needs to reach the frontline. There are a number of commitments in the Long Term Plan to improve children's mental health, which fit with the improvements I want to see. I want a clear four-week waiting time target to be set and met, with the necessary increase in specialist mental health workers to ensure access is provided for all children and young people who need it. I am also endorsing the continued positive involvement from schools in mental health. Bullying and academic pressure can lead to poor mental health, but it is an environment where children can be as many as ten times more likely to access help. To encourage the latter, I would like to see an NHS-funded counsellor in every school, alongside clear school mental health policies, peer support and the cultivation of a positive language and ethos around mental wellbeing.

It is vital that the internal, often silent suffering of thousands of children does not continue unnoticed. From earliest infancy to young adulthood, it is imperative that we cultivate an environment that supports and empowers children to talk about their mental health and to seek help when needed. It is important for us all to recognise the central importance of childhood mental health and to give a voice to those children who are still in need of support.

I hope that this book will go a long way towards providing front-line workers with the knowledge and skills to recognise children and young people's mental health needs.

Introduction

Paula Lavis, Theodosiou Louise, Pookie Knightsmith and Sue Bailey

Children and young people's mental health is higher on the policy agenda than ever, and with good reason. A new prevalence survey has shown that 1 in 8 children and young people aged 5-19 years old have a mental health condition. This indicates an increase from the 2004 survey, which found a prevalence of 1 in 10. For the first time the survey has looked at the prevalence of health conditions in 2-5-year-olds and in 16-19-year-olds. This confirmed what we already knew, which is that some children under 5 already have mental health problems, and there is a significant, higher prevalence in older teenagers.

We have made considerable progress in children and young people's mental health over the last ten years; there is now greater awareness of the issue and the importance of prevention and early intervention. However, at the same time, life generally is arguably now more complicated for children and young people. We hear they are more stressed at school, and when they leave, making the transition to adulthood can be more difficult and extend beyond late teens and early twenties. Those who have mental health problems often have to wait far too long to access specialist mental health services, and preventative services are often not available. This is why, despite some really good practice across the country, some people refer to a mental health crisis taking place.

The CYPMHC vision

This is the second edition of what was formerly titled *Children and Young People's Mental Health Today*. The editors of this book are all in some way connected to the Children and Young People's Mental Health Coalition (CYPMHC). The CYPMHC was set up in 2010 and brings together leading organisations, forming a powerful voice to campaign on issues around children and young people's mental health. Our vision is of a nation where mental health is prioritised, positive mental health is promoted and early intervention practice are in place to secure mentally healthier futures for our children and young people.

Who is this book for?

The book is aimed at people working with children and young people, but who do not necessarily have much or any training in mental health. It aims to give a good overview of mental health and wellbeing, outline the policy context across the UK, identify key risk and protective factors, and give an overview of the prevalence of mental health conditions in children and young people.

What's new?

At the time of writing, the policy context in the UK as a whole is progressive, but we know that many children and young people still have to wait too long to access mental health support. In England for the first time, policy is talking about mental health provision for 0–25-year-olds. As in the first edition of this book, we have focused on all stages of childhood and adolescence. Mental health issues do not happen in isolation. A number of factors put children and young people at increased risk of developing mental health problems. Issues within the family or the wider society, physical health issues and so on, all increase the risk. With this in mind, a number of the chapters in the book address issues such as the mental health of young people who are at a higher risk of developing mental health issues.

This book is not just an updated version, but includes new chapters about current and emerging issues, such as values-based practice, adverse childhood experiences (ACE), the impact of social media, the mental health of children and young people who are lesbian, gay, bisexual or transgender, and how physical health impacts on mental health and vice versa.

We tend to refer to children and young people's mental health services, which suggests something singular and possibly health-orientated. The reality is that it is a system rather than a service, and we need all agencies to work in an integrated way. We all need to use the best available evidence, have a shared set of values and work together with children, young people and their families to truly transform services and achieve good outcomes.

Chapter 1: What is Mental Health?

Mike Shooter and Louise Theodosiou

Key learning points

■ Children and young people (CYP) have a right to have their voice heard in decisions and interventions that affect their wellbeing and mental health.

■ Most mental ill health experienced in adulthood originates in childhood.

■ A CYP's wellbeing is significantly influenced by the social circumstances they experience, including the mental health of their parents and carers.

■ Mental health needs are a complex mix of genetics, environment and life events.

■ Mental health is more than the absence of mental illness; it is a positive sense of psychological wellbeing.

■ Lasting recovery from mental ill health and behavioural needs requires more than medical treatment for the surface symptoms; the lives of the CYP we work with are complex and challenging and must be acknowledged.

Keywords

Mental health; wellbeing; biological causes; environmental influences; children's rights

What do we mean by wellbeing, mental health and resilience?

The World Health Organization (2014) has defined wellbeing – their words capture the challenge and the importance of this concept:

'Mental health is defined as a state of wellbeing in which every individual realizes his or her own potential, can cope with the normal stresses of life, can work productively and fruitfully, and is able to make a contribution to her or his community.'

YoungMinds (2017) notes that schools can be key to developing the resilience and wellbeing of CYP. Pupils spend a large amount of time in the classroom and teachers are often the first agency that parents will approach when they are concerned about their CYP. Alongside increasing investment in child and adolescent mental health services, the Green Paper from the Department of Health and the Department of Education (2017) outlines the plan to ensure that all schools and colleges have strong links to wellbeing and mental health services, and this is now being operationalised across the UK.

Recent campaigns have raised awareness about mental illness (Time To Change, 2018). However, stigma still remains, and appears to start developing in childhood (Kaushik *et al*, 2016). One in eight CYP have a mental health need (NHS Digital, 2018a). Mental illness is now the biggest cause of days off work in the western world; increasingly, companies have policies to address it, and governments are investing in services to help people with mental health problems. Many agencies have worked to campaign for 'no health without mental health' (YoungMinds, 2007; Royal College of Psychiatrists, 2010) and this is enshrined in law by the Health and Social Care Act (2012) which emphasises the need for a parity of esteem between physical and mental health needs.

It is well established that the antecedents of most adult and adolescent mental illness begin in childhood (Smith, 2006), thus early intervention is a key and expanding part of the services offered to CYP. Early intervention requires early recognition of possible mental health needs, programmes to enhance wellbeing and resilience and pathways to specialist care. There is increasing recognition that the promotion of mental health is an essential component of total wellbeing. Training programmes to raise awareness about mental health are helping to address this unmet need. These need to be accompanied by staff with the training to work with different levels of complexity and need and systems that allow CYP to access the different components of care that they need.

Chloe

Chloe is a 15-year-old girl who moved to live with her grandmother at 2½ years old. Her mother has a history of significant physical and mental health problems; social care had tried to support her mother to care for Chloe but there were increasing concerns about Chloe's wellbeing as a toddler and her mother now has supervised visits with her daughter. Chloe struggled to settle into school, and was identified as having dyslexia. The local authority undertook an Education and Health Care Plan to support her learning. Chloe had the same friend throughout primary school; this girl transitioned to a different high school, and Chloe was noted to become increasingly withdrawn and isolated.

Chloe's attendance started to reduce in the first year of her GCSEs and she was noted to smell of cannabis. When this was carefully explored in a confidential space, she reported that she had started to smoke to reduce her anxiety. She was tearful and subdued, disclosing feelings of loneliness and low mood.

Models of mental health, wellbeing and resilience

Normally, a child's wellbeing is the product of healthy individual development within a sympathetic environment. Physical maturation is matched by the successful completion of cognitive, emotional, social and spiritual 'tasks' appropriate to each age group. This is empowered by good relationships with family, peers, communities and education systems, in a mutually reinforcing cycle. From it, the resilient child emerges with a clear sense of identity and self-worth, effective problem-solving skills, motivational drive, the ability to recognise, label and manage his or her own emotions, and a respect for the feelings of others. We can see that Chloe may have difficulties with attachment and experienced a disruption in her early care. She may benefit from the opportunity to enhance her wellbeing and resilience.

What do we know about the rates of mental health needs of CYP?

NHS Digital (2018a) notes that overall rates of mental health conditions have risen slightly from 9.7% in 1999 to 10.1% in 2004 and 11.2% in 2017. This rise was related to an increase in emotional conditions. Furthermore, rates of emotional conditions were seen to rise throughout childhood in the 2017 survey with rates of anxiety conditions being over three times higher in 17–19-year-olds than in 2–4-year-olds. For girls aged 17–19, over 22% experienced an emotional conditions. This echoes the findings from NHS Digital (2018b) which identified a rise in the number of CYP who were admitted to hospital after an episode of self-harm, for girls this rise was greater than the increase in the population.

What are the challenges to the wellbeing of CYP?

Chloe illustrates some of the factors which have been known for many years to impact on the wellbeing of CYP. We know that after housing costs have been deducted, about 40% of children are living in low income households (House of Commons Library, 2018) and this figure is set to rise. It is not revelatory to say that accessing education, healthcare and enjoyable activities are all challenged by poverty, but this truism must be acknowledged.

Furthermore, in the modern world, we know that things are changing rapidly. In the past two decades there have been considerable changes in the available technology and the way that this is used by young people. The Centre for Mental Health (2018) discusses the potential impact, both positive and negative, of social media on CYP. There does seem to be evidence that the mental health of some CYP can be negatively affected by social media, the internet and digital gaming (NHS Digital, 2018c). While a causal relationship between technology use and mental health needs has not yet been identified, Chapter 21 discusses in more detail the possible impact on CYP of social media, depending on the intensity of use, and also of the information that can be accessed via the internet. Chapter 21 also discusses the ways that CYP can be vulnerable online.

How can we think about mental illness?

Prevention of mental illness is complicated by different perspectives on the causes of mental illness, each with their own evidence base. The biological model focuses on inherited chemical imbalances within the brain with impaired transmission of nerve impulses, and can be treated, at least partly, by drugs designed to restore those balances (Nutt, 2007).

Others point out that what we are born with – 'nature' – can only account for some of our vulnerability, even in these illnesses. The rest is down to 'nurture' – our life experiences and the way we are brought up. Psychodynamic models identify the origins of mental health conditions in a conflict between the various developing parts of our psychology, the defences we erect against those conflicts, the abnormal patterns of behaviour this can cause, and the way they interfere with human relationships.

Mental health problems can rarely be accounted for by one of these models alone. They are more likely to be complex jigsaws of interlocking factors in which the emotional and behavioural consequences are the final common outcome, rather than specific symptoms identifiable by fine diagnosis and laboratory tests. Treatment would therefore require the combined efforts of many people with a diverse range of medical, therapeutic, social and educational skills. So, if mental illness is so complicated, where does that leave mental health?

How can we enhance the wellbeing and resilience of CYP?

What is clear is that we need to make sure that all CYP have the chance to reach their potential. This needs to be done through ensuring that universal services such as education are supported to enhance the wellbeing of all CYP. Innovations such as the Mentally Healthy Schools website (2018), which is partnered with YoungMinds and the Anna Freud Centre, has resources to help primary schools maintain the wellbeing of their pupils. Universal services also need to be trained and supported to recognise CYP who may have more complex needs, for example, depression requiring CBT or developmental conditions such as ADHD. If such conditions are recognised early, CYP can receive the care they need and be supported to maintain their wellbeing. There are a number of signs that Chloe needs additional support, and that the sooner this is implemented the better the outcomes will be for her.

How can we support CYP with mental health needs?

A key international challenge is ensuring that services working to support the mental health of CYP have enough staff with the right training. The Green Paper (Department of Health and Education, 2017) outlines ways that education staff can be supported in developing wellbeing in school. Furthermore, Thrive (Wolpert *et al*, 2014) and its implementation iThrive, provide a model which can bring together education, the voluntary sector and health providers to ensure that CYP are supported to meet their mental health needs whether that involves wellbeing support in school or the management of complex risk.

Future in Mind (2015) gave a voice to CYP, they used it to outline the challenges of transition, to reiterate the message of Crisis Care Concordat (2014) in that they do not want to tell their story more than once, especially when in crisis, and spoke about their desire to be involved in their healthcare at all levels. This document emphasised the need for more funding of health and wellbeing services and the need for services to offer joined up care with a wider focus than the purely clinical. Finally, Future in Mind (2015) emphasised the need for early intervention, which of course means ensuring that we have a seamless system working with parents from the time of birth through to adulthood. Some parents will need support from early years services and this will enhance the resilience of their children, other families will need to move from general early years services into wellbeing and mental health services to support CYP with developmental needs.

Mental health problems are caused by many factors, acting together on vulnerable CYP. Even where the problem is a clearly defined mental illness with a biological basis and a strong genetic component, that illness will be affected by the stresses in life to which CYP are subjected – nature and nurture. Help therefore needs to combine many approaches in a package tailored to the circumstances of the individual child. None of the theoretical models is an answer in itself. They are merely tools in a kit from which that package can be constructed.

Ideally, this would require services that are comprehensive in every sense (Kurtz *et al*, 2006). The many different agencies involved with the welfare of children, both professional and voluntary, should act in concert to tackle the particular profile of problems in their area. They should be jointly commissioned, jointly resourced and jointly implemented. They should be universal in scope, rather than targeted at particular problem groups. And they should offer support to the whole trajectory of a vulnerable child's life, both in crisis and in long term development. This is enshrined in the guidance from the Joint Commissioning Panel for Mental Health (2011).

CYP have a right to a voice and to have that voice heard in the design and practice of anything that affects their life (Future in Mind; 2015). YoungMinds (2018) spoke to children and families about their experiences of mental health services. CYP and their families fed back that they wanted to be involved in maintaining their wellbeing, but that they needed information to do so, they wanted information about the services they could access and they wanted to get support from trained staff when they needed to. Some CYP fed back that they had not had the experiences that they wanted; the need for flexible, rapidly accessible care that was linked to education was emphasised. They wanted to participate in the design, implementation and development of services, and they wanted to be able to play a role when their mental health allowed and to be able to step in and out of this role when they felt less well. Finally, CYP and their families wanted the stigma around mental health needs to be tackled.

Recent years have brought recognition of the fact that mental health services for CYP have received less than 1% of the health budget overall (Dubicka & Bullock, 2017). The government has pledged that by 2020, at least 35% of CYP who would be recognised to have a mental health condition will be treated (HM Government, 2017). By increasing awareness of wellbeing and mental health needs at all levels, this investment can reach as many CYP as possible, hopefully as early as possible to ensure that CYP can reach their potential and enjoy the wellbeing they deserve.

How can we support the wellbeing of staff who work with CYP?

Working with CYP with wellbeing and mental health needs is both rewarding and challenging. *Health Committee Contents* (2014) notes that there 'is increasing sickness, a lot of burnout' in CAMHS, while *Children and Young People Now* (2018) notes that 62.3% of children's social workers want to leave their jobs in the next 16 months. The situation for teachers is much the same (Tapper, 2018). People working in these roles genuinely want to enhance the lives of CYP, but they must be supported to do so. Staff must be supported to work flexibly and creatively, they need the resources and the colleagues to work safely. Think about the people working with you and for you, try to remember their own mental health needs and think about your own needs too. The children and young people that we work with deserve that.

Conclusion

This book has drawn contributions from young people and professionals in a wide range of roles. This reflects the theme of wellbeing needed to be held in mind by everyone. Collaborative working is key to developing the services that will support the current and future generations of CYP.

References

Centre for Mental Health (2018) *Briefing 53: Social Media, young people and mental health* [online]. Available at: https://www.centreformentalhealth.org.uk/publications/social-media-young-people-and-mental-health (accessed 30 June 2019).

Children and Young People Now (2018) *Two Thirds of Children's Social Workers Want to Leave Current Job, Study Finds* [online]. Available at: https://www.cypnow.co.uk/cyp/news/2005995/two-thirds-of-childrens-social-workers-want-to-leave-current-job-study-finds (accessed 30 June 2019).

Department of Health (2015) *Future in Mind: Promoting, protecting and improving our children and young people's mental health and wellbeing* [online]. Available at: https://assets.publishing.service.gov. uk/government/uploads/system/uploads/attachment_data/file/414024/Childrens_Mental_Health.pdf (accessed 30 June 2019).

Department of Health and the Department of Education (2017) *Transforming Children and Young People's Mental Health Provision: A Green Paper* [online]. Available at: https://assets.publishing. service.gov.uk/government/uploads/system/uploads/attachment_data/file/664855/Transforming_ children_and_young_people_s_mental_health_provision.pdf (accessed 30 June 2019).

Dubicka B and Bullock T (2017) Mental health services for children fail to meet soaring demand. *British Medical Journal* **358** j4254.

Health Committee Contents (2014) *Children's and Adolescents' Mental Health and CAMHS* [online]. Available at: https://publications.parliament.uk/pa/cm201415/cmselect/cmhealth/342/34208.htm (accessed 30 June 2019).

House of Commons Library (2018) *Poverty in the UK: Statistics* [online]. Available at: https:// researchbriefings.parliament.uk/ResearchBriefing/Summary/SN07096 (accessed 30 June 2019).

HM Government (2014) *Mental Health Crisis Care Concordat: Improving outcomes for people experiencing mental health crisis* [online]. Available at: https://assets.publishing.service.gov.uk/ government/uploads/system/uploads/attachment_data/file/281242/36353_Mental_Health_Crisis_ accessible.pdf (accessed 30 June 2019).

HM Government (2017) *Response to the Five Year Forward View for Mental Health* [online]. Available at: https://www.gov.uk/government/uploads/system/uploads/attachment_data/file/582120/ FYFV_mental_health__government_response.pdf (accessed 30 June 2019).

Joint Commissioning Panel for Mental Health (2011) *Ten Key Messages for Commissioners: Child and adolescent mental health services* [online]. Available at: https://www.jcpmh.info/wp-content/ uploads/10keymsgs-camhs.pdf (accessed 30 June 2019).

Kaushik A, Kostaki E and Kyriakopoulos M (2016) The stigma of mental illness in children and adolescents: a systematic review. *Psychiatry Research* **243** 469–494.

Mental Health Workforce Strategy (2016) *Five Year Forward View* [online]. Available at: https://www. england.nhs.uk/wp-content/uploads/2016/02/Mental-Health-Taskforce-FYFV-final.pdf (accessed 30 June 2019).

NHS Digital (2018a) *Mental Health of Children and Young People in England, 2017: Summary of key findings* [online]. Available at: https://files.digital.nhs.uk/C9/999365/MHCYP%202017%20 Behaviours%20Lifestyles%20Identities.pdf (accessed 30 June 2019).

NHS Digital (2018b) *Mental Health of Children and Young People in England, 2017: Behaviours, lifestyles and identities* [online]. Available at: https://files.digital.nhs.uk/C9/999365/MHCYP%20 2017%20Behaviours%20Lifestyles%20Identities.pdf (accessed 30 June 2019).

NHS Digital (2018c) *Hospital admissions for self-poisoning or self-harm in young people* [online]. Available at: https://digital.nhs.uk/data-and-information/find-data-and-publications/supplementary- information/2018-supplementary-information-files/hospital-admissions-for-self-poisoning-or-self-harm- in-young-people (accessed 30 June 2019).

Nutt D (2007) Medication. In: R Persaud (ed) *The Mind: A user's guide*. London: Royal College of Psychiatrists/Bantam Press.

Office for National Statistics (2016) *Selected Children's Wellbeing Measures by Country* [online]. Available at: https://www.ons.gov.uk/peoplepopulationandcommunity/ wellbeing/adhocs/005283selecte dchildrenswellbeingmeasuresbycountry (accessed November 2018).

Royal College of Psychiatrists (2010) https://www.rcpsych.ac.uk/pdf/No%20Health%20-%20%20the%20 evidence_%20revised%20May%202010.pdf

Tapper J (2018) *Burned out: why are so many teachers quitting or off sick with stress?* [online]. Available at: https://www.theguardian.com/education/2018/may/13/teacher-burnout-shortages-recruitment-problems-budget-cuts (accessed 30 June 2019).

UNICEF (1992) *United Nations Convention on the Rights of the Child*. Geneva: United Nations. Available at: www.unicef.org/crc (accessed June 2019).

UNICEF (2007) *Child Poverty in Perspective: An overview of child wellbeing in rich countries*. Florence: UNICEF Innocenti Research Centre.

Wolpert M, Harris R, Jones M, Hodges S, Fuggle P, James R, Wiener A, Mckenna C, Law D and Fonagy P (2014) *THRIVE The AFC–Tavistock Model for CAMHS* [online]. Available at: http://www.implementingthrive.org/wp-content/uploads/2016/03/Thrive.pdf (accessed 30 June 2019).

World Health Organization (2014) *Mental health: A state of wellbeing* [online]. Available at: http://www.who.int/features/factfiles/mental_health/en/ (accessed 30 June 2019).

YoungMinds (2007) *No Health Without Mental Health. Annual report 2006–2007*. London: YoungMinds.

YoungMinds (2017) *Wise Up: Prioritising wellbeing in schools* [online]. Available at: https://youngminds.org.uk/media/1428/wise-up-prioritising-wellbeing-in-schools.pdf (accessed 30 June 2019).

YoungMinds (2018) *Your Voices Amplified* [online]. Available at: https://youngminds.org.uk/youngminds-professionals/our-projects/amplified-hub/amplified-insights-survey/ (accessed 30 June 2019).

Websites

Time To Change: https://www.time-to-change.org.uk/about-us
Mentally Healthy Schools: https://www.mentallyhealthyschools.org.uk

Chapter 2: Children and Young People's Mental Health Structure and Policy

Prathiba Chitsabesan, Bernadka Dubicka, Elaine Lockhart, Alka Ahuja and Richard Wilson

Key learning points

- Mental health is an integral part of children and young people's general health and wellbeing and therefore children and young people's mental health (CYPMH) provision needs to be embedded in a wide range of services for young people.

- Delivering good outcomes for children and young people requires a values-based, systems-wide approach working collaboratively across agencies and with children, young people and their families.

- Children and young people should have easy access to the right support from the right service at the right time, and as close to home as possible.

- Delivering evidence-based interventions requires a workforce with the relevant skills and competencies across a range of agencies from infancy to young adults.

- Aim to improve transparency and accountability across the system through the use of data and outcome metrics, with a focus on outcomes that matter to children, young people and their families.

Keywords

CAMHS, systems wide approach, Future in Mind, Five Year Forward View, NHS long-term plan, collaborative working, values, co-production

Introduction

Children and young people's mental health services continue to remain a high priority for government and the NHS. Delivering good outcomes for young people will require coordinated action across different parts of government including health, education, third sector, local government and justice and between national and local bodies. There are opportunities through increased investment and more collaborative commissioning and service delivery arrangements to deliver a systems-wide approach to providing care for children and young people.

This chapter will briefly describe how children and young people's mental health services are structured, and outline relevant policy across the four nations.

Children and young people mental health services in context

Recent statistics from NHS Digital (2018) indicate that 12.8% of 5–19-year-olds and 5.5% of 2–4-year-olds have a mental health condition, with rates particularly high for 17–19-year-old women (NHS Digital, 2018).

Children and young people's mental health services (previously called CAMHS: Child and Adolescent Mental Health Services) refers to a range of services that provide assessment and treatment to children and young people (CYP) who are experiencing mental health needs.

Services to support child and adolescent mental health have grown from diverse roots. It is now well established that mental health is an integral part of children and young people's general health and wellbeing and therefore children and young people's mental health (CYPMH) provision needs to be embedded in a wide range of services for young people. This includes universal health promotion and prevention programmes to services provided in education and community settings, including targeted provision for vulnerable groups of young people such as those in local authority care or in contact with the criminal justice system.

Universal services (services available to everybody, such as Sure Start Children's Centres, schools, colleges, primary care and youth centres) can be important in preventing mental health problems. Education provision, particularly schools, can play an important role in early identification and support to children and young people with mental health needs. In England all schools will be required to teach pupils about maintaining mental wellbeing. Local authorities play an important role in promoting children's and families physical and mental wellbeing, in part through their statutory duties relating to public health.

However, differences in language and culture between the wider systems (health, education, social care), as well as within systems (adult versus child and adolescent services) make systems working difficult and co-ordinating service delivery challenging. Attempts have been made to describe children and young people's mental health services. The most well-known framework was a model dividing service provision into four tiers. This model helped differentiate between the different forms of services that might be available to children and young people. However, more recent models including Thrive (see later), focus on the needs of children and young people and include a systems-wide framework in considering how support can be delivered by a range of different practitioners and agencies, including the role of parents and carers.

Following the Health and Social Care Act (2012), the government has increased its focus on mental health services, and has now committed to providing 'parity of esteem' for mental and physical health services. Parity of esteem means that mental health is valued as much as physical health, including equal access to care and allocation of resources proportionate to need.

Data and outcome metrics

Data is important in providing transparency within the system with regard to commissioning and service delivery. Within England, NHS-commissioned services provide anonymised patient-level data through the Mental Health Services Data Set (MHSDS). MHSDS brings together key information including activity and access data from community and hospital-based services for children and young people in contact with mental health services. The NHS, as a whole, aims to prioritise the recording and use of data based on outcomes. There are a range of patient- and clinician-rated outcome measures (PROMs and CROMs) and patient-rated experience of services measures (PREMs) that can be used in routine clinical practice. Commonly used measures include the Strengths and Difficulties Questionnaire (SDQ), Health of the Nation Outcomes Scales for Children and Adolescents, HONOSCA and Revised Children's Anxiety and Depression Scale (RCADS).

The Child Outcomes Research Consortium (CORC) learning collaboration aims to aid alignment and integration of data and outcomes across agencies and organisations.

Workforce development and training

Transforming the mental health workforce is fundamental to creating sufficient capacity to deliver accessible, quality services and good outcomes for children and young people. Developing new care models means building flexible teams working across organisational boundaries and ensuring they have the full range of skills and expertise to respond to service-user needs in different settings. Professionals supporting children with mental health needs may work in a variety of different settings from community-based teams providing support in schools, youth offending teams or local authority settings, to those working within specialist settings including hospital-based outpatient and inpatient services. Subsequently, practitioners may come from a variety of different backgrounds including nurses (paediatric or mental health), mental health practitioners, psychologists, psychiatrists, and allied professionals such as social workers, speech and language therapists and occupational therapists. There is also increasing recognition of the important role of practitioners working in third and voluntary sector organisations, as well as other frontline youth practitioners, in supporting children and young people with mental health needs. Therefore, consideration needs to be given to the training of the wider workforce within communities as well as those working in specialist mental health settings. Access to regular supervision and consultation for staff is essential in providing effective services. Managers working within services should also ensure that the wellbeing of staff is a primary concern and that staff are provided with the necessary training and support to deliver evidence-based quality care.

The Children and Young People's Improving Access to Psychological Therapy (CYPIAPT) programme is an important part of training the workforce in England. Health Education England delivers the CYPIAPT programme though a number of national learning collaboratives. It aims to increase the range of evidence-based therapies available, deliver outcome-focused care, and promote young people's participation in their treatment and in-service design and delivery.

MindEd is a free educational resource developed for professionals working across community and specialist settings. It provides information on a range of mental health needs in CYP, key principles in providing assessment and support, as well as information for families.

Approaches to service delivery

Children and Young People Improving Access to Psychological Therapy (CYP IAPT) is being rolled out across England and seeks to combine evidence-based practice with user involvement and outcome evaluation to embed best practice in child mental health. It includes 5 key principles underlying transformation: participation, increasing mental health awareness and reducing stigma, improving access and engagement, delivering evidence-based therapy and demonstrating outcomes and accountability through data collection.

Thrive aims to replace the tiered model with a conceptualisation of a whole system approach. The THRIVE categories are needs-based groupings (Wolpert *et al.*, 2015). The THRIVE framework conceptualises five needs-based groupings for young people with mental health difficulties and their families:

- thriving
- getting advice
- getting help
- getting further help
- getting risk support.

Each of the five groupings is distinct in terms of:

- the needs and/or choices of the individuals within each group
- skill mix required to meet these needs
- dominant metaphor used to describe needs (wellbeing, ill health, support)
- resources required to meet the needs and/or choices of people in that group.

The groups are not distinguished by severity of need or type of problem. Rather, groupings are primarily organised around different supportive activities provided by children and young people mental health services in response to mental health needs and influenced by client choice.

Choice and Partnership Approach (CAPA) is a clinical service transformation model that brings together collaborative practice, goal setting with regular reviews and demand and capacity management including lean thinking. It is an approach based on the key principles of shared decision making and clarity of choice. CAPA focuses on helping people make explicit choices about what may most benefit them and links this with evidence-based packages of care. One of CAPA's key components is to change language to one which promotes strengths-based, collaborative work, thinking about skills needed, rather than access to a particular professional discipline. In particular, CAPA segments work so that skills and capacity can be considered within a job planning process.

Values-based practice, working in partnership with evidence-based practice, can help to provide the skills and other resources needed to support balanced decision-making between stakeholders, within a framework of shared values. While all stakeholders have a shared values base for promoting good outcomes for children and young people's mental health, they have different perspectives on what matters or is important in achieving these. Unaddressed, such differences can lead to barriers to providing joined-up care. However, when acknowledged, it is possible to develop a framework of shared values within which balanced decisions can be made in partnership.

Transition and services 0–25 years

The majority of CYPMH services have been commissioned to provide services for CYP up to 18 years of age. It is well recognised that transition to adult mental health services (AMHS) can be challenging, with many young adults failing to access services. More recently, services for young people up to the age of 25 have been developed in some areas bringing together CYPMHS, AMHS and youth services to try to address some of the challenges of fragmented commissioning and differences in culture between CYP and adult services. NICE transition guidance (2016) emphasises the need for transition to be multi-agency and to involve service users in the design and development of services.

Structures and policy

England

The Department for Health and Social Care is responsible for mental health policy, while NHS England is responsible for overseeing the commissioning of NHS-funded services, either directly or through clinical commissioning groups (CCGs). Various other government departments and arm's-length bodies including Department for Education, Public Health England, Health Education England and Youth Justice Board also have a role in funding and/or delivering these services through a number of work programmes to support commissioners and service providers.

In 2015, the government set out its vision for children and young people's mental health services in its Future in Mind strategy (Department of Health, 2015). The strategy identified challenges within the current system from fragmentation to lack of investment, and collaborative working across agencies. It set out a broad vision of how children's and young people's services should be improved and included themes such as resilience and early intervention, access and workforce development. The strategy identified a range of stakeholders (NHS, public health, local authorities, social care, schools and youth justice services) as having an important role to play in supporting children and young people's mental health. Each of these has distinct and different accountability mechanisms.

The government has launched a number of initiatives supported by additional funding to take forward its vision for improving CYPMH services including:

- **Five Year Forward View for Mental Health (2016)** programme which covers all NHS mental health services in England, but with specific objectives to improve children and young people's mental health services. Through local transformation plans (LTP), each CCG working alongside other stakeholders is expected to set out the local offer for children and young people including how the needs of the most complex and vulnerable groups would be met.

- **Stepping Forward to 2020/21 (2017)**, an accompanying mental health workforce development programme, led by Health Education England; and

- **Transforming Children and Young People's Mental Health Provision: A Green Paper (2017)**, jointly published by the Department for Health and Social Care and the Department for Education (2017) and due to be implemented from the end of 2019. It has a focus on developing the links between schools and health services. The Green Paper sets out plans for two new roles linked to education: mental health leads in schools and mental health support teams. The former will be responsible for overseeing the use of the 'whole school approach to mental health and wellbeing' and helping to identify children at risk of, or showing signs of, mental ill health. The mental health support teams will provide interventions to support CYP with mild to moderate mental health needs, supervised by local specialist CYPMH teams.

- **NHS Longterm Plan (2019)** continues investment in CYPMH services including expansion of services in schools, crisis care and eating disorder services as well as improving services for young adults working in partnership with adult mental health services.

Local transformation plans contribute to larger scale regional Sustainability and Transformation Plans (STPs). Both STPs and Integrated Care Systems (ICS) provide an opportunity to change in how care is delivered moving away from a system defined in terms of the services organisations towards greater collaborative working across a number of health and local authority partners.

Various other initiatives also contribute to the delivery of Future in Mind. As Future in Mind is a cross-government strategy, some sit outside the remit of the NHS England. Some initiatives aim to support children and young people's mental health, rather than have it as their primary focus, for example, the Troubled Families programme run by the Ministry of Housing, Communities & Local Government.

In England, the Care Quality Commission (CQC) regulates healthcare services to ensure they meet safety and quality standards, and has published two thematic reports on mental health services for children and young people in 2017 and 2018. The Commission raised concerns that complexity and fragmentation in mental health services were contributing to challenges for some children and young people in accessing the support they needed.

Scotland

Scotland's population is 5.5 million and CYPMH is delivered through 14 Health Boards which are now part of Health and Social Care Partnerships that provide a variable degree of integration at children's services level, with considerable variation in local funding. Sharing best practice and the development of community intensive treatment teams has allowed the adolescent in-patient units to reduce the length of stay and improve access to beds.

A national secure CYPMH unit is being developed and there is ongoing work regarding the development of specialist in-patient provision for children and young people with learning disability and mental health needs. Scotland has a national 18-week referral to treatment target for referrals to CYPMHS, although most areas are struggling to meet this with the increase in referrals over the last 5 years and variation in service provision.

All the actions from the 2017 Mental Health Strategy relating to children and young people, the Rejected Referrals audit, Audit Scotland report and the Programme for Government in 2018 have been brought together in the newly established Children and Young People's Mental Health and Wellbeing Taskforce. This has been jointly commissioned by Scottish Government and the Convention of Scottish Local Authorities (COSLA) to take a whole system approach to children and young people's mental health. It will bring together input from partners across a range of sectors and will focus on services for CYP aged 0–25 years. It will run until the end of 2020.

This will build on the national multi-agency approach underpinning all children's services in Scotland, Getting It Right For Every Child (GIRFEC). There are four strands of work focusing on:

- generic services
- neurodevelopmental services
- specialist services
- children and young people at risk.

There will be accompanying work on the development of the workforce, improving data quality and the promotion, prevention and support for mental health within schools.

This work will be supported by the established training and workforce development within NHS Education Scotland (NES), data collection by the Information Statistics Division (ISD) and the Mental Health Access Improvement Support Team (MHAIST) hosted by Healthcare Improvement Scotland.

Wales

In Wales, the **Local Health Boards (LHBs)** are responsible for commissioning primary and secondary healthcare in close conjunction with their partners in local authority. Specialist services, including all Tier 4 CYPMH and planning of Tiers 2 and 3 is done nationally on behalf of health boards by Welsh Health Specialised Services Committee (WHSCC). Most areas of Wales have a specialist CYPMH out-of-hours service but the comprehensiveness of these services varies from nursing cover to consultant cover.

The **Wales CAMHS/ED Network** is hosted by the NHS Wales Health Collaborative and is funded by the Welsh Government. The network acts as an advisory body to all seven Health Boards on the implementation of Welsh Government policy for CAMHS/ED services. As an advisory body for CAMHS to all seven health boards in Wales, the network additionally advises on an all-Wales perspective on the planning of eating disorder services across the full age range, in line with Welsh Government policy. It has a specific focus on the requirements at 'transition age' of eating disorder services in Wales. Other network programmes include the development of gender identity services, standardising CAMHS data requirements, CITT crisis teams provision, review of out-of-area (Wales) placements for tier 4 services and a review of CAPA implementation in Wales.

T4CYP (Together for Children and Young People), the Welsh Government multi-agency service improvement programme, was launched in 2015. It aims to reshape, remodel and refocus the emotional and mental health services provided for children and young people in Wales, in line with the principles of prudent healthcare. The programme's 'Windscreen Model' provides the context of a continuum of support enabling the programme to focus on supporting early years' development, and the promotion of wellbeing and resilience in all young children, early identification and intervention and then more specialist services.

T4CYP priority work streams include resilience, wellbeing and early years; early intervention and enhanced support; neurodevelopmental issues and comorbid learning disabilities and specialist CYPMHS. The three cross-cutting work streams are Workforce, Education and Training; Care Transitions; and Health Needs Assessment and Evidence Review.

Welsh Government's focus on a 'whole school' approach to mental health and wellbeing for children and young people supports the wider and ongoing reform of mental health support. A Joint Ministerial Task and Finish Group has been set up to accelerate work on this approach. It will look at the new curriculum being developed and consider issues such as staff training. The work of the group will be informed by the report *Mind over Matter*, which called for emotional and mental wellbeing and resilience to be a stated national priority.

Northern Ireland

In Northern Ireland, children and young people's mental health services are provided by five local Health Care Trusts according to policy determined by the NI Health & Social Care Board (HSCB) & Public Health Agency (PHA). Northern Ireland experiences particular challenges to good mental health and wellbeing due to high rates of poverty, very poor general health indices (State of Child Health Report 2017) and the legacies of societal post-conflict adjustment.

The Regional Strategy for CAMHS Improvement was formulated via the *Bamford Northern Ireland Report 2005* (Department of Health, 2005) recognising the need for substantial investment and modernisation of services across all of the steps of care from prevention, through early intervention to highly specialised services for those young people in most substantial need.

Since 2012, **Mental Health Crisis Resolution Teams** are now established in all Trust areas and consistent evidence-based pathways are in evolution for a range of needs including eating disorder services, therapeutic services for looked-after children, young people with substance-using problems, and developmental needs with mental health consequences. In addition, Childhood Early Intervention Services are well established in some areas and under development in others.

Because of the small size of the Northern Ireland region (1.8 million population) there is an opportunity to develop services in a coherent and integrated manner. The HSCB Lead in partnership with clinicians and senior service managers has secured funding to embed an effective leadership structure to carry out further rationalisation and improvements, particularly to acute provision. A Regional

CAMHS Clinical Director and Operational Lead will be appointed in 2020. The emphasis will be on person-centred care based on best evidence and in facilitating this through sound investment and partnership.

Conclusion

In recent years, there has been an unprecedented focus on mental health within the NHS providing greater transparency regarding the needs of children and young people as well as commissioning and service delivery required to meet those needs. Important principles in delivering effective CYPMH services include the need to:

- build resilience, promote good mental health and wellbeing, prevention and early intervention

- improve access so that children and young people have easy access to the right support from the right service at the right time and as close to home as possible

- develop a clear joined-up approach linking services through care pathways

- deliver evidence-based interventions – this requires a workforce with the relevant skills and competencies across a range of agencies from infancy to young adults

- improve transparency and accountability across the system through the use of data and outcome metrics, with a focus on outcomes that matter to children, young people and their families

- deliver good outcomes for children and young people – this requires a values-based, systems-wide approach working collaboratively across agencies and with children, young people and their families.

References and key policy documents

Betts J and Thompson J (2017) *Mental Health in Northern Ireland: Overview, Strategies, Policies, Care Pathways, CAMHS, and Barriers to Accessing Service*. Belfast: Northern Ireland Assembly Research and Information Service.

Department for Health and Social Care and Education (2017) *Transforming Children and Young People's Mental Health Provision: A Green Paper*. London: The Stationery Office.

Department of Health (2015) *Future in Mind: Promoting, protecting and improving our children and young people's mental health wellbeing*. London: DoH. London: DoH.

Health Education England (2017) *Stepping Forward to 2020/21*. London: HEE.

National Assembly for Wales, Children, Young People and Education Committee (2018) *Mind Over Matter: A report on the step change needed in emotional and mental health support for children and young people in Wales*. Cardiff: National Assembly for Wales.

NHS Digital (2018) *National Study of Health and Wellbeing: Children and Young People*. London: NHS Digital. Available at: https://digital.nhs.uk/data-and-information/publications/statistical/mental-health-of-children-and-young-people-in-england/2017/2017 (accessed 5 August 2019).

NHS England (2015) *Five Year Forward View for Mental Health*. London: NHS England.

NHS England (2019) *NHS Long-term Plan*. London: NHS England.

NICE (2016) *Transition from children's to adults' services for young people using health or social care services*. Available at: https://www.nice.org.uk/guidance/ng43 (accessed 5 August 2019).

Royal College of Paediatrics and Child Health (2017) *State of Child Health: 2017 recommendations for Northern Ireland*. Belfast: RCPCHealth.

Scottish Government (2017) *Mental Health Strategy 2017–2027*. Edinburgh: Scottish Government. Available at: https://www.gov.scot/publications/mental-health-strategy-2017-2027/ (accessed 26 June 2019).

Wolpert, M, Harris R, Hodges S, Fuggle P, James R, Wiener A, McKenna C, Law D, York A, Jones M, Fonagy P, Fleming I and Munk S (2015) *Thrive Elaborated*. London: CAMHS Press.

Websites

MindEd: www.minded.org.uk.

The Child Outcomes Research Consortium (CORC): www.corc.uk.net

Getting it Right for Every Child: https://www.gov.scot/policies/girfec/

Thrive: www.thriveapproach.com.

Choice and Partnership Approach (CAPA): www.capa.co.uk

Values based practice: www.valuesbasedpractice.org.

Chapter 3: Working Together for Children and Young People's Mental Health

Barbara Rayment and Leo Kroll

Key learning points

- Working together is key to good outcomes but can be a challenge in both clinical and multi-agency work.

- Values-based practice (VBP) is an established method to deliver integrated health care; providing a person-centred approach based on values and the evidence-base.

- Similar values-based practice models are available, such as Youth Access's Young People's Charter, values, and competency framework.

- VBP and other models are available for use at a commissioning and practice-based level to deliver multi-disciplinary and multi-agency work.

- There are different training platforms for VBP and person-centred care and shared decision-making, (e.g. online, face-to-face). Team and personal reflection are also helpful and encouraged.

Keywords
Person-centred; multi-agency; cross-sector professional practice; active involvement of young people

Introduction

This chapter will explore the practical application of a values-based approach to everyone working together for children's and young people's mental health.

The last three decades have seen a growing awareness of the need to implement policy and practice that facilitates a whole system and person-centred approach to working with children, young people and their families. From *Every Child Matters* (2004) and the *National Service Framework* (2004), to the more recent *Future in Mind* (2015), there is widespread agreement amongst policymakers and professionals of the need for everyone to work together. It is only by working together that we will succeed in offering the integrated support that young people have repeatedly said they want.

This chapter will show how a focus on what matters (our values) has the potential to enable us all to work within a common framework of shared values, rather than the things – for example, goals, ideas, and opinions – which have the potential to divide us. By encouraging thinking about shared values at three levels – planning and commissioning; service; and practice – we seek to demonstrate how these can lead to both a better service experience and outcomes for children, young people and families.

Difficulties and solutions

Despite the outlined agreements and aspirations to integrate services and work clinically in line with client values, it is difficult to do. Why is this? Answers from professionals, children, young people and families include resource shortages, poor understanding of evidence-based practice by non-health agencies, inappropriate medicalisation of childhood and suffering, and a need to diagnose first, and listen to what matters second.

 A review of Children and Young People's Mental Health Services (CYPMHS) by the Care Quality Commission (CQC) (2018) supports these views. It found that despite good intentions to transform services, in too many instances experience did not match policy aspirations for person-centred care. A lack of flexibility, failure to inform, consult and involve young people impacted not just on their experience of services, but also the outcomes of their care.

A key barrier identified by CQC to creating better and more 'joined up' responses between services was the ongoing difference in the language and understanding of mental health across different parts of the system. NHS-provided services were often perceived as focused only on biological/medical interpretations, while local authority-led provision was seen as only interpreting need through a social and economic lens. Other gaps and barriers focused on data and the fragmented nature of planning and commissioning services. Without good local leadership and the will to collaborate and join up commissioning, CQC found that the resulting picture of local provision militated against the delivery of person-centred care and support. Too often, practitioners worked well with children and young people despite the system, rather than because it supported the delivery of services they need and deserve.

The Values-Based CAMHS Commission report (2016) and complementary work by Youth Access, the advice and counselling services network, offer a response to CQC's findings.

Values-based practice provides a framework about how practice can be implemented at three levels:

- planning and commissioning
- service delivery
- clinical practice.

What follows is a brief overview of VBP and how it could help with the practicalities of working with children, young people and families using a person-centred, shared decision making, and evidenced-based approach. We also suggest VBP can help 'oil the machinery' of integrated and multi-disciplinary working by first articulating the common purpose and values of different organisations, and then using skills to drive mutually respectful decisions about next steps, paying attention to the values of both organisations and service users. This process includes thinking about what works (evidence) and practising within a safe and ethically sound framework.

We also highlight Youth Access's development of a similar framework 'from the ground up', through consultation with young people and professionals about their views of what matters, and the evidence of what works.

History of values-based practice

Values-based practice arose through a collaboration between educators, philosophers and clinicians and was supported by Warwick University and a number of funding organisations (Woodbridge & Fulford, 2004). It now has a rich and varied international life and has become part of the recovery approach for people who have (or have had) a severe mental illness, with its remit covering all aspects of health care at both commissioning and provider level. Further details and a resource wiki of training materials and publications are available at https://www.valuesbasedpractice.org/.

Values-based practice (VBP) consists of:

- four skills areas
- two aspects of clinical relationships
- three principles linking values and evidence
- partnership in decision-making.

Together, these result in balanced 'dissensual' decisions made within frameworks of shared values. Dissensual can mean 'agreeing to disagree', where the underlying values e.g. to improve depression (a goal) so as to lead a more autonomous and fulfilled life (value), are recognised and understood. The means to achieve this may vary depending on the ideas and opinions of those involved.

A summary of the ten essential components of values-based practice (VBP) is included in *Essentials of Values-based Practice: Clinical stories linking science with people* (Fulford *et al*, 2012). One of the key items is the 'two feet' principle of basing decisions on both values and evidence (Williams & Fulford, 2007).

Linking values to evidenced-based practice is incorporated both in Sackett's (2000) original definition, and in the introductory sections of every NICE guidelines.

NICE guidelines include the following phrase:

'When exercising their judgment, professionals are expected to take this guideline fully into account, alongside the individual needs, preferences and values of their patients or service users.'

And Sackett, in the original evidence-based practice book (ibid), writes:

'By patient values we mean the unique preferences, concerns and expectations each patient brings to a clinical encounter and which must be integrated into clinical decisions if they are to serve the patient.'

The VBP training manual (Chevinsky *et al*, 2015) describes values and VBP in the following way:

'Values are highly complex and differ among populations, cultures, religions, and individuals. They are universal in that everyone has them – the team members you will work with and the patients you will serve are no exception. It is important to recognize the diversity of values and the basis of Values-Based Practice is the

respect we have and show for the differences in these values. In fact, the application of Values-Based Practice is reliant on the notion of respect for patients' views, needs, values, and expectations, including their race, religion, culture, gender, age, sexual orientation, and any disability. It is for this reason that sexism, racism, homophobia, and other kinds of values that devalue and marginalize people are explicitly excluded from this framework.'

Hindley and Whittaker (2017) (with funding from the Dinwoodie Settlement, the Royal College of Psychiatry Faculty of Child and Adolescent Psychiatry, the Children and Young People's Mental Health Coalition and Young Minds) reviewed values in CYPMHS and convened a commission (the Values-Based CAMH System Commission) to explore the role of values-based practice in all parts of the UK. The 2016 report detailed 'what really matters' to people involved in CYPMHS (previously known as CAMHS). Services should be person-centred, accessible, responsive, non-judgemental, respectful, confidential, involve children and young people and families and communicate well. The Commission recommended implementation via training, education and research.

Service planning and commissioning

Commissioning values-based, outcomes-focused, evidence-based CYPMHS is key to the provision of accessible and integrated pathways of care and support. Various enablers have been identified to support effective local practice (Youth Access, 2014), including:

- cross sector commitment to a shared, long-term strategic vision
- strong joint commissioning structures, e.g. integrated commissioning hubs
- clear and influential leadership
- effective communication with all stakeholders
- robust evidence, e.g. needs, service take-up, outcomes, interventions
- willingness to be flexible, loosen control and take informed risk(s).

At the centre of values-based commissioning is an emphasis on the views and values of potential and existing service users. For local areas to truly commission well and meet the mental health needs of children and young people, values-based commissioning requires not just principled statements about the commitment to involve service users, but observable practice that enables and ensures effective partnership working (see boxed text).

> ## Box 3.1: Examples of young people's involvement in commissioning
>
> As part of work to transform local mental health provision, Newcastle and Gateshead CCG (2018) listened to young people's views, as well as professionals, to help re-model their services. Young commissioners now work alongside commissioning staff to develop the new service model.
>
> Sheffield made a similar commitment to involving young people. This resulted in a number of 'asks' from young people, which were incorporated into local plans.
>
> (Sheffield CCG, 2017)

Involving young people can be challenging, since it relies on the practice of co-production, collaboration and shared decision-making. It demands a shift in the power dynamics of the relationships between commissioners, service providers and young people. Essentially, the adoption of a 'doing with,' rather than a 'doing to' approach. However, executed well, the potential benefits of putting service user participation and involvement at the centre of planning and commissioning are significant, including:

- commissioning becomes a more dynamic and creative process
- service design is better focused on person-centred delivery, since provision is shaped by those the provision is aimed at
- more responsive service planning and delivery offers opportunities for improved access, engagement and outcomes, resulting in greater efficiency and cost effectiveness
- the whole system becomes more accountable to users
- those involved acquire additional benefits, e.g. increased knowledge, confidence and skills.

YoungMinds offer various resources and support to local areas wishing to improve their commissioning practice with young people.

Implementing values at a service level

Youth Access's work with young people's information, advice and counselling services (YIACS) illustrates opportunities for embedding a values-based approach at the service level. With their early development in the 1960s, informed by Carl Rogers's work and the person-centred counselling movement, and further influenced by youth work and advice work principles, YIACS have long been described as offering a young person-centred model of health and wellbeing.

Following Future in Mind, and with Department of Health funding, Youth Access consulted professionals and young people to enable a refreshment of its values and principles and the development of new resources and tools, including a competency framework; *Delivering Better* (2018), and a service charter; *Altogether Better* (2017), co-produced with young people. Primarily intended for YIACS, these resources also have value to others wanting to embed person-centred and integrated approaches to young people's mental health and other needs.

Youth Access's competency framework comprises four clusters:

- positive relationships
- integrated support
- performance and accountability
- influence and innovation.

These four are further divided into two levels of competencies that are closely aligned, where possible, to other nationally agreed competencies. The framework can support training, supervision and whole organisation reviews, as well as helping organisations wishing to meet the 'Altogether Better' charter.

'Altogether Better' sets out seven priorities (see Box 3.2) agreed by young people as key to the delivery of young person-centred provision. The charter offers providers a tool to check the quality of young people's service experience; Youth Access is developing digital and in-person mechanisms for collecting their feedback.

Box 3.2: 'Altogether Better': A charter created by young people for person-centred mental health and wellbeing services

The seven priorities:

1. Treat us with respect.
2. Make it easy for us to access the service.
3. Have all the help we need in one place.
4. Provide a welcoming and age appropriate setting.
5. Provide support for young people up to the age of 25.
6. Have skilled workers who take us seriously.
7. Involve us in decision making.

Clinical implementation

When thinking about implementing values-based practice within clinical practice, you may find it helpful to consider the following case study about Maria.

Maria

You are a therapist from a youth service commissioned by the NHS to work in schools. You are seeing for the second time, a 14-year-old girl, Maria, who has low mood, and has harmed herself by cutting her arms. She is being bullied at school, and her mother has problems with excessive drinking. Maria is not sleeping well, and has a friend with low mood who takes anti-depressant medication which Maria says helps her friend. What matters to Maria is her mum and how to get her to drink less, and her own low mood and poor sleep which is affecting her school work. She wants to try medication, like her friend. You, her therapist, are not sure that medication is needed (and you don't believe medication works that well). What matters to you is her self-harm, the bullying at school which seems a big problem to you, and her mother's apparent neglect of Maria because of her excessive drinking. No other agencies are involved at present, and you think there are safeguarding concerns.

What areas do you agree on? How do you work together in partnership with Maria, her mother, and other agencies to reach a (dissensual) decision about next steps? 'Dissensual' meaning a decision that is based on shared values, even if some disagreement is present about how to work towards those values.

Valued living areas can be divided into four: health, relationships, work and leisure interests. Maria's priority valued living areas are relationships (her mum's health), her own health (mood and sleep), and achieving (school). Yours are Maria's health (self-harm, mood), relationships (bullying and Maria being concerned about her mother).

Thus, there are some values that overlap and others that do not and are of a lower priority. In the busy world of clinical work, and living (as a young person), often quick decisions happen without reflecting on underlying values, priorities, and solutions to try. Using the 10 parts of VBP (Table 3.1, Fulford *et al*, 2012) enables clinicians and teams to slow this process and also structure reflection.

Three VBP skills can come into play here: awareness, communication (including agreeing to disagree on value prioritisation), and reasoning. The relationship area 'person- and values-centred care' is also in action, as well as the area of 'partnership'.

Maria – next steps

You, as the therapist, are person and values-centred, and explain that you agree with Maria that her health (sleep, mood, self-harm) needs further assessment, especially as Maria's solution is to try medication. You suggest that there may be other solutions too, and that you will work together with her, and the CAMHS team to explore options and make a joint decision with Maria. Maria replies that she is pretty set on wanting medication, rather than therapy, or talking, and would prefer to carry on seeing you.

You also agree that you and Maria share values about being concerned about her mum, though for different reasons, and this needs further work. You say that she might not be entirely happy with your decision, but you have to discuss how well her mum is able to look after her (Maria) and look after herself. You need to talk to her teacher about this, and possibly social services too. Maria is not happy with this, though understands.

Finally, you agree that school is important, and that the above problem areas (health and home relationships) seem to get in the way of Maria doing her best. You also wonder whether being bullied stops her achieving. Maria definitely disagrees on this, and spontaneously says she does not want any help with this area. You agree to leave this, though you both also agree to 'check-in' about it.

Thus, working in partnership with Maria and hopefully the system, is the VBP work that flows from and supports this conversation. Sharing the valued-living areas, and prioritising subsidiary goals and solutions results in a better understanding of shared values, as well as reaching a balanced decision about plans.

Maria – moving forward

You attend the CAMHS service with Maria and her mother, and Maria is started on medication. The service also advises that she has a structured programme of activities that align with her values (other than caring for her mother). This includes going to leisure activities (dance, yoga, walking the neighbours' dog) that she used to do. This programme of 'behavioural activation' has a developing evidence-base, and you say you are interested in knowing more about this. Maria agrees to work on this activity programme with you, and states again that she does not want 'therapy'.

You talk to the school as well, and they say Maria seems well cared for and is getting into school every day. They also say that her mum has recently →

agreed to self-refer herself to the alcohol service, after they had a school meeting with mum and Maria about Maria's deteriorating school performance. The school say that when mum is not drinking she seems a 'good mother', and they don't have concerns when she is not drinking. They and Maria think she has been drinking for about the last six months.

So, a positive end to this story, with the 'two feet' principle for VBP coming into play:

■ Evidence for the treatment of depression (good clinical care by the system, a reasonable use of medication), and:

■ Structured values-focused activities (behavioural activation principles).

There are many less positive stories, and you can reflect on whether the principles and practices within this chapter could move care towards more positive results at all three levels, as well as help understand and address barriers (resources, time and service thresholds), that can sometimes hinder clinical outcomes.

The MindEd e-learning platform has a module on VBP that uses parts of Maria's story. The VBP module is part of the combined therapies package (MindEd, 2018), whose principles are of collaborative care, good integration of services, and awareness of 'blind spots' that may act as barriers to making progress and helping people work towards their own goals that lie within their values and valued living areas.

Conclusion

There are resources and reports (Royal College of Psychiatrists CR215; CR204, 2018) that link to the themes of this chapter, particularly the collaborative care model (McNally & Nixon, 2014), guidance from Children and Young People's Improving Access to Psychological Therapies (CAMHS Press, 2014), the 'Me first' materials http://www.mefirst.org.uk/ and person-centred approaches (HEE/SfH/SfC, 2017).

We hope this chapter has stimulated your interest about how values-led services and evidenced-based practice link together. Also, how understanding values and key components of good clinical care and commissioning practices lead to more integrated services, and the principles of 'working together'.

References

CAMHS Press (2014) *CYP IAPT Principles in Child and Adolescent Mental Health Services Values and Standards: Delivering With and Delivering Well* [online]. Available at: https://www.england.nhs.uk/wp-content/uploads/2014/12/delvr-with-delvrng-well.pdf (accessed 30 June 2019).

Chevinsky J, Fulford KWM, Peile E and Monroe A (2015) *Who Needs Values? Approaching values-based practice in medical education – instructors manual.*

Fulford KWM, Peile E and Carroll H (2012) Values-based practice teaching framework. In: Fulford, KWM, Peile E and Carroll H. *Essentials of Values-based Practice: Clinical stories linking science with people* (pp208 – 210). Cambridge: Cambridge University Press.

Health Education England/ Skills for Health/Skills for Care (2017) *Person-Centred Approaches: Empowering people in their lives and communities to enable an upgrade in prevention, wellbeing, health, care and support. A core skills education and training framework.* London: HEE/SfH/SfC. Available at: http://www.skillsforhealth.org.uk/services/item/146-core-skills-training-framework Person centered and mental health frameworks (accessed 1 July 2019).

Hindley P and Whitaker F (2017) Editorial: Values based child and adolescent mental health systems. *Child and Adolescent Mental Health* **22** (3) 115–117. Available at: https://onlinelibrary.wiley.com/doi/full/10.1111/camh.12235 (accessed 1 July 2019).

McNally D and Nixon B (2016) *Collaborative Care Model.* London: MindEd. Available at: https://www.minded.org.uk/Component/Details/447850 (accessed 25 June 2019).

MindEd (2018) *Combining Therapies: Fundamentals of combining therapies.* London: MindEd. Available at: https://www.minded.org.uk/Catalogue/Index?HierarchyId=0_38403_38404&programmeId=38403 (accessed 25 June 2019).

Newcastle and Gateshead CCG (2018) *2018 Review of Children and Young People's Mental Health & Emotional Wellbeing Transformation Plan 2015-2020).* Available at: https://www.newcastlegatesheadccg.nhs.uk/get-involved/children-young-people-families/children-and-young-people-mental-health/transformation-plan-refresh-2018/ (accessed 19 September 2019).

Richards V and Lloyd K (2017) *Core Values for Psychiatrists: College Report CR204.* London: RCPsych. Available at: https://www.rcpsych.ac.uk/docs/default-source/improving-care/better-mh-policy/college-reports/college-report-cr204.pdf?sfvrsn=5e4ff507_2 (accessed 25 June 2019).

Royal College of Psychiatrists (2018) *Person-centred Care: Implications for training in psychiatry. College report CR215* [online]. Available at: https://www.rcpsych.ac.uk/improving-care/campaigning-for-better-mental-health-policy/college-reports/cr215 (accessed 25 June 2019).

Sheffield CCG (2017) *Sheffield's Emotional Wellbeing and Mental Health Strategy for Children and Young People [online].* Available at: https://www.sheffield.gov.uk/content/dam/sheffield/docs/public-health/health-wellbeing/Local%20Transformation%20Plan.pdf (accessed 19 September 2019).

Values-based CAMHS Commission (2016) *What Really Matters in Children and Young People's Mental Health; Report of the values-based child and adolescent mental health system commission.* London: Royal College of Psychiatrists. Available at: https://valuesbasedpractice.org/wp-content/uploads/2015/04/Values-based-full-report.pdf (accessed 25 June 2019).

Williams R and Fulford KWM (2007) Evidence-based and values-based policy, management and practice in child and adolescent mental health services. *Clinical Child Psychology and Psychiatry* **12** (2) 223–242. Available at: https://journals.sagepub.com/doi/pdf/10.1177/1359104507075926 (accessed 25 June 2019).

Woodbridge K and Fulford KWM (2004) *'Whose Values?' A workbook for values-based practice in mental health care.* London: The Sainsbury Centre for Mental Health.

Youth Access (2017) *Altogether Better: A charter created by young people for person centred mental health and wellbeing services*. London: Youth Access. Available at: http://www.youthaccess.org.uk/downloads/altogether-better-charter-web.pdf (accessed 25 June 2019).

Youth Access (2018) *Delivering Better: A competency framework for YIACS* [online]. Available at: http://www.youthaccess.org.uk/downloads/delivering-better-competency-framework-for-yiacs.pdf (accessed 25 June 2019).

Chapter 4: Delivering Culturally Competent Services

Yvonne Ayo, Dinah Morley and Steven Walker

Key learning points

- Children and young people from black and minority ethnic (BAME) communities living in the UK are at disproportionate risk of mental illness. There are significant differences across ethnic groups.

- They experience significant barriers to accessing services, including culturally inappropriate models of diagnosis and provision, language barriers, poor access to primary care services and stigma, and are more likely to disengage with mainstream services.

- Child and adolescent mental health services (CAMHS) need to offer readily accessible, non-stigmatising environments and culturally diverse staff who understand the context in which their young clients live, as well as actively engaging children and young people and their parents and carers in service design and delivery.

Keywords

Cultural competence; black and minority ethnic (BAME) communities; children and young people; accessibility; mixed race; spirituality; asylum seekers/ refugees; gangs

Summary

'Culture affects the way people label illness, identify symptoms, seek help, decide whether someone is normal or abnormal, set expectations for clients, give themselves personal meaning and understand morality.'
(Black and Ethnic Minority Working Group, 2010)

'Cultural competence is... the capacity to provide effective health and social care, taking into account people's cultural beliefs, behaviours and needs...'
(BMEWG Hackney, 2010; CSIP, 2007a)

Principles of cultural diversity should underpin all services. Understanding the impact of societal pressures and individual cultures is central to ensuring accessible care. In this chapter we make reference to gangs, religion, asylum seeker and refugee young people and spirituality, issues that have a particular bearing on the mental health of black and minority ethnic young people.

A note on terminology: The term 'mixed race' is used throughout as being the term most used and preferred by those who were consulted to inform the 2001 census (Aspinall *et al*, 2006). This term is used here to include mixed heritage, bi-raciality, multiple heritage and mixed ethnicity.

Background

We live in an increasingly multicultural society: 14% of the UK population of 56 million (2011 UK census data) are from minority ethnic groups – a total of 7.8 million people. Children and young people under 18 years old from black and minority ethnic backgrounds make up approximately 2.5 million of this population.

Between 2001 and 2011 there was a disproportionately large growth in the numbers of children of mixed race. The 2011 census data indicated that there are now around 603,000 children of mixed race under the age of 18 in the (UK) population, compared with approximately 338,000 in 2001. Providing CAMHS that are appropriate and acceptable to all these children, young people and families from different cultures and backgrounds is a key challenge for services.

As noted by Street (2008) there is limited research into the mental health needs of young people from minority ethnic groups, with much of the literature in this field concerning adults. However, this shows that people from minority ethnic groups often experience problems accessing services and, when they do, may have poorer treatment and care experiences than white people. This situation is very powerfully described in *Breaking the Circles of Fear*, a report on adult mental health services published by the Sainsbury Centre for Mental Health (2002), and is acknowledged in the National Institute for Mental Health in England (NIMHE) report *Inside Outside: Improving mental health services for black and minority ethnic communities in England* (NIMHE, 2003).

The mental health needs of different ethnic groups

Understanding the prevalence of mental illness among different ethnic groups and variations in help-seeking behaviour is widely acknowledged to be a complex issue. Fernando and Keating (2009) point out that caution is needed because many studies are based on very small sample sizes. There is a lack of consistency in how ethnicity is defined and studies often use measures of mental health developed from white populations.

Ethnicity is not a static concept; it can change over relatively short periods of time, and how it is defined is influenced by social, political, historical and economic circumstances. Individuals can perceive themselves as having a number of different ethnic identities that may be based on sharing a common lifestyle or religion, or their ethnic identity may be informed by a geographical association with a region or country. There may be differences between generations in terms of the influence of the country of origin and it is important to think about the stages of the development of cultural identity (Malek, 2002).

A breakdown by ethnicity of the prevalence of severe mental health problems, based on 2012 SDQ scores for total difficulties, shows that percentages of 11-year old children with severe mental health problems are significantly higher for children of mixed race, followed by white children and then black children. Percentages of mixed race girls with severe mental illness is even more disproportionate. (Guttman *et al*, 2015)

Disproportionate numbers of young black men are being labelled as mentally ill and subjected to restrictive or medication-based treatment. South Asian young women have higher rates of eating disorders than their white equivalents and disproportionate numbers of Bangladeshi children are not accessing CAMH services (Walker, 2019).

A recent important review (de Haan *et al*, 2018) concluded that since ethnic minority youth are treated less often for mental health conditions than other youth, it is important to analyse their risk for dropout and to determine if there are ethnicity-specific determinants. It shows that ethnic minority patients have a higher risk of treatment dropout than ethnic majority patients and that dropout rates are ethnically specific. The review indicates that to prevent dropout, therapists should pay attention to variables such as ethnic background, therapist–patient ethnic match, and the quality of the therapeutic relationship.

In other studies, very high rates of mental health conditions have been found among young refugees and asylum seekers (Vostanis, 2014). Increased levels of self-harm among minority ethnic children and young people have been reported (Bhui *et al*, 2007). A recent study found that of all suicides of young people under 20 years of age 11% were from BAME groups (Rodway *et al*, 2016.)

In addition to research on prevalence rates, we know from other areas of research that young people from black and minority ethnic groups are disproportionately exposed to many of the known 'risk factors' linked with mental health problems. These include being excluded from school, being looked after by the local authority, being involved in the justice system, and being homeless.

In Birmingham, for example, a Commission for Racial Equality investigation report found that African-Caribbean pupils were four times more likely to be excluded from school for fewer and less serious offences than white children, and were less likely to later re-enter mainstream education (Ofsted, 2001). Similarly, data on income and job prospects indicates that families from minority ethnic groups fare badly in comparison with white people from the same class, with a resulting increased risk of adverse impact on children's health and psychological development (Dwivedi, 2002).

Barriers to accessing help

Alongside a growing awareness of the differences in the rates of mental health conditions between people from minority ethnic groups and those from white backgrounds, in the last few years the issue of health inequalities has become more prominent.

Breaking the Circles of Fear (Sainsbury Centre for Mental Health, 2002) found that not only were black service users not treated with respect and their voices not heard, but services were not accessible, welcoming, relevant or well-integrated within the community for which they were meant to be providing. Primary care was seen to be limited; service user, family and carer involvement was lacking, and black-led community initiatives were not valued; nor, crucially, were they provided with secure funding on which to build capacity in the longer term.

Similar concerns are expressed in *Inside Outside* (NIMHE, 2003), which famously found the NHS mental health services to be 'institutionally racist', and that to change this required:

'... *progressive community-based mental health at the centre of service development and delivery. Those who use mental health services are identified, first and foremost, as citizens with mental health needs, which are understood as located in a social and cultural context.*'

The Department of Health's *Delivering Race Equality* strategy and action plan (Department of Health 2005), adopts many of the *Inside Outside* proposals, as well as some of those put forward in the report of the Inquiry into the death of David (Rocky) Bennett (Blofeld, 2003). In particular, it calls for:

- more appropriate and responsive services
- community engagement of BAME communities in the design and delivery of appropriate and accessible mental health services
- better information about the needs of BAME communities.

We know from the smaller research field that does exist that some of the barriers that have been identified for BAME adults hold true for children and young people too – not least, the lack of service user involvement, the sense of services not being appropriate or accessible to them, and the fear of the stigma surrounding mental health that can make young people very wary of approaching mental health services. A tendency to only seek help when at crisis point is also apparent.

These were all prominent themes in the *Minority Voices* study undertaken by YoungMinds in 2005 (Street *et al*, 2005). This explored the experiences of young people and their families from a range of different ethnic groups, and found that many young people:

- had little or no understanding of formal mental health services and how to get themselves referred to them (once they had realised they needed help)
- were very reluctant to talk about their concerns unless it was to someone they knew and trusted
- were deterred by long wait times for appointments, the need to often travel some distance to a service and the inflexibility of service provision in terms of only being open at times that were difficult for young people
- encountered difficulties with a lack of interpreting support and a lack of cultural understanding among many staff when they did successfully access a service.

Many of the findings from *Minority Voices* echo those in other studies of young people's perspectives on mental health, including work by the Mental Health Foundation (Smith & Leon, 2001), and an earlier study by YoungMinds, *Where Next?* (Street & Svanberg, 2003), which looked at Tier 4 inpatient CAMHS. The *Minority Voices* findings add a specific cultural dimension, in particular in relation to the influence of the local community and of parents.

Several of the interviewees suggested that in many CAMHS and other mental health services, the limited understanding of the different family dynamics in minority ethnic families can make it hard for professionals to engage with them.

An inability to offer interventions in any language other than English, and a widespread lack of funds with which to develop and deliver services appropriate to the needs of local BAME communities was noted. It was also apparent that staff skills, experience and training in working with young people from BAME backgrounds varied considerably, which impacted on staff confidence. Some staff and workers highlighted limitations in existing training: in particular they said that professional mental health training remains very Eurocentric and does not sufficiently address cross-cultural contexts (Kurtz & Street, 2006).

The characteristics of a service for BAME children and adolescents with mental health problems which aspires to better accessibility can be described as composing of three elements:

1. '*Consultation with individual black families and their communities is required to ensure service provision meets their needs and to identify gaps in services. A pro-active community-orientated practice offers a practical and effective way of achieving this.*
2. *Information needs to be provided about rights and responsibilities in the context of childcare and mental health legislation. Jargon-free material should be accessible in different formats and languages about child and adolescent mental health needs.*
3. *Competence – Staff competence in child and adolescent mental health is not enough if this is not matched with demonstrable knowledge and skills required to practice in an ethnically diverse society.*'

(Walker, 2019)

Children and young people of mixed race

There are also disproportionately high numbers of mixed race children featuring in the known risk areas. These young people will have very different experiences of childhood depending on where they have grown up; what they look like i.e. their skin colour; and the way in which their family, school and community supports or undermines their 'mixedness'. The group's extreme heterogeneity does not allow for a one-size-fits-all assessment of their needs and this is another challenge for practitioners.

Box 4.1: Examples of good practice

The Young Influencers: https://www.healthwatchtowerhamlets.co.uk/our-work/projects/

300 Voices: https://www.mashhub.org.uk/300-voices

YoungMinds Welcome: youngminds.org.uk/.../youngminds-welcome

The Manchester Multiple Heritage project: www.multipleheritage.co.uk

Mosaic in Brighton: www.mosaicbrighton.org.uk

CAMHS cultural competence resource tool: galyic.org.uk/docs/occa_workbook.doc

A number of research studies have pointed to the racism these young people suffer at the hands of both black and white peers; the difficulties they experience in seeking a safe identity; the negative school experiences, as well as the stigma against mixed relationships in wider society (Guy, 2018). All of these are often quite subtle and/or hidden experiences, and are set in the context of tensions they may face within their families as well as the wider communities in which they live (Morley & Street, 2013).

The population of the UK, particularly in the large conurbations, is increasingly 'mixed' and increasingly intergenerationally mixed. A child who will look, and identify as, black or white may well have grandparents or other wider family members who will be of a different racial heritage. This heritage is likely to have great importance for the child and will be part for the search for an identity which acknowledges this fact. The mixed race young person can feel s/he has no group to belong to and may elect to be black or white, often depending on epidermal appearance. Practitioners have a tendency to default to 'black' when working with a mixed race child or young person. (It is interesting to observe that the press more or less exclusively refer to Barack Obama as the first black president when he is clearly of mixed parentage.)

Gangs

Membership of a gang, assumptions of gang membership, and frequent stopping by the police play an important part in the lives of BAME adolescents. Previously, gangs were defined as localised groups which claimed and patrolled particular territories, engaged in criminal activity, had particular visual identifications and were often in conflict with other gangs known as postcode wars. Status was achieved in displays of physical violence in streets which occurred temporally and within a particular location. The rise of social media and the availability of illicit drugs has precipitated a number of changes in gang behaviour. For example, digital technology permits perceived insults and taunts to be replayed indefinitely, witnessed by a large audience of friends and followers. Gang violence is increasingly more about the protection of drug markets than defending the reputation and honour of the gang.

The murder of a 14-year-old boy in 2019 in north east London by three men raised increasing concerns about the vulnerability of young people who are pressurised by criminals to participate in crime. The reduced visibility of gangs and their online 'business' activities may mean that more violence is gang-related than previously realised (Whittaker & Densley, 2019).

Addressing the relationship between poor mental health and gang behaviour requires a collaborative approach across a wide range of services which include: health, local authorities, schools, criminal justice and voluntary agencies (Madden, 2013).

Religion and spirituality

Sin is defined variously in many religions and for a child or young person the word and concept come with the sense of failing to be satisfactory, for example, from early toileting experiences through to exam performance or adolescent sexuality. The sense of sin and failure is quickly transformed into guilt and shame resulting in feelings of depression, distress and despair unless there is some balancing influence. Some young people may believe that their problem/s are the result of divine intervention – a punishment for a sin or misdemeanor of some kind.

Among some cultures there is a potent belief system that spirits can possess people and make them unwell or be invoked to help them with a problem. In the case of a child or young person who is causing concern among teachers, social workers or health professionals, there may be a simple diagnosis or assessment of the cause of the problem but this may not fit with the family's beliefs about the cause. If therapists are unable or unwilling to explore this aspect of belief then they may be missing a vital component of the individual or family's overall belief system about how the world works and how problems arise; more importantly, what is likely to be effective treatment (Walker, 2019). Multicultural counselling and therapy effectiveness are enhanced when the worker uses flexible methods and defines goals consistent with the life experiences and cultural values of the young person. (See Box 4.2: Case studies.)

Box 4.2: Case studies

Ms B

Ms B is a depressed young Albanian Muslim woman with three children under 5 years of age exhibiting disturbed behaviour, and a 10-year-old at primary school with poor attendance. The family are refugees and have experienced severe trauma in recent years. Her partner, who is ten years her senior has been involved with drug and alcohol abuse and is suspected of abusing her. She is terrified her children will be removed because she is unable to care for them properly or protect them from the violence of her partner. Ms B is hostile to social workers, health visitors and teachers who have expressed concerns about the welfare of all four children. She feels persecuted, does not want any involvement and resents any interference in her life. The plan summary could look something like this:

- Younger children to attend nursery daily.
- Ms B to play with the younger children once a day.
- Ms B to attend a domestic violence survivors group.
- Ms B to take 10-year-old to school.
- Partner to attend anger management course.
- Partner to attend drug counselling.
- Family network to visit Ms B weekly.

Iraqi family

A family of Iraqi asylum seekers have been referred to your service. The father claims he was tortured and had death threats made against his wife and three children who are of Kurdish origin. The children are all under 8 years of age and his wife is a nursery teacher. Some of the children speak very little English. The family have been relocated to a small town where there are very few families from Middle Eastern countries. The housing office have reported racist incidents and a teacher has expressed concern about one of the children who is wetting and soiling in class provoking bullying from other children.

Commentary

Remember that the family are likely to be suspicious of your motives and will require a lot of genuine evidence that they should trust you. Their naturally defensive behaviour may come across as hostile/uncommunicative and you need to deal with this in a non-confrontational manner. A translator/interpreter should accompany you having been fully briefed beforehand about your task. Do not assume that every interpreter is the same, and try to evaluate their beliefs/attitudes and whether there may be ethnic or religious differences between them and the family. Strict translation of words and terms will be unhelpful therefore time ➜

needs to be spent on the interpretation of the translation. You can better engage with the family by: enabling everyone to have their say, sensitive questioning, reinforcing the integrity of the family system, noting patterns of communication and structure.

Your networking skills can mobilise the statutory agencies to provide what is required to attend to the immediate areas of concern and clarify roles and responsibilities. A case conference or network meeting can formalize this with an action check list for future reference to monitor the plan. One option may be to plan some family sessions together with a colleague from another agency.

This could combine assessment and intervention work to ascertain medium term needs whilst using therapeutic skills to help the family establish their equilibrium. The key is to enable them to re-establish their particular coping mechanisms and ways of dealing with stress, rather than trying to impose an artificial solution. Maintaining a systems-wide perspective can help you evaluate the factors and elements building up to form a contemporary picture of their context. Working with them as a family and demonstrating simple things like reliability and consistency will provide them with an emotional anchor – a secure enough base to begin to manage themselves in due course (Elliot, 2007).

Asylum seekers and refugee children

Refugees and asylum-seeking young people can find the experience of migration and re-location very challenging. Often from a background of trauma these young people have to adjust to new cultures, languages, settling into schools and integrating themselves into their new lives with their past. Over 90% of refugee and asylum seeker children require mental health services which they often do not receive (Ellis, 2011). The main barriers to lack of mental health support are lack of service accessibility and stigma. Within the refugee communities stigma surrounding mental health increases the reluctance to access mental health services (Fazel *et al*, 2016).

Anxieties about how others perceive them, particularly in schools, or the possibility of becoming educationally disadvantaged if they are diagnosed with a mental health condition, adds to this reluctance. Refugee and asylum seeker families may not know of the services available in the areas to where they have been re-located. Specialist services for these young people and community-based support within the local area are essential.

Good practice developments

In recent years CAMHS have developed more flexible services for black and minority ethnic children and young people and families. Awareness of the possible stigmatisation of attending clinics has promoted the development of services that are locally based in communities e.g. schools, family centres, GP surgeries.

Schools play an increasingly significant role, and joint work with attendance officers, learning mentors, educational psychologists and others enables consideration of the individual cultural needs of students and their families, referring them on to other services when appropriate.

Delivery of outreach interventions such as individual and family work, groups for students and parents, parenting programmes and drop-in services, organised by schools, and training for school staff, all increase opportunities for access by black and ethnic minority children and young people. Multi-agency working between different services which include mental health, social care, education and other specialist services come together, i.e. the 'team around the child' to consider appropriate whole family approaches, sensitive to culture and ethnicity.

Whilst these approaches are beneficial to all children and young people with mental health problems and conditions, they allow for a flexibility of approach and engagement with voluntary groups which support the mainstream services in making them more accessible to young people from black and minority ethnic communities.

To help CAMHS to develop culturally competent provision, in 2007 the National CAMHS Support Services (NCSS) and the Centre for Transcultural Studies at Middlesex University produced a tool for service providers to review their performance in this respect (CSIP, 2007b).

Conclusion

Although this is a complex topic and there are significant deficits in current data, recent research gives some useful pointers for how CAMHS might be developed to ensure they are culturally competent. Attitudes of practitioners at all levels to working across cultures are critical. Practitioners must acknowledge their own prejudices to ensure effective communication across a range of cultures. For commissioners of services, this will include forging new partnerships with voluntary sector organisations that are well embedded within minority ethnic populations to develop new community-based service models. For staff, there are new tools and resources which help develop practice that is flexible and works within a young person's context and, perhaps most crucially, promotes the active participation of the young person in the treatment process.

Working across cultures can be hard work for all involved. Practitioners need to work with sensitivity and a willingness to learn from the young person and family about the meaning of mental health in the cultural context of the child.

References

Aspinall P, Song M and Hashem F (2006) *Mixed Race in Britain: A survey of the preferences of mixed race people for terminology and classifications*. Canterbury: University of Kent.

Blofeld J (Chair) (2003) *Independent Inquiry into the Death of David Bennett*. Cambridge: Norfolk, Suffolk and Cambridgeshire Strategic Health Authority.

Bhui K, McKenzie K and Rasul F (2007) Rates, risk factors and methods of self-harm among minority ethnic groups in the UK: a systematic review. *BMC Public Health* **7** (336). Available at: https://bmcpublichealth.biomedcentral.com/articles/10.1186/1471-2458-7-336 (accessed 26 June 2019).

Black and Ethnic Minority Working Group (2010) *Cultural Competency Toolkit: Health and social care*. London: London Borough of Hackney.

Byron T (for Department for Children, Schools and Families and the Department for Culture, Media and Sport) (2010) *Safer Children in a Digital World*. London: HMSO.

Care Services Improvement Partnership (CSIP) (2007a) *The Papadopoulos, Tilki and Taylor model for developing cultural competence / CAMHS Cultural Competence Tool*. London: Department of Health/CSIP.

Care Services Improvement Partnership (CSIP) (2007b) *CAMHS Cultural Competence Resource Tool*. Middlesex University: The Centre for Transcultural Studies.

de Haan A, Boon, A, de Jong J and Vermeiren R (2018) A review of mental health treatment dropout by ethnic minority youth. *Transcultural Psychiatry* **55** (1) 3–30.

Department of Health (2005) *Delivering Race Equality in Mental Health Care: An action plan for reform inside and outside services and the Government's response to the independent inquiry into the death of David Bennett*. London: Department of Health.

Dwivedi K (2002) *Meeting the Needs of Ethnic Minority Children*. London: Jessica Kingsley.

Elliot V (2007) Interventions and Services for Refugee and Asylum-Seeking Children and Families. In P Vostanis (Ed) *Mental Health Interventions and Services for Vulnerable Children and Young People*. London: Jessica Kingsley.

Ellis B (2011) New directions in refugee and youth mental health services: Overcoming barriers to engagement. *Journal of Child and Adolescent Trauma* **4** 69–85.

Fazel M, Garcia J and Stein A (2016) The right location? Experiences of refugee adolescents seen by school-based mental health services. *Clinical Psychology and Psychiatry* **21** (3) 368–380.

Fernando S and Keating F (2009) *Mental Health in a Multi-Ethnic Society: A multidisciplinary handbook*. (2nd edition). London: Routledge.

Guttman l, Joshi H, Parsonage M and Schmoon I (2015) *Children of the New Century: Mental health findings for the Millennium Cohort Study*. London: Centre for Mental Health.

Guy S (2018) *Breaking Stereotypes With Data: A report on mixed race children and families in the UK.* London: People in Harmony.

Kurtz Z, Stapelkamp C, Taylor E, Malek M and Street C (2005) *Minority Voices: A guide to good practice in planning and providing services for the mental health of black and minority ethnic groups.* London: YoungMinds.

Kurtz Z and Street C (2006) Mental health services for young people from black and minority ethnic backgrounds: the current challenge. *Journal of Children's Services* **1** (3) 40–49.

Madden V (2013) *Understanding the Mental Health Needs of Young People Involved in Gangs.* Westminster: Joint Health and Wellbeing Board.

Malek M (2002) Developing culturally appropriate services. In: *FOCUS: Bridging the Gap Between Policy and Practice in Child and Adolescent Mental Health Services. Conference proceedings.* London: Royal College of Psychiatrists' Research Unit.

Morley D and Street C (2013) *Mixed Experiences: Growing up mixed race – mental health and wellbeing.* London. National Children's Bureau.

National Institute for Mental Health in England (NIMHE) (2003) *Inside Outside: Improving mental health services for black and minority ethnic communities in England.* London: Department of Health.

Office for National Statistics (2018) *Population Estimates.* London: ONS.

Ofsted (2001) *Improving Behaviour and Attendance in Schools.* London: Ofsted.

Rodway C, Tham G, Saied I, Turnbull P, Windfhur K, Shaw J, Kapur N and Appleby L (2016) Suicide in children and young people in England: a consecutive case series. *The Lancet* **3** (8) 751–759.

Sainsbury Centre for Mental Health (2002) *Breaking the Circles of Fear: A review of the relationship between mental health services and African and Caribbean communities.* London: Sainsbury Centre for Mental Health.

Secretary of State for Health and Secretary of State for Education (2017) *Transforming Children and Young People's Mental Health Provision: A Green Paper.* London HMSO.

Smith K and Leon L (2001) *Turned Upside Down: Developing community-based crisis services for 16–25-year-olds experiencing a mental health crisis.* London: Mental Health Foundation.

Street C (2008) Developing accessible and culturally competent services. In: *Child and Adolescent Mental Health Today: A handbook.* Brighton: Pavilion Publishing & Media.

Street C and Svanberg J (2003) *Where Next? New directions in the provision of in-patient mental health services for young people.* London: YoungMinds.

Street C, Stapelkamp C, Taylor E, Malek M and Kurtz Z (2005) *Minority Voices: Research into the access and acceptability of services for the mental health of young people from black and minority ethnic groups.* London: YoungMinds.

Vostanis Y (2014) Meeting the mental health needs of refugees and asylum seekers. *British Journal of Psychiatry* **204** (3) 176–177.

Walker S (2019) *Supporting Troubled Young People: A practical guide to helping with mental health problems.* St. Albans: Critical Publishing.

Whittaker A, Cheston L, Tyrell T, Higgins M, Felix-Baptiste C and Havard T (2018) *From Postcodes to Profit: How gangs have changed in Waltham Forest.* London: South Bank University.

Whittaker A and Densley J (2019) London's gangs have changed and it is driving a surge in pitiless violence. *The Guardian.* Available at: https://www.theguardian.com/commentisfree/2019/jan/10/london-gangs-changed-violence-waltham-forest-drugs (accessed 26 July 2019).

Chapter 5: Infant Development Within Early Relationships

Jane Barlow and Angela Underdown

Key learning points

- Early relationships are essential to the emotional and neurological development of the infant.

- The parents or primary caregivers are one of the most important parts of the infant's early environment.

- The sensitivity of interactions between babies and their main caregivers influences whether a baby is securely attached.

- Securely attached infants develop the confidence to use the main caregiver as a secure base from which to explore the world.

- Insecurely attached infants may limit their explorations of the wider world, or deploy defensive strategies to cope with aroused or distressed emotional states.

- Parents who are anxious, angry or depressed may not be able to help their baby to regulate their emotional states.

Keywords

Parent–infant interaction; attachment; emotional development; neurological development

Introduction

Warm, sensitive relationships are key for healthy emotional development. Although it was once thought that development was a biological unfolding of inherited characteristics, it is now accepted that environmental experience plays a major part in influencing the way in which the brain develops. Furthermore, the parents or primary caregivers are one of the most important parts of the baby's early environment, and their capacity to support the infant's development is crucial. Less than optimal parenting during this period can have a significant effect on the baby's immediate and long-term development. Supporting parents to provide infants with the best start in life is therefore particularly important.

This chapter will describe the infant's neurological and emotional development, the key environmental factors that support this development, and the ways in which the absence of particular types of environmental support can have a significant impact on the long-term development of the infant during these important early years. Chapter 6 will look in detail at the range of ways in which services can support parenting, so as to ensure children are enabled to reach their full potential.

Prenatal bonds

Research suggests that the relationship with the unborn baby is as important as the relationship that is established following birth. Pregnancy is a critical phase in the lives of expectant parents when they are reorganising the relationships around themselves as well as forging the bond with their new baby. It is both a period of vulnerability and an opportunity for transformation and change (Slade & Sadler, 2019).

During pregnancy women usually begin to imagine what their unborn baby will be like. A mother might say for instance: 'He is very active at night time when the comedy programmes are on, so we think he will be quite a cheeky little thing…'.

Such prenatal mental imaginings (also known as 'maternal mental representations') are shaped not only by the biological changes taking place, but also by a range of psychological and social factors, such as the mother's memories of her own early relationships, her family traditions, her hopes, her fears and her fantasies.

A significant link has been found between the richness of these prenatal maternal representations and the quality of the interaction with the baby in the first six months of life (Foley & Hughes, 2018). However, research also suggests that, typically, only around half of women experience the type of mental representations in pregnancy that are optimal, with the remaining women being classified as 'disengaged' or 'distorted' (Theran *et al*, 2005). A range of factors have been found to influence such representations including domestic abuse, with women who have experienced such abuse having significantly more negative representations of their infants and themselves, and their babies being more likely to be insecurely attached (Huth-Bocks *et al*, 2004).

In addition to having an impact on the bonding process, high levels of maternal stress can affect a number of aspects of fetal development and have a long-term impact on the emotional and behavioural development of the child (Glover, 2018). It is, as such, crucially important to support the emotional wellbeing of expectant mothers.

The social infant

Following birth, the infant's interactions with primary caregivers are important to a number of key aspects of their later development. Infants are unique individuals, and close observations (Beebe & Lachman, 2004; Murray & Andrews, 2000) have revealed the many ways in which they influence and respond to their changing environments as they seek interaction with others. Indeed, it is now accepted that the earliest years of life are a key period in terms of infants learning how to make emotional attachments and forming the first relationships that lay many of the foundations for future mental health (Bowlby, 1969, 1988; Stern, 1985; Sroufe, 2005; Fonagy *et al*, 2004). Infants need opportunities to attune to others, to learn to regulate or manage their emotions and behaviour, and to attach to their main carers, who in turn reflect and respond to them as an individual.

The importance of early relationships

The infant experiences a range of states of arousal, and one of the key tasks during the first year of life is learning to manage or regulate his or her emotions and behaviour. Parents play a crucial role in supporting the baby to 'co-regulate' emotional states by responding appropriately so that the infant does not become overwhelmed (Stern, 1985; Rosenblum *et al*, 2019). Attuned parents are able to act as sensitive moderators or accelerators of infant emotion. Specifically, early interactions between the caregiver and baby play a significant role in influencing the chemical neurotransmitters that have a direct effect on the brain (e.g. neuropeptides such as dopamine), thereby setting the thermostat for later control of the stress response. Excessive stress during infancy results in the baby's brain being flooded by cortisol for prolonged periods, and an eventual lowering of the threshold for activation of fear/anxiety, resulting in the child experiencing more fear/anxiety and difficulty dampening this response (for an overview see Schore, 1994 or Gerhardt, 2015).

This early relationship is also important because it is now recognised that the day-to-day interactions that take place between the caregiver and baby 'indelibly influence the evolution of brain structures responsible for the individual's socio-emotional functioning for the rest of the lifespan' (Schore, 1994). Indeed, it is the unique wiring of a baby's brain that plays a key role in shaping how that particular baby behaves, thinks, feels, and shapes his or her developing sense of 'self'. The importance of these interactions reflects the fact that although the structural development of the brain is practically complete before birth (Berens & Nelson, 2019), much functional development takes place during the brain's growth spurt during the first and second years of life, with a proliferation of nerve pathways conducting electrical messages across fluid-filled synapses that rapidly increase (synaptogenesis) in response to interpersonal and intrapersonal experiences. The infant brain over-produces synapses in response to sensory experiences and then 'prunes' away those that are unused, leaving neurons intact and eliminating unused synapses (Berens & Nelson, 2019).

Infant attachment

The development of a baby's brain occurs at the interface of relationships with key 'attachment' figures. Through day-to-day interactions infants usually begin to build a sense of security and trust that gradually helps them to develop the confidence to use the caregiver as a 'secure base' (Bowlby, 1969) from which to start exploring the environment.

Attachment is an affective or emotional bond between infant and caregiver (Bowlby, 1969), the role of which is the co-regulation of infant emotion and arousal (Rosenblum *et al*, 2019). Babies who receive sensitive, emotionally responsive care during their first year are more likely to become securely attached, while babies receiving insensitive, inconsistent or unresponsive care are more likely to become insecurely attached.

Securely attached infants develop the confidence to use the main caregiver as a 'secure base' from which to explore the world. Insecurely attached infants lack this secure base, and so may limit the explorations of the environment that are a key part of their learning, or deploy defensive strategies to cope with aroused or distressed emotional states.

Attachment relationships are also recognised to be a prototype for later relations because the attachment relationship is internalised (i.e. becomes what is known as an 'internal working model' or IWM), which is effectively a 'representational model' of themselves, and themselves with other people. This provides the child with a set of expectations in terms of what to expect from others. Physically and emotionally neglected children, for example, may expect others to be unresponsive, unavailable and unwilling to meet their needs. As Barrett (2006) describes:

'For some children who have been rejected, abused, humiliated or treated in ways that have left them feeling confused about what to expect from other people... such children will not be able to use their attachment figures as a secure base and will be more likely to be pessimistic both about the chances of people liking them and about the way people will treat them.'

Overall, infants who have a secure attachment are more able to be independent, relate to their peers and engage in more complex and creative play (Finelli *et al*, 2019; Sroufe, 2005), while infants with an insecure or disorganised attachment may experience a range of long-term problems including:

- externalising disorders (i.e. conduct and behaviour problems) (Fearon *et al*, 2010)

- personality disorder (i.e. mental health problems characterised by enduring maladaptive patterns of emotional regulation, relating and behaviour) (Steele & Siever, 2010)

- an increased likelihood of experiencing symptoms that meet clinical criteria (Borelli *et al*, 2010).

The parent's attachment

One of the factors affecting a child's attachment status is the parents' attachment (i.e. their own internal working models – IWM), which can be assessed using the Adult Attachment Interview (Fonagy *et al*, 1995) to indicate how a parent perceives and reflects on their own early care. The research suggests that insecurely attached adults may be more likely to produce insecurely attached babies, most probably because the parent's IWMs influence their parenting behaviours (De Wolff & van IJzendoorn, 1997). Such behaviours may be underpinned by changes in their physiology. For example, one study involving MRI scans found that securely attached mothers when shown images of their babies face (i.e. sad and happy) showed greater activation of brain reward regions (e.g. oxytocin-associated hypothalamus/pituitary region), while insecure/dismissing mothers showed greater activation of parts of the brain (i.e. insular cortex) that are associated with less positive feelings, in response to their baby's sad face (Strathearn *et al*, 2009).

Infants may, as such, have different attachment relationships with different caregivers and a range of other factors are now recognised to be associated with secure attachment. These include the parents' capacity to 'tune in' to their infant's emotional states and to think about and respond to the infant as an individual with his or her own likes, dislikes and feelings and behaviours, which is known as reflective functioning.

Reflective functioning

Reflective function refers to 'the capacity of the parents to experience the baby as an 'intentional' being rather than simply viewing him or her in terms of physical characteristics or behaviour. This supports the infant's developing sense of self and lays the foundations for the child's understanding of mental states in other people (i.e. known as mentalisation), and their capacity to regulate their own 'internal experiences' (Fonagy *et al*, 2004). Another group of researchers refer to this as 'mind-mindedness', or the mother's capacity to both tune into, and correctly interpret, her baby's moods or feelings (Meins *et al*, 2002). A number of studies have now shown that such mind-mindedness is strongly associated with her child's development at two years of age (Meins *et al*, 2002; 2012).

Although the child's perception of mental states in him or herself and others initially depends on representations from attachment figures, as the infant grows, other adults and older siblings increasingly play a role:

'If the child's perception of mental states in himself and others depends on his observation of the mental world of the care-giver, then this sets a target for optimizing the facilitative power of early experience. Clearly, children require a number of adults with whom an attachment bond exists – who can be trusted and have an interest in their mental state – to support the development of their subjectivity from a pre-mentalizing to a fully mentalizing model.'
(Allen & Fonagy, 2006).

Some adults may have less capacity for reflective function than others, particularly if they themselves have not experienced sensitive, warm relationships or if they are experiencing severe difficulties such as mental health problems, addiction to alcohol or drugs, or domestic violence (e.g. Stover & Coates, 2015). Adverse childhood experiences (ACEs) of this sort then impact on the child's later functioning (Thompson *et al*, 2019; Murray *et al*, 2019).

Factors affecting parenting

A range of other factors have been found to affect parenting, perhaps the most important being poverty (Katz *et al*, 2007); this can have an direct effect on parenting by making it difficult for parents to provide for their baby, but it also has an indirect effect by increasing parental stress, and the likelihood that the parent(s) will experience mental health problems.

Mental health problems such as anxiety and depression are common and affect around 15–20% of women in the first year after childbirth (NICE, 2014), and around 5–10% of men (Paulson & Bazemore, 2010). Anxiety and depression in both mothers and fathers can independently affect the interaction with the infant, and thereby the infant's longer term development. For example, research shows that depression affects the sensitivity of interactions with the infant, with depressed mothers being either more remote and distant with the infant or more intrusive (Murray *et al*, 1996), the long-term impact being an increased likelihood of depression in adolescence (Murray *et al*, 2019). The research also shows that other less common mental health problems such as borderline personality disorder (Laulik *et al*, 2013), eating disorders (Stein *et al*, 2006), and problems such as domestic violence (Huth-Bocks *et al*, 2004) and substance misuse (Hatzis *et al*, 2017), are also associated with a range of compromised forms of interaction with the baby, thereby reducing the likelihood of the infant becoming securely attached.

Therefore, in order to support parenting during infancy, early years professionals need to bear in mind that the ability of parents to provide the sort of parenting that is key to them achieving their developmental goals, may be affected by their wider circumstances, and that these need to be addressed in addition to their problems with the interaction.

Early parenting tasks

Babies begin to show a preference for particular attachment figures at around seven months of age, and there are a number of important parenting tasks that contribute to this. These include the sensitive meeting of the baby's needs from moment to moment, the containing of the baby's anxieties, and the turn-taking exchanges that form the basis of much interaction between caregiver and baby. By two months, the face is the primary source of visual-affective communication, and face-to-face interactions at this age are highly arousing and affect laden, and expose infants to high levels of cognitive and social information, and stimulation (Schore, 1994). The infant and his/her caregivers regulate the intensity of these interactions through a pattern of interaction in which the infant and carer are at first attuned (synchrony), following which the baby breaks away to look elsewhere (rupture), after which an attuned parent waits in order to re-engage the infant (repair). (This type of interaction can been seen at the following website: https://aimh.org.uk/getting-to-know-your-baby/ – see the section on early interactions). Adults who have difficulty 'tuning in' and repairing ruptures are either consistently too passive or too intrusive, and are also likely to raise infants who are unable to co-regulate their emotional and physical arousal (Beebe *et al*, 2012).

Other important parenting tasks in the first few months of life include 'marked mirroring' (Fonagy *et al*, 1995). Mirroring occurs, for example, when a baby is aroused or upset, and a mother unconsciously provides a signal (verbal or facial) that resonates with what the baby is feeling. The caregiver 'marks' this by using exaggerated voice tones, or by opening his or her eyes wide so that the infant knows the emotion is understood but also manageable because the parent is not overwhelmed by the feeling (Gergely & Watson, 1996). (This type of interaction can also be seen at: https://aimh.org.uk/getting-to-know-your-baby/. The child then internalises what has been reflected back to him.

Thus, by mirroring the infant's emotional state the caregiver shows empathy, but also subtly ensures that the baby knows that it is his or her feelings that are being mirrored back (Fonagy *et al*, 1995). The parent thereby provides a response that is congruent with their infant's feelings, and that reflects back to him in ways that allow the infant to feel 'contained' by the parental response (see next paragraph for further explanation), not overwhelmed. For example, in one study 8-month-old infants were soothed after immunisation most effectively when their mothers rapidly reflected the upset but also added some other emotional display, such as smiling or questioning to 'dilute' the upset feeling (Fonagy *et al*, 1995). From this, infants learn about what they are experiencing, and that such experiences are not overwhelming. This process results in the infant building up what we call second or higher order representations of interactions that come to represent him or herself in interaction with other people. These serve as internal maps that guide future interactions.

Containment (Bion, 1962) refers to the way in which a parent takes on the powerful or overwhelming feelings of their baby, and by communicating with touch, gesture or speech, 'returns them' in a more manageable form. Winnicott (1960) described how parents 'hold in mind' the needs of the baby so the infant actually experiences a sense of security with someone who understands their needs, responds to distress signals, and contains their difficult feelings. Parents who are anxious, angry or preoccupied with their own emotional state may not be able to help the baby manage difficult feelings, leaving the infant overwhelmed.

Conclusion

A number of aspects of parenting are particularly important because they influence the baby's later capacity for affect regulation, and the rapidly developing soft wiring of the brain. As such, where they are functioning well, they enable the baby to successfully negotiate important developmental tasks. However, there are a range of factors that influence the way in which parents interact with their baby, and these reflect past (e.g. their own attachment and capacity for reflective functioning) and current life experiences (e.g. poverty, mental health problems etc). These are therefore the aspects of parenting that we should be aiming to support, and the next chapter examines some of the ways in which this might be done.

References

Allen JG and Fonagy P (2006) *Handbook of Mentalization-based Treatment*. Chichester: John Wiley.

Barlow J (2017) The Importance of the relationship with the unborn baby. In P Leach (ed) *Transforming Infant Wellbeing: Research, Policy and Practice for the First 1001 Critical Days* (pp37–46). London: Routledge.

Barrett H (2006) *Attachment and the Perils of Parenting: A commentary and critique*. London: NFPI.

Beebe B and Lachman F (2004) Co-constructing mother–infant distress in face-to-face interactions: contributions of microanalysis. *Zero to Three* **May**, 40–48.

Beebe B, Lachmann F, Markese S, Buck KA, Bahrick LE, Chen H, Cohen P, Andrews H, Feldstein S and Jaffe J (2012) On the origins of disorganized attachment and internal working models: paper ii. an empirical microanalysis of 4-month mother-infant interaction. *Psychoanalytic Dialogues* **22** (3) 352–374.

Berens A and Nelson C (2019) Neurobiology of fetal and infant development: implications for infant mental health. In C Zeanah (Ed) *Handbook of Infant Mental Health* (4th edition), pp41–62. New York: Guilford Press.

Bion W (1962) *Learning from Experience*. London: Heinemann.

Borelli JL, David DH, Crowley MJ and Mayes LC (2010) Links between disorganized attachment classification and clinical symptoms in school-aged children. Journal of Child and Family Studies 19 (3) 243–56.

Bowlby J (1969) *Attachment. Attachment and loss series (Vol I)*. New York: Basic Books.

Bowlby J (1988) *A Secure Base: Parent–child attachment and healthy human development*. London: Routledge.

De Wolff MS and van IJzendoorn MH (1997) Sensitivity and attachment: a meta-analysis on parental antecedents of infant attachment. *Child Development* **68** (4) 571–591.

Fearon RP, Bakermans-Kranenburg MJ, Van Ijzendoor MH, Lapsley AM and Roisman GI (2010) The significance of insecure attachment and disorganization in the development of children's externalizing behavior: a meta-analytic study. *Child Development* **81** (2) 435–56.

Finelli J, Zeanah CH Jr and Smyke A (2019) Attachment Disorders in Early Childhood. In C. Zeanah (Ed) *Handbook of Infant Mental Health* (4th edition), pp452–466. New York: Guilford Press.

Foley S, and Hughes C (2018) Great expectations? Do mothers' and fathers' prenatal thoughts and feelings about the infant predict parent-infant interaction quality? A meta-analytic review. *Developmental Review* **48** 40-54.

Fonagy P, Gergely G, Jurist E and Target M (2004) *Affect Regulation, Mentalization and the Development of the Self*. London: Karnac.

Fonagy P, Steele M, Steele H, Leigh T, Kennedy R, Mattoon G and Target M (1995) Attachment, the reflective self, and borderline states: the predictive specificity of the Adult Attachment Interview and pathological emotional development. In: S Goldberg, R Muir and J Kerr (Eds) *Attachment Theory: Social, Developmental and Clinical Perspectives*, pp233–278. New York: Analytic Press.

Gergely G and Watson J (1996) The social biofeedback model of parent-affect mirroring. *International Journal of Psycho-Analysis* **77** 1181–1212.

Gerhardt S (2015) *Why Love Matters: How affection shapes a baby's brain*. Hove: Routledge.

Glover V (2018) Stress in pregnancy can change fetal and child development. In P Leach (Ed) *Transforming Infant Wellbeing: Research, Policy and Practice for the First 1001 Critical Days*, pp98–106. London: Routledge.

Hatzis D, Dawe S, Harnett P and Barlow J (2017) Quality of caregiving in mothers with illicit substance use: a systematic review and meta-analysis. *Substance Abuse*, **11**. Available at: https://doi.org/10.1177/1178221817694038 (accessed 26 June 2019).

Huth-Bocks A, Levendosky A, Theran S and Bogat A (2004) The impact of domestic violence on mothers' prenatal representations of their infants. *Infant Mental Health Journal* **25** (2) 79–98.

Katz Il, Corlyon J, La Placa V and Hunter S (2007) *The Relationship Between Parenting and Poverty*. York: Joseph Rowntree Foundation.

Laulik S, Chau S, Browne K and Allam J (2013) The link between personality disorder and parenting behaviors: a systematic review. *Aggression and Violent Behavior* **18** (6) 644–655.

Meins E, Fernyhough C, deRosnay M, Arnott B, Leekam SR and Turner M (2012) Mind-mindedness as a multidimensional construct: appropriate and nonattuned mind-related comments independently predict infant–mother attachment in a socially diverse sample. *Infancy* **17** (4) 393–415.

Meins E, Fernyhough C, Wainwright R, das Gupta M, Fradley E and Tuckey M (2002) Maternal mind-mindedness and attachment security as predictors of theory of mind understanding. *Child Development* **73** (6) 1715–1726.

Murray L and Andrews L (2000) *The Social Baby*. London: The Children's Project.

Murray L, Fiori-Cowley A, Hooper R and Cooper P (1996) The impact of postnatal depression and associated adversity on early mother-infant interactions and later infant outcome. *Child Development* **67** 2512–2526.

Murray L, Halligan S and Cooper P (2019) Postnatal depression and child development. In C Zeanah (Ed) *Handbook of Infant Mental Health* (4th edition), pp172–186. New York: Guilford Press.

NICE Guidelines CG 192 (2014) (updated 2018) *Antenatal and Postnatal Mental Health: Clinical management and service guidance*. Available at https://www.nice.org.uk/guidance/cg192/ (accessed 26 June 2019).

Paulson J and Bazemore S (2010) Prenatal and postpartum depression in fathers and its association with maternal depression: a meta-analysis. *Journal of the American Medical Association* **303** 1961–196.

Rosenblum K, Dayton C and Muzik M (2019) Infant Social and Emotional Development in a Relational Context. In C. Zeanah (Ed) *Handbook of Infant Mental Health* (4th edition), pp95–119. Guilford: New York.

Schore AN (1994) *After Regulation and the Origin of the Self: The neurobiology of emotional development*. New Jersey: Erlbaum.

Slade A and Sadler L (2019) Pregnancy and Infant Mental Health. In C Zeanah (Ed) *Handbook of Infant Mental Health* (4th edition), pp25–40. Guilford: New York.

Sroufe LA (1995) *Emotional Development: The organization of emotional life in the early years*. Cambridge: Cambridge University Press.

Sroufe LA (2005) Attachment and development: a prospective, longitudinal study from birth to adulthood. *Attachment & Human Development* **7** (4) 349–367.

Steele H and Siever L (2010) An attachment perspective on borderline personality disorder: advances in gene-environment considerations. *Current Psychiatry Reports* **12** (1) 61–7.

Stein A, Woolley H, Cooper S, Winterbottom J, Fairburn CG and Cortina-Borja M (2006) Eating habits and attitudes among 10-year-old children of mothers with eating disorders: longitudinal study. *British Journal of Psychiatry* **189** 324–9.

Stern D (1985) *The Interpersonal World of the Infant: A view from psychoanalysis and developmental psychology*. New York: Basic Books.

Stover CS and Coates EE (2015) The relationship of reflective functioning to parent child interactions in a sample of fathers with concurrent intimate partner violence perpetration and substance abuse problems. *Journal of Family Violence* **31** (4) 433–442.

Strathearn L, Fonagy P, Amico J and Read Montague P (2009) Adult attachment predicts maternal brain and oxytocin response to infant cues. *Neuropsychopharmacology* **34** 2655–2666.

Theran SA, Levendosky AA, Bogat GA and Huth-Bocks AC (2005) Stability and change in mothers' internal representations of their infants over time. *Attachment and Human Development* **7** (3) 253–68.

Thompson S, Kiff C and McLaughlin K (2019) The Neurobiology of Stress and Adversity in Infancy. In C Zeanah (Ed) *Handbook of Infant Mental Health* (4th edition), pp81–94. Guilford: New York.

Winnicott D (1960) The theory of the parent–child relationship. *International Journal of Psychoanalysis* **41** 585–595.

Chapter 6: Supporting Parenting During Infancy

Jane Barlow and Angela Underdown

Key learning points

■ A number of models of intervention have been developed to support positive parenting; these include universal provision for all parents, selective provision targeted at parents in need of further support and indicated models where problems are already present.

■ Such support has been shown to have benefits both for the individual parent and child and in terms of savings in later demands on health, social and criminal justice services.

■ Skilling up of the workforce to enable them to provide these different levels of support should involve the development of observational skills in terms of parent-infant interaction, and ability to deliver standardised interventions that are explicitly aimed at improving the infant relationship.

Keywords
Parenting support; attachment; observational and intervention skills

Introduction

The preceding chapter showed that warm, sensitive relationships are a prerequisite for the infant's healthy emotional development. How then do we ensure that parents' roles are acknowledged, understood and properly supported? This chapter starts by examining the different levels of support that can be provided to parents of infants, and goes on to examine the ways in which the early years and primary care workforce can be 'skilled up' in terms of both observational and intervention practices, to work most effectively with this group of parents. It will be suggested that this work involves a range of professionals who can recognise the importance of early relationships, understand how current stresses and the 'ghosts from the nursery' may impact on caregiving, and who have the skills to support all parents, including identifying and intervening with parents experiencing significant problems.

Intervening to support parenting

Three levels of provision are available in terms of intervening to support parenting during infancy – universal, selective and indicated. A universal model consists of the provision of support to all parents, irrespective of need; midwifery and health visiting services are, for example, provided on a universal basis.

A selective model of provision consists of services that are provided to parents who are at increased risk as a result, for example, of the fact that they live in socioeconomically deprived parts of the country. The Family Nurse partnership programme is an example of this form of provision in the UK.

Indicated models of provision consist of interventions or services that are provided to parents who are experiencing difficulties such as problems with bonding, severe postnatal depression or other mental health problems, or where there are child protection concerns. There is a range of specialist services of this nature that are provided to a small number of parents and babies experiencing such difficulties.

Progressive universalism

In order to be able to offer early support that is appropriately targeted in terms of the level of need, it is necessary to identify when parents and infants are experiencing difficulties. The concept of progressive universalism (HM Treasury & DfES, 2007) was developed to define a model in which some level of support is available to all families (i.e. universal), but more support is provided to those who need it most (selective or indicated). One of the key features of progressive universalism, in addition to its recognition of the importance of prevention and of early intervention, is the possibility of using the universal service component to identify families who are in need of more intensive support.

Working with parents of infants

This section describes some of the promising methods of working to support parents of infants, focusing in particular on models that support the parent to provide the type of care that promotes the development of a secure attachment in the infant. The section is organised in terms of the different levels of provision described above, and we look at what programmes are available at each of the different levels.

Universal support

A number of promising universal group-based **preparation for parenthood programmes** have been developed in the UK; these are, typically, delivered during the perinatal period for two hours weekly over 8-9 weeks, and are provided by qualified professionals. For example, The Solihull five-week 'Journey to Parenthood' programme focuses on 'understanding pregnancy, labour, birth and your baby'; it combines traditional antenatal information with helping to prepare families to have a relationship with their baby (https://solihullapproachparenting. com/product/antenatal-journey-to-parenthood-resource-pack/).

Similarly, the Family Links 'Welcome to the World' programme involves an eight-week group for expectant couples, delivered weekly from around 22 weeks of pregnancy. Topics include empathy and loving attentiveness, infant brain development, healthy choices, managing stress and promoting self-esteem and confidence, and effective communication (https://familylinks.org.uk/what-we-do#welcome-to-the-world). Both of these courses have online materials available, and preliminary evaluation (i.e. using pre- and post-tests only) suggests a range of potential benefits, including the relationship with the developing baby.

The identification of parents in need of additional support is ideally done through the use of routine service delivery (i.e. progressive universalism, described in the section on the previous page). For example, ante and postnatal promotional interviews, are recommended as part of the Healthy Child Programme (Shribman & Billingham, 2009), and involve a visit by the health visitor at 28 weeks antenatal and eight weeks postnatal. 'Promotional guides' are used to help the practitioner to explore key areas, and to support the things that are going well, and to identify things that may not be going so well.

Mariam

During a 28-week antenatal visit to Mariam, a prospective mother with a history of an eating disorder, the health visitor discovered that Mariam didn't like to touch her bump or think about the baby. Through conversation, it emerged that she felt that although she would look after her baby, she didn't think that she could love him. This gave the health visitor the opportunity to provide Mariam with some additional support to help her to address the physical and emotional changes that were taking place in pregnancy.

The postnatal visit can be used to explore how the birth went, the changing roles within the family, the emotional adjustment of both parents (i.e. whether they are anxious and/or depressed), and the interaction between the parents and the baby. This provides the health visitor with the opportunity to deliver appropriate additional support (see next section).

In terms of supporting parents at a universal level, practitioners can use routine exchanges to model good practice and to share knowledge. Practices that can be easily recommended during routine exchanges between professional and parent include the use of infant carriers (Anisfeld *et al*, 1990) and helping parents to introduce books, songs and music (PEEP) (Street, 2006). There is also a growing number of media-based interventions that can assist professionals to share knowledge of this sort. For example, *Baby Express* is a newsletter that has been shown to improve some aspects of early parenting (e.g. perceived hassles, appropriate expectations) that are associated with attachment security. Other media-based resources available include apps, such as Baby Buddy, and combined apps and online resources, such as *Getting to Know Your Baby* (https://aimh. org.uk/getting-to-know-your-baby/). Although the evidence is still limited, the potential of this approach is considerable given its low cost and universality.

Helping parents to recognise their baby's cues and signals, whether they are very subtle behavioural cues such as avoidance of eye contact or more obvious cues such as arching of the back and screaming, can also be done using tools such as the Brazelton Newborn Behavioural Observations (NBO) system and Neonatal Behavioral Assessment Scale (NBAS) (https://www.brazeltontouchpoints.org/ offerings/nbo-and-nbas/). This approach is also aimed at helping parents to recognise their baby's areas of strength and to support the areas in which he or she is less strong. Recent findings from a systematic review showed that the NBO was potentially more effective than the NBAS in improving sensitivity, although further research is still needed to evaluate its effectiveness with parents facing challenging circumstances (Barlow *et al*, 2018a).

Selective support

Selective support is typically provided using one of a number of formats – home visits or group-based programmes. For example a number of selective group-based 'preparation for parenthood' programmes are now available, such as Mellow Mums and Mellow Dads (https://www.mellowparenting.org/our-programmes/ mellow-mums/) and Baby Steps (https://learning.nspcc.org.uk/services-children-families/baby-steps/). 'Baby Steps' (NSPCC) is an interactive group programme based on theory and research into the transition to parenthood and infant mental health for use with targeted groups of parents facing increased challenges, and in some areas of socioeconomic disadvantage.

Example – Baby Steps

Baby Steps starts with a home visit in the seventh month of pregnancy followed by six weekly group sessions before the baby is born. After the baby is born, the family is visited again at home, and a video of interaction is taken, if parents wish, and a reflective review is offered so parents can identify their baby's cues; this is followed by three more group sessions. Groups are led by a practitioner from health and one from children's services (e.g. health visitor or midwife and a family support worker). The interactive sessions include films, group discussions and creative activities designed to build confidence and communication skills. There is a strong focus on building relationships between couples and between parents and their babies (Underdown, 2017). Baby Steps covers six themes:

- The development of my/our unborn baby.
- Changes for me and us.
- My/our health and wellbeing.
- Giving birth and meeting my/our baby.
- Caring for my/our baby.
- Who is there for us? – people and services.

Early evaluation shows promising outcomes in terms of quality of the interaction with the child, and a number of aspects of parental functioning including anxiety and depression, although the intervention has not yet been subject to evaluation using a random controlled trial.

In-vivo techniques

Some of the best methods available for supporting parents at risk of poor parenting or who may be experiencing problems such as postnatal depression, use techniques that involve working directly with the mother and baby, and include infant massage and the use of video feedback. For example, teaching groups of parents who are experiencing distress (e.g. postnatal depression) how to use infant massage may help an intrusive mother to become more sensitive, or may help an irritable baby to relax and sleep thereby facilitating more relaxed and sensitive parenting (Galanakis et al, 2015). Similarly, video feedback involves a professional videotaping up to 10 minutes of interaction between the carer and baby/child, returning subsequently to examine the tape with the parent, and using the videotape to point out examples of positive parent-infant interaction. Standardised versions of such programmes, such as VIPP-SD, also include sessions that focus on the delivery of sensitive discipline (e.g. Van Zeijl et al, 2006). The research suggests that these can improve the sensitivity of diverse groups of parents in terms of their interaction with the baby (O'Hara et al, forthcoming).

Home visiting programmes

Home visiting programmes are also sometimes used with parents who are at risk of poor outcomes. Core features of the many available home visiting programmes are an intensive series of home visits beginning prenatally (e.g. Family Nurse Partnership) or soon after the child's birth (e.g. Family Action) and continuing during the child's first two years of life. They are typically delivered by specially trained personnel – usually professionals but sometimes volunteers – who provide information, support and training regarding child health, development, and care. Programmes vary in terms of the issues they address, and common themes include early infant care, infant health and development, and parenting skills, but they may also include maternal health and wellbeing, diet, smoking, drug/alcohol use, exercise, transition to parenthood, and the parent's relationship with their partner. Overall, the programmes place a strong emphasis on building good relationships within the family, tailoring the intervention to the needs of the family, and developing the parents' social support network. Numerous systematic reviews have summarised the available evidence on the effectiveness of home visiting programmes, most of which conclude overall that the impact of home visiting is variable, with some programmes showing no evidence of effectiveness, and other programmes being effective for some outcomes (see https://pediatrics. aappublications.org/content/101/3/486). The Nurse Family Partnership programme is possibly one of the best-evidenced programmes to date (Olds *et al*, 1998; Olds, 2005), and although there was limited evidence effectiveness in the UK (https://www.cardiff.ac.uk/centre-for-trials-research/research/studies-and-trials/view/building-blocks), a programme of adaptation to rapidly adapt, test and improve the Family Nurse Partnership programme in England is currently being undertaken in 20 local authority areas (https://fnp.nhs.uk/fnp-next-steps/adapt/).

Indicated support

Families in need of indicated level support may be experiencing a range of problems and be in need of referral to perinatal mental health teams, drug and alcohol workers, or teams working with women experiencing domestic violence. They may also need to be referred to children's social care.

Specialist practitioners may also be able to work 'dyadically' with the parent and baby together. Recent programmes that have been developed are based on research about the importance of the mother's capacity for mentalisation and involve a holistic approach. 'Minding the Baby' is a US interdisciplinary community-based programme that uses specially-trained nurses and social workers to visit high-risk pregnant women over a two-year period. While intensive support is offered in all areas – such as relationship difficulties, domestic violence, budgeting etc – the focus is on the development of mentalisation (Sadler *et al*, 2006; 2013), although there is currently limited evidence of its effectiveness in the UK (NSPCC, forthcoming).

Parent under Pressure (PUP) is another programme that is delivered on a one-to-one basis in the home by specially trained practitioners. The PUP programme provides expertise in the delivery of 20 modules that can be used selectively as appropriate by the practitioner. For example:

- Module 6: 'Connecting with Your Baby or Child' provides structure and a series of activities whereby a parent is able to reflect on their own relational experience with their infant or child. There is an emphasis on learning their baby's language and 'mindful play', in which a parent is taught to use mindfulness constructs to observe, describe and participate during play and at special times.

- Module 4: 'How to Manage Your Emotions Under Pressure – Increasing Mindful Awareness' provides opportunities for parents to reflect on their ability to manage mood and impulsive behaviours through the incorporation of mindfulness-based strategies.

PUP has been shown to be effective in reducing child abuse potential and improving a number of aspects of parental functioning (Barlow *et al*, 2018b). It may also be helpful to refer the parent to other specialist services such as parent-child psychotherapy, which one systematic review showed can improve attachment security although overall there was no evidence of its benefits in terms of other outcomes, and no evidence to show that it is more effective than other types of treatment for parents and infants (Barlow *et al* 2015). Despite the limited evidence, parent-infant/child psychotherapy is now being used to support a wide range of parent-infant problems, ranging from attachment difficulties to infant feeding problems and faltering growth, to hostility toward the infant. It is also being used to support the parenting of infants on the child protection register. This approach is underpinned by the belief that once the mother has been helped to 'recognise the ghosts in the nursery' and to link them to her own history and present, changes to the mother's representational world can take place, facilitating new paths for growth and development for both mother and infant. Much more recently this representational approach has been combined with a more behavioural approach (see box overleaf).

> ## Watch, Wait and Wonder
>
> 'Watch, Wait and Wonder' is an 'infant-led' parent-infant psychotherapy that involves the mother spending time observing her infant's self-initiated activity, accepting the infant's spontaneous and undirected behaviour, and being physically accessible to the infant. The mother then discusses her experiences of the infant-led play with the therapist with a view to examining the mother's internal working models of herself in relation to her infant (Cohen *et al*, 1999).

Developing new skills

The final section of this chapter describes some of the skills that are required by core groups of practitioners to enable them to work effectively with parents of new babies. In the UK there are a range of highly accessible and affordable training programmes available, and these should be undertaken as part of a practitioners continuing professional development (CPD).

Two key types of training are available. First, there are a number of online courses now available to enable practitioners to get a better understanding of some of the core issues related to infant mental health. These include:

- Babies in Mind (https://www.futurelearn.com/courses/babies-in-mind/0/steps/7781), a four-week online course that is free and can be done in the participants' own time), and

- Infant Mental Health Online (IMHOL) (https://warwick.ac.uk/fac/sci/med/about/centres/wifwu/training/), which is a 12-week online course run by Warwick Infant and Family Wellbeing Unit.

In addition to these, there are a range of courses that will provide practitioners with up-to-date and evidence-based observational and intervention skills (see overleaf).

Core skills

If we are to achieve the goal of helping parents to promote the type of care during the early years that will help the baby to develop regulatory capacities that we now recognise to be central to effective later functioning (including the management of anger and stress) (Schore, 2003), we need to provide core groups of professionals with the expertise to work in partnership with families; this involves a range of skills in terms of sensitivity and communication. The **Family Partnership Model** is one of a number of UK-based training programmes, and is 'based upon an explicit model of the helping process that demonstrates the specific helper qualities and skills, which enable parents and families to overcome their difficulties, build strengths and resilience and fulfil their goals more effectively' (http://www.cpcs.org.uk/index.php?page=about-family-partnership-model).

The **Solihull Approach** is another model that provides practitioners with core skills to enable them to work with families through the use of understanding about 'containment', 'reciprocity' and 'behavioural management' to enable them to address a wide range of problems that parents experience during the first two years of their child's life, many of which focus on difficulties in relation to infant regulation (i.e. eating and sleeping) (https://solihullapproachparenting.com).

Motivational interviewing is another technique that can be used to enable practitioners to work effectively with parents by providing them with the fundamental clinical skills to work in partnership with parents to bring about change (https://www.apt.ac/motivational-interviewing-training-courses.html).

Observational skills

Professionals should also have the observational skills necessary to recognise when things are not going well between a mother and baby. This means being able to observe interactions between a mother and her baby and assess from them how well the relationship is developing. Training in the use of the **PIIOS (Parent-Infant Interaction Observation Scale)** (https://warwick.ac.uk/fac/sci/med/study/cpd/cpd/piios/), a method of coding a brief period of mother-infant interaction (three minutes of normal play), could for example, provide professionals with the skills to identify when mothers are 'intrusive' in their interactions with their baby, or when they are 'passive'. This training also provides practitioners with the skills to feed back the findings to the parent in a positive manner (i.e. identifying things that are going well), and also providing parents with an opportunity to identify how they would like things to be different (Svanberg *et al*, 2013). Where parents and infants are experiencing greater difficulties in establishing healthy interactions – for example, where the passivity is bordering on neglect or where the intrusiveness has elements of aggression directed at the baby – the skills of specialist mental health professionals, such as parent-infant psychotherapists (see overleaf), and sometimes child protection services, may be required.

In addition to being able to observe the interaction, professionals need the skills to be able to identify the parents to whom they can provide intervention (i.e. parents experiencing minor difficulties), and to know the specialist services to which to refer other families.

Intervention skills

In the UK there is a range of highly accessible and affordable training programmes available, and these should be undertaken as part of practitioners' continuing professional development (CPD). The **Infant Mental Health Competencies Framework (IMHCF)** (https://aimh.org.uk/infant-mental-health-competencies-framework/) should be used by all practitioners who are working with parents during the perinatal period to enable them to identify their strengths, and the areas in which they need further training. In addition, practitioners need further training in some of the methods of working that were described earlier. For example, video interaction guidance training is an inexpensive and accessible model of training in the UK (https://wwww.videointeractionguidance.net/). Similarly, the NBO (https://mellowparenting.org/our-training/) and group-based programmes such as Mellow Babies (https://www.mellowparenting.org/our-training/) and Parents Under Pressure (http://www.pupprogram.net.au) training can be easily accessed as part of continuing professional development.

Practitioners delivering these programmes should be in receipt of supervision to enable them to be reflective practitioners, and to address the complex issues that may arise when delivering such programmes. The delivery of such programmes should also involve an assessment as to whether the intervention has produced change using one of the many available standardised parent-report measures. For example, evaluation of infant massage for parents who are depressed and experiencing interaction problems should involve the use of the EPDS (https://www.fresno.ucsf.edu/pediatrics/downloads/edinburghscale.pdf) and the MORS (Mother-Object Relations Scale) (https://www.bristol.ac.uk/media-library/sites/sps/documents/c-change/mors-sf.pdf).

Conclusion

Supporting parenting during the perinatal period involves recognising that the first few years of life are particularly important if a baby is to develop their true potential. There are a range of informal ways in which early years and primary care professionals can do this as part of their daily interactions with parents. They can also use CPD to acquire new skills in some of the evidence-based methods of working to support families that have been described in this chapter.

References

Anisfeld E, Casper V, Nozyce M (1990) Does infant carrying promote attachment? An experimental study of the effects of increased physical contact on the development of attachment. *Child Development* **61** 1617–1627.

Barlow J, Bennett C, Midgley N, Larkin SK, Wei Y (2015) Parent-infant psychotherapy for improving parental and infant mental health. Cochrane Database of Systematic Reviews 1.Barlow J, Parsons J and Stewart-Brown S (2005) Systematic review of the effectiveness of group-based parenting programmes for infants and toddlers. *Child: Care, Health and Development* **31** (1) 33–42.

Barlow J, Herath NINS, Bartram Torrance C, Bennett C, Wei Y (2018a) The Neonatal Behavioral Assessment Scale (NBAS) and Newborn Behavioral Observations (NBO) system for supporting caregivers and improving outcomes in caregivers and their infants. *Cochrane Database of Systematic Reviews* **3**. Available online at: CD011754. DOI: 10.1002/14651858.CD011754.pub2. (accessed 26 June 2019).

Barlow J, Sembi S, Parsons H, Kim S, Petrou S, Harnett P and Dawe S (2018b) A randomized controlled trial and economic evaluation of the Parents Under Pressure program for parents in substance abuse treatment. *Drug and Alcohol Dependence* **194** 184–194.

Brazelton TB and Nugent JK (1995) *Neonatal Behavioral Assessment Scale*. Cambridge: Cambridge University Press.

Cohen NJ, Lojkasek M, Muir E, Muir R and Parker CJ (2002) Six-month follow-up of two mother–infant psychotherapies: convergence of therapeutic outcomes. *Infant Mental Health Journal* **23** 361–380.

Cohen NJ, Muir E, Lojkasek M, Muir R, Parker CJ, Barwick M and Brown M (1999) Watch, wait and wonder: testing the effectiveness of a new approach to mother–infant psychotherapy. *Infant Mental Health Journal* **20** 429–451.

Douglas H and Ginty M (2001) The Solihull approach: evaluation of changes in the practice of health visitors. *Community Practitioner* **74** 222–224.

Feinberg ME and Kan ML (2008) Establishing family foundations: impact of a transition to parenting program on co-parenting, depression, parent-child relationship, and infant regulation. *Journal of Family Psychology* **22** 253–263.

Fraiberg S (1980) *Clinical Studies in Infant Mental Health*. New York: Basic Books.

Fraiberg S, Adelson E and Shapiro V (2004) Ghosts in the nursery: a psychoanalytic approach to the problems of impaired infant–mother relationships. Cited in: J Raphael-Leff (ed) *Parent–infant psychodynamics*. London: Whurr.

Galanakis M, Ntaouti E, Tsitsanis G and Chrousos G (2015) The effects of infant massage on maternal distress: a systematic review. *Psychology* **06** (16) 2091–2097.

HM Treasury and Department for Education and Skills (2007) *Aiming High for Children: Supporting families*. London: The Stationery Office. Available at: https://dera.ioe.ac.uk/7755/1/PU188.pdf (accessed 26 June 2019).

O'Hara L, Barlow J, Livingstone N and Macdonald G (forthcoming) Video feedback for improving parental sensitivity and attachment. *Cochrane Database of Systematic Reviews* **9**. Available at: https://www.cochrane.org/CD012348/BEHAV_video-feedback-improving-parental-sensitivity-and-attachment (accessed 26 June 2019).

Olds D (2005) The nurse–family partnership: foundations in attachment theory and epidemiology. Cited in: L Berlin, Y Ziv, L Amaya-Jackson and M Greenberg (eds) *Enhancing Early Attachments: Theory, research, intervention and policy*. New York: Guilford Press.

Olds D, Eckenrode J, Henderson C Jr, Kitzman H, Luckey D, Pettitt L, Sidora K, Morris P and Powers J (1998) Long-term effects of nurse home visitations on children's criminal and anti-social behaviour: 15 year follow-up of randomised trial. *Journal of the American Medical Association* **280** 1238–1244.

Sadler LS, Slade A, Close N, Webb DL, Simpson T, Fennie K and Linda Mayes LC (2013) Minding the baby: enhancing reflectiveness to improve early health and relationship outcomes in an interdisciplinary home visiting program. *Infant Mental Health Journal* **34** (5) 391–405.

Sadler LS, Slade A and Mayes LC (2006) Minding the baby: a mentalization based parenting program. In: P Fonagy and J Allen (eds) *Handbook of Mentalization-based Treatment*. Chichester: Wiley.

Schore AN (2003) *Affect Dysregulation and Disorders of the Self*. New York: WW Norton.

Shribman S and Billingham K (2009) *Healthy Child Programme – Pregnancy and the first five years*. London: Department of Health. Available at: https://assets.publishing.service.gov.uk/government/uploads/system/uploads/attachment_data/file/167998/Health_Child_Programme.pdf Accessed 26 June 2019.

Street A (2006) *The role of singing within mother–infant interactions*. Unpublished PhD thesis. London: Roehampton University.

Svanberg PO, Barlow J and Tigbe W (2013) The effectiveness of training in the Parent-Infant Interaction Observation Scale for health visitors. *Journal of Health Visiting* **1** (3) 162–166.

Underdown A (2017) Baby Steps: a relationship-based perinatal group programme. In: M Celebi (Ed) *Weaving the Cradle. Facilitating Groups to Promote Attunement and Bonding between Parents, their Babies and Toddlers*, (pp 156–167). London: Singing Dragon.

Van Zeijl J, Mesman J, Van IJzendoorn MH, Bakermans-Kranenburg MJ, Juffer F, Stolk MN, Koot HM and Alink LR (2006) Attachment-based intervention for enhancing sensitive discipline in mothers of 1- to 3-year-old children at risk for externalizing behavior problems: a randomized controlled trial. *Journal of Consulting and Clinical Psychology* **74** (6) 994–1005.

Chapter 7: Adversity and Trauma-Informed Practice (ATIP) for Children and Young People

Marc Bush

Key learning points

- Adverse childhood experiences (ACEs) are highly stressful, and potentially traumatic, events or situations that occur during childhood and/or adolescence.

- Not all CYP who face childhood adversity go on to develop trauma-related symptoms, or wider mental health problems.

- Childhood adversity and trauma impacts a CYP's development, their relationships with others, and increase the risk of engaging in health-harming behaviours, and experiencing poorer mental and physical health outcomes in adulthood.

- These experiences directly affect the CYP and their environment, and require significant social, emotional, neurobiological, psychological or behavioural adaptation.

- Adaptations are CYP's attempts to survive in their immediate environment, find ways of mitigating or tolerating the adversity by using the resources available to them, establish a sense of safety or control and make sense of the experiences they have had.

- Personal, structural and environmental factors can help to protect against adverse outcomes, and professionals can support CYP best by becoming adversity and trauma-informed. This includes reflecting on the six principles of 'adversity and trauma-informed care' (ATIC) and embedding them into their everyday practice.

Keywords
Adverse childhood experiences (ACEs); adversity; trauma

Introduction

We all face emotionally distressing and challenging situations during our childhood and adolescence, however for some people the very environments they grow up in and the people they relate to are extremely adverse to their mental health and wellbeing. These adverse experiences have a potentially traumatic and lifelong impact. This chapter explores the impact of adversity and trauma on a child and young person's (CYP) social, emotional, psychological and interpersonal development, as well as their mental health. It provides an alternative way of understanding trauma-related behaviours that professionals will be confronted with, and advocates for an approach that aims to establish safety and build the resilience of CYP through the six principles of adversity and trauma-informed care (ATIC).

The six principles of adversity and trauma-informed practice (ATIP)

1. Adverse childhood experiences (ACEs)

Adverse childhood experiences (ACEs) are defined as highly stressful, and potentially traumatic, events or situations that occur during childhood and/ or adolescence. It can be the experience of a single event, or prolonged threats to, and breaches of, the CYP's safety, security, trust or bodily integrity (Bush, 2018). These ACEs are exacerbated by wider social conditions and circumstances that create inequalities in the ways that CYP live, and are treated by those around them (WHO & CGF, 2014). These inequalities include levels of material deprivation or child poverty and institutional prejudice in state and support services (Bellis *et al*, 2014c; McLaughlin, 2017; Ayre, 2016).

ACEs are more common than you might think. Almost half of all adults living in the UK report experiencing at least one form of adversity in their childhood or adolescence (Bellis *et al*, 2014a; Bellis *et al*, 2016). This broadly reflects the picture of childhood adversity in other developed countries (Kessler & McLaughlin, 2010; McLaughlin *et al*, 2012).

A wide range of experiences can be described as adverse, including: maltreatment, violence and coercion, inhuman treatment, prejudice, household or family adversity, adjustment, adult responsibilities, bereavement and survivorship.

In reality, there are significant overlaps in people's experiences of these adversities. For example, a study from England suggests that 16% of adults experience two or three ACEs, and almost 1 in 10 experience four or more (Bellis *et al*, 2014a). This means that many children experience the cumulative impact from different forms of ACEs on their health and wellbeing outcomes in adolescence and adulthood (Schilling *et al*, 2008; NCI, 2017).

2. Experiencing trauma

The terms 'adversity' and 'trauma' are often used interchangeably, however, there are subtle differences between the two. Whilst adversity describes the situation and experience that a person has been confronted with, trauma refers more commonly to the impact it has on their mental health. More specifically, experiences of adversity can result in a number of different forms of emotional distress and mental health conditions, some of which are specifically related to traumatic stress. This can involve the diagnosis of post traumatic stress disorder (PTSD) (APA, 2013; WHO, 2016), and more recently van der Kolk and colleagues (2005) proposed the introduction of a new classification of 'developmental trauma disorder' (DTD), which would specifically recognise trauma resulting from interpersonal and developmental trauma.

While all CYP will experience some form of emotional distress, and neurobiological, neuroceptive and neurocognitive changes as a result of the adversity, not all of these will result in enduring mental health conditions, nor will they necessarily lead to a trauma-related diagnosis. A recent study found that almost a third of CYP have been exposed to trauma by the age of 18 years, with one in 13 having experiences that would meet the thresholds for PTSD (Lewis *et al*, 2019).

As professionals we need to be well attuned and sensitive to presenting patterns of behaviour, relationships or thought that might indicate an emerging trauma-related response and the presence of a current or historic adversity, whether diagnosed or not. McCrory and colleagues have found common neurocognitive alterations in adults who have experienced adversity (whether or not they have a diagnosed mental health condition), and suggested that they can be used to predict future psychiatric symptoms and mental health problems (McCrory *et al*, 2017). As a result, they propose the idea of 'latent vulnerability', arguing that more attention needs to be given to pre and sub-clinical symptoms of mental ill health resulting from adversity (McCrory & Viding, 2015).

In contrast, some CYP find ways of surviving and overcoming the adversity they have faced by drawing on the internal or external resources and support available to them. In this way it does not have a substantive or long-term impact on their everyday life, relationships with others or social functioning. However, around one in three CYP who have a traumatic experience will go on to develop symptoms that could lead to a traumatic stress-related psychiatric diagnosis.

(For more information visit: http://www.nhs.uk/conditions/post-traumatic-stress-disorder/pages/introduction.aspx)

Trauma-related symptoms that you may see amongst CYP could include:
- intrusive memories or flashbacks to traumatic experience(s)
- symbolic and nonverbal enactment of traumatic experiences or sensations through the use of play or in relationships with significant others
- distressing dreams and reoccurring night terrors where features of the dream relate to the traumatic experience
- avoiding situations, or people in authority, who trigger memories of these traumatic experiences
- intense feelings of detachment, disassociation or estrangement from others
- perceiving threats from those in authority and an exaggerated suspicion about the motives or intentions of those in authority who offer support
- becoming quickly irritable or angry towards people or objects with little provocation
- becoming engaged in reckless, risk-inducing or self-destructive behaviours.

For example, a CYP might respond to trauma with disassociation, by which a CYP might try to separate their emotions from the overwhelming feelings of distress they experienced at the time of the adversity. These CYP may feel unconnected with their body or a specific body region or area associated with the (for example sexual) trauma. They may also feel an emotional numbness and significant cognitive fatigue if they try to recall or remember anything related to the experience (Bremner, 2006) – this is also known as being in a state of hypoarousal. Sometimes, it seems as if the child has spaced out or is emotionally absent (Minton *et al*, 2006). Some of these CYP are consequently unable to experience pleasure as a result of activities that would usually be pleasurable, such as music, social interaction or sexual encounters (Frewen *et al*, 2012; DePierro *et al*, 2014).

3. Impact on development, health and mental health

Experiencing childhood adversity fundamentally alters the course of a CYP's development and has a substantive impact across the lifecourse (Bellis *et al*, 2014a; 2014b). These experiences increase the risk of poorer physical (Mental Health Taskforce and NHS England, 2016) and mental health outcomes in adolescence and adulthood (Centre for Public Health and Public Health Wales, 2015; Brown, 2009; Ford, 2010). One major US study uncovered a strong relationship between ACEs and risk factors for ill health and poor wellbeing. (Further information on the Adverse Childhood Experiences (ACEs) studies coordinated by the Centers for Disease Control and Prevention is available at: http://www.cdc.gov/violenceprevention/acestudy/index.html). Research in England, Wales and Scotland replicated these findings and suggest that ACEs are strongly associated with adverse behavioural, health and social outcomes in childhood, adolescence, adulthood and later life (Bellis *et al*, 2015; Bellis *et al*, 2016; Couper & Mackie, 2016; Smith *et al*, 2016).

At least one in three diagnosed mental health conditions in adulthood are known to directly relate to adverse childhood experiences that have subsequently impacted on their psychological development and wellbeing (Kessler, 2010). Furthermore, childhood adversity is accompanied by lower levels of mental wellbeing and life satisfaction in adolescence and adulthood (Hughes, 2016), as well as an increased risk of enduring mental health problems; including experiencing psychosis (Bebbington, 2011; Larkin & Read, 2008; Varese, 2012). Subsequently, CYP who have faced adversity are more likely to use psychiatric medicines that have an additional adverse impact on their physical health in the longer term (Anda, 2007).

Furthermore, experience of adversity and trauma is associated with higher rates of avoidable death from natural causes; including from the leading causes of early adult deaths, such as heart disease, respiratory disease and cancer (Bellis *et al*, 2014a; Felitti *et al*, 1998). Kelly-Irving *et al* (2013) found women who had experienced one adversity had a 66% increased risk of premature death, and those who had experienced two or more adversities had an 80% increased risk compared to their peers. In contrast, men who had faced two or more adversities in childhood have a 57% increased risk of early death compared to their peers (Kelly-Irving *et al*, 2013).

YoungMinds updated an international model to describe the impacts of adversity and trauma to young people's mental and physical health over their lifetime (Bush, 2018).

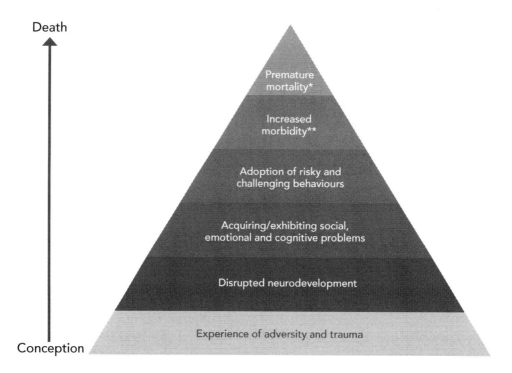

Figure 7.1: The impact of adversity and trauma on CYP

* Dying earlier than would otherwise be expected
** Living with physical and/or mental ill health

It is important to remember that the relationships between experiences of adversity and mental health outcomes are very complex (Hambrick et al, 2018). As professionals, we should never reduce a child to the number of ACEs they have had, nor should we believe that all CYP are fated to poor mental health over their lifetime (Science and Technology Committee, 2018). We continue to develop throughout our lives, and by building healthy, enriching, nurturing, growthful, and trusted relationships and environments, we can move beyond adversity and trauma (Herman, 2015 [1992]; Education Scotland, 2018; Sweeney & Taggart, 2018).

4. Understanding adversity and trauma-related behaviour

In the face of adversity, many CYP adopt risky behaviour or behaviours that challenge professionals working with them i.e. highly sexualised behaviours and the use of substances. For example, the study of ACEs in England found that those adults who had experienced four or more adversities in their childhood, were twice more likely to binge drink, and 11 times more likely to have gone on to use illicit drugs (Bellis *et al*, 2014a). The chances of developing a dependence on substances doubles if a CYP has also experienced sexual abuse (Simpson & Miller, 2002) or other forms of violence (Douglas *et al*, 2010).

CYP who have had adverse experiences can frequently exhibit self-destructive and self-defeating behaviours. These are attempts by the CYP to make sense of their experiences (Singer *et al*, 1995) and cope with trauma they have acquired, and is a way of communicating something that is not yet conscious, or that perhaps cannot yet be verbalised (Nicholson *et al*, 2010). Other behavioural responses might include CYP attempting to self-calm and self-soothe, but in a self-harming or regressive way (Greenwald, 2015). This might include violent rocking, chanting, scratching their face or body or biting themselves, or banging their hands against walls or objects. These behaviours can quickly become labelled as problematic by professionals and families. Some are problematically seen as signs of being 'anti-social', having a problem with one's 'conduct', and being oppositional, defiant or disruptive towards a parent, a carer or authority figure (i.e. a parent, teacher, doctor or social worker).

CYP who engage in significant risk-taking should be seen as both finding ways to make sense of adversity and trauma they have experienced, as well as avoiding the need to address and resolve the trauma. Such children are at additional risk of being labelled as having a clinical condition (such as 'oppositional/defiant disorder', 'hyperactivity' and 'conduct disorder'), rather than having the adversity and trauma-related symptoms identified (Greenwald, 2015). Additionally, these children are more likely to be known to the authorities, because they are engaging in alienating, anti-social or criminal behaviour. (For wider description of groups of children who may be known to authorities because of an additional risk of harm, see HM Government, 2015.)

As previously mentioned, experiences of adversity and trauma directly affect the CYP and their environment, and require significant social, emotional, neurobiological, psychological or behavioural adaptation. We can best understand these adaptations to be people's attempts to:

■ survive in their immediate environment

■ find ways of mitigating or tolerating the adversity by using the resources available to them

■ establish a sense of safety or control

■ make sense of the experiences they have had.

As such, these behaviours and ways of thinking should be regarded as creative adaptations and adjustments that the CYP is using to survive in an adverse environment. It is very difficult to predict what a CYP's response to adversity and trauma might be (reflected in the wide range of trauma-stress symptoms, for example), and whether the behaviours and ways of thinking that they adopt will successfully mitigate the impact of the adversity they face.

5. Adversity and trauma-informed practice (ATIP)

It is clear that we need to move beyond a purely diagnostic model of adversity and trauma, and instead place greater emphasis on creating safe environments and practices, building individual resources and wider resiliency, as well as restoring connection to supportive and safe communities (Herman, 2015 [1992]; Bloom, 2013).

Professor Peter Fonagy (2018) proposes that we see this resilience as an 'outcome of the quality of the social network surrounding the child and the child's capacity to access that network', rather than a quality or characteristic of the individual child. From this standpoint, he makes a compelling case to focus on the 'systems of care' in the social environment around the CYP, as well as providing the specialist support a CYP will need to make sense of their trauma.

At an individual level, building resilience allows the CYP to protect the developing brain and body from adverse neurobiological and neurocognitive changes. At a social level, it ensures the CYP can re-establish the safety, connection and support they will require to recover from the adverse experience(s), and to mitigate the feelings of isolation, hopelessness and meaninglessness that can arise from adversity and trauma. Reflecting this, research suggests that the following can protect against adverse outcomes or mitigate their onset, intensity and escalation:

- positive and supportive family environments
- safe and mutual relationships with peers
- access to a wider supportive and understanding community
- ability to regulate emotions and manage emotional distress
- acquisition of practical problem-solving skills
- compassionate, attuned and supportive responses from professionals
- early intervention from support, therapeutic or safeguarding services
- trauma-informed policies and systems that addressing bullying, harassment or victimisation.

YoungMinds have synthesised existing principles of adversity and trauma-informed practice (ATIP), which actively promote this resilience. This new framework for services and professionals has been informed by the lived experience of CYP, and includes their own collective articulation of the principles (Bush, 2018).

Table 7.1: Putting adversity and trauma-informed approaches into practice. From Bush (2018).

| 1. Prepared | <ul><li>Creates and maintains a priority in addressing the causes and mental health consequences of childhood adversity and trauma. This includes having this priority embedded in local commissioning, service and transformation plans.</li><li>Analyses available data on prevalence, and possible local need, at both a pre-/sub-clinical and clinical level.</li><li>Anticipates mental health needs arising from childhood adversity and trauma, by embedding knowledge, expertise and informed interventions in local commissioning and service pathways.</li></ul> | 'When you notice, or I tell you that I need help, you should already know what the next step is – sometimes I feel like people are making it up as they go along.'

→ |

2. Aware	■ Ensures local agencies and partners have a good understanding of childhood adversity and trauma, and the associated symptoms and responses. ■ Has a common framework for identification and routine enquiry about adversity and trauma in childhood and adolescence. ■ Understands and responds to the cultural, identity and gendered contexts of the CYP and the community in which they live – including situations where a CYP continues to live in adverse circumstances.	'Don't label me with the experiences I've had – I'm not a label, I am me. Everyone's experiences are different, and it doesn't define who I am.' 'Recognise all of my needs – I don't think of my life as school, family, medication; all of the different parts of my life are connected, see me as a whole person.' 'Understand my behaviour – when I'm shouting, crying, hiding, stealing, hitting out at myself or others I'm just trying to make sense of everything I've gone through. I'm not 'wrong', 'damaged', 'mad' or 'bad'.'
3. Flexible	■ Provides stepped support to CYP who face adversity or trauma at both a pre- / sub-clinical and clinical level. ■ Provides models of care that enable alternative and more flexible forms of access and engagement (i.e. through street triage). ■ Provides targeted models of care to excluded groups of CYP who live in adverse and traumatic environments .	'Find a way that we can both understand each other – we might communicate in different ways, make sure you use a way that works for me.' 'Shape your support around me – getting care is already hard work, so don't make it harder by giving me the wrong person, in a place I don't feel comfortable in, or at a time that doesn't work for me.'

4. Safe and responsible	
■ Intervenes early to prevent an escalation of need and avoid preventable exposure to additional adversity and trauma in CYP's lives. ■ Puts in place policies, practices and safeguarding arrangements that avoids re-traumatising the CYP and stigmatising their behavioural or emotional response to trauma. ■ Ensures that safeguarding procedures are in place, are seen as part of interventions in childhood adversity, and work in a way that supports the CYP to recover from the adversity or trauma they have faced. ■ Ensures that CYP receive coordinated support from knowledgeable, qualified, trustworthy and well-trained professionals who have suitable supervision and workforce support that can address vicarious or secondary trauma that may occur.	'Keep me safe and don't betray my trust – tell me what you will need to do next and who you will be talking to, and make sure you include me in the process and keep me updated.' 'Know where I'm coming from – I may not be or feel safe back where I live. If people know about what is going on, they could use it against me.' 'The way you treat me matters – to recover I need you to treat me with respect and understand why I'm behaving this way. Make sure I'm not in the care of someone who will make things worse. I want someone who is on my side.'

5. Collaborative and enhancing	
■ Meaningfully engages and involves CYP who have faced adversity and trauma in decisions about their treatment, care and the design of interventions. ■ Adopts a strengths-based approach, recognising the resources and resilience that CYP have drawn upon in the past, and creating positive and additional strategies for symptom mitigation and recovery – including self-soothing, emotional and regulation and the promotion of self-care. ■ Ensures models of care recognise and harness (where possible) families, care-giving, peer and community assets as part of treatment and recovery.	'Include me in decisions about my life – ask me what I want to happen, I have the right to be involved in decisions about my life.' 'I've survived this long… – build on my strength and help me find new ways to recover.' 'I want to talk to someone who has been through the same thing – it helps me make sense of what I've experienced and shows me I am not alone.'

<table>
<tr>
<td rowspan="3">6. Integrated</td>
<td>

- Enables effective communication and data-sharing between agencies to ensure that the whole of the CYP's needs are identified and met.
- Co-commissioned (possibly with a lead agency) to ensure that there is a continuity of care and consistency of pathways across, and within, the services and interventions that CYP will receive.
- Ensuring smooth transitions between stepped care models, providing timely referral and treatment to specialist services, and proving access to enhanced mental health, adversity and trauma knowledge and expertise when required (i.e. through outreach and liaison models of care).

</td>
<td>

'Stop asking me to repeat myself – it's a hard thing for me to talk about, and if it's going to help me I'd rather you told the right professional so that I don't have to.'

'Don't pass me from person to person – I have to start from scratch each time. I don't want to be thrown between services, and it's going to screw with my recovery.'

</td>
</tr>
</table>

You can read more about adversity and trauma-informed practice (ATIP) in a free guide for frontline professionals by YoungMinds, Anna Freud National Centre for Children and Families, and Body & Soul (see Brennan et al, 2019).

References

American Psychiatric Association (2013) *Diagnostic and Statistical Manual of Mental Disorders (Fifth edition – DSM-5)*. Washington DC: American Psychiatric Publishing.

Anda RF, Brown DW, Felitti VJ Bremner JD, Dube SR and Giles WH (2007) Adverse childhood experiences and prescribed psychotropic medications in adults. *American Journal of Preventative Medicine* **32** (5) 389–94.

Ashton K, Bellis MA, Davies AR, Hardcastle K and Hughes K (2016) *Adverse Childhood Experiences and their association with chronic disease and health service use in the in the Welsh adult population*. Cardiff: Public Health Wales. Available at: http://www.wales.nhs.uk/sitesplus/documents/888/ACE%20 Chronic%20Disease%20report%20%289%29%20%282%29.pdf (accessed 26 June 2019).

Ayre D (2016) *Poor Mental Health: The links between child poverty and mental health problems*. London: The Children's Society. Available at: http://www.childrenssociety.org.uk/sites/default/files/ poor_mental_health_report.pdf (accessed 26 June 2019).

Bebbington P, Jonas S, Kuipers E, King M, Cooper C, Brugha T, Meltzer H, McManus S and Jenkins R (2011) Childhood sexual abuse and psychosis: data from a cross-sectional national psychiatric survey in England. *British Journal of Psychiatry* **199** (1) 29–37.

Bellis MA, Hughes K, Leckenby N, Perkins C and Lowey H (2014a) National household survey of adverse childhood experiences and their relationship with resilience to health-harming behaviors in England. *BMC Medicine* **12** (72) 1–10.

Bellis MA, Hughes K, Leckenby N, Jones L, Baban A, Kachaeva M, Povilaitis R, Pudule I, Qirjako G, Ulukol B, Ralevah M and Terzici N (2014b) Adverse childhood experiences and associations with health-harming behaviours in young adults: surveys in eight eastern European countries. *Bulletin of the World Health Organization* **92** 641–655.

Bellis MA, Lowey H, Hughes K and Harrison D (2014c) Adverse Childhood Experiences: Retrospective study to determine their impact on adult health behaviours and health outcomes in a UK population. *Journal of Public Health* **36** (1) 81–91.

Bellis MA, Hughes K, Leckenby N, Hardcastle KA, Perkins C and Lowey H (2015) Measuring mortality and the burden of adult disease associated with adverse childhood experiences in England: a national survey. *Journal of Public Health* **37** (3) 445–454.

Bloom SL (2013) *Creating Sanctuary: Toward the evolution of sane societies (revised edition)*. New York: Routledge.

Bremner JD (2006) Traumatic stress: effects on the brain. *Dialogues in Clinical Neuroscience* **8** (4) 445–461.

Brennan R, Bush M and Trickey D with Levene C and Watson J (2019) *Adversity and Trauma-Informed Practice: A short guide for professionals working on the frontline*. London: YoungMinds, Anna Freud National Centre for Children and Families, and Body & Soul. Available at: https://youngminds.org.uk/media/3091/adversity-and-trauma-informed-practice-guide-for-professionals.pdf (accessed 26 June 2019).

Brown DW, Anda RF, Tiemeier H *et al* (2009) Adverse childhood experiences and the risk of premature mortality. *American Journal of Preventive Medicine* **37** (5) 389–396.

Bush M (2018). *Addressing Adversity: Prioritising adversity and trauma-informed care for children and young people in England*. London: YoungMinds and Health Education England. Available at: http://youngminds.org.uk/addressingadversity (accessed 26 June 2019).

Couper S and Mackie P (2016) *'Polishing the Diamonds': Addressing Adverse Childhood Experiences in Scotland (Scottish Public Health Network)* [online]. Glasgow: Scottish Public Health Network and NHS Health Scotland. Available at: https://www.scotphn.net/wp-content/uploads/2016/06/2016_05_26-ACE-Report-Final-AF.pdf (accessed 26 June 2019).

DePierro JM, D'Andrea W and Frewen P (2014) Anhedonia in trauma related disorders: the good, the bad and the shutdown. In M Ritsner (ed) *Anhedonia: A Comprehensive Handbook Volume II (Neuropsychiatric and Physical Disorders)*, pp175–189. London: Springer.

Douglas KR, Chan G, Gelernter J, Arias AJ, Anton RF, Weiss RD, Brady K, Poling J, Farrer L, Kranzler HR (2010) Adverse childhood events as risk factors for substance dependence: partial mediation by mood and anxiety disorders. *Addictive Behaviors* **35** 7–13.

Education Scotland (2018) *Nurture, Adverse Childhood Experiences and Trauma Informed Practice: Making the links between these approaches*. Livingston: Education Scotland.

Felitti VJ, Anda RF, Nordenberg D, Williamson DF, Spitz AM, Edwards V, Koss MP and Marks JS (1998) Relationship of childhood abuse and household dysfunction to many of the leading causes of death in adults. The Adverse Childhood Experiences (ACE) Study. *American Journal of Preventative Medicine* **14** (4) 245–258. Available at: http://www.ncbi.nlm.nih.gov/pubmed/9635069 (accessed 26 June 2019).

Fonagy P (2018) Meeting the mental health needs of looked-after children and care leavers. In: M Bush (ed) *Addressing Adversity: Prioritising adversity and trauma-informed care for children and young people in England*. London: YoungMinds and Health Education England. Available at: http://youngminds.org.uk/addressingadversity (accessed 26 June 2019).

Ford JD (2010) Complex adult sequelae of early exposure to psychological trauma In RA Lanius, E Vermetten and C Pain (eds) *The Impact of Early Life Trauma on Health and Disease: The hidden epidemic*, pp69–76. Cambridge: Cambridge University Press.

Frewen PA, Dean JA and Lanius RA (2012) Assessment of anhedonia in psychological trauma: development of the Hedonic Deficit and Interference Scale. *European Journal of Psychotraumatology* **3** 8585.

Greenwald R (2015) *Child Trauma Handbook: A guide for helping trauma-exposed children and adolescents*. London: Routledge.

Hambrick EP, Brawner TW, Perry BD, Brandt K, Hofmeister C and Collins, JO (2018) Beyond the ACE Score: examining relationships between timing of developmental adversity, relational health and developmental outcomes in children. *Archives of Psychiatric Nursing* **33(3)** 238-247.

Herman J (2015 [1992]) *Trauma and Recovery: The aftermath of violence – from domestic abuse to political terror*. PA: Basic Books.

HM Government (2015) *Working Together to Safeguard Children: A guide to inter-agency working to safeguard and promote the welfare of children*. London: The Stationery Office. Available at: https://www. gov.uk/government/publications/working-together-to-safeguard-children--2 (accessed 26 June 2019).

Hughes K, Lowey H, Quigg Z and Bellis MA (2016) Relationships between adverse childhood experiences and adult mental wellbeing: results from an English national household survey. *BMC Public Health* **16**, 222. Available at: http://www.ncbi.nlm.nih.gov/pmc/articles/PMC4778324/ (accessed 1 July 2019).

Kelly-Irving M, Lepage B, Dedieu D, Bartley M, Blane D, Grosclaude P, Lang T and Delpierre C (2013) Adverse childhood experiences and premature all-cause mortality. *European Journal of Epidemiology* **28** (9) 721–734.

Kessler R (2010) Childhood adversities and adult psychopathology in the WHO World Mental Health Surveys. *British Journal or Psychiatry* **197** (5) 378–385.

Kessler RC and McLaughlin KA (2010) Childhood adversities and adult psychopathology in the WHO World Mental Health Surveys. *British Journal of Psychiatry* **197** (5) 378–385.

Larkin W and Read J (2008) Childhood trauma and psychosis: evidence, pathways, and implications. *Journal of Postgraduate Medicine* **54** (4) 287–293.

Lewis SL, Arseneault L, Caspi A, Fisher HL, Matthews T, Moffitt TE, Odgers CL, Stahl D5, Teng JY, Danese A (2019) The epidemiology of trauma and post-traumatic stress disorder in a representative cohort of young people in England and Wales. *Lancet Psychiatry* **6** (3) 247–256.

McCrory EJ and Viding E (2015) The theory of latent vulnerability: reconcetualizing the link between childhood maltreatment and psychiatric disorder. *Development and Psychopathology* **27** 495–505.

McCrory EJ, Gerin MI and Viding E (2017) Annual Research Review: Childhood maltreatment, latent vulnerability and the shift to preventative psychiatry – the contribution of functional brain imaging. *Journal of Child Psychology and Psychiatry* **58** (4) 338–357.

McLaughlin KA (2017) The long shadow of adverse childhood experiences. *Psychological Science Agenda (April)*. Available at: http://www.apa.org/science/about/psa/2017/04/adverse-childhood.aspx (accessed 26 June 2019).

McLaughlin KA, Green JG, Gruber MJ, Sampson NA, Zaslavsky AM and Kessler RC (2012) Childhood adversities and first onset of psychiatric disorders in a national sample of adolescents. *Archives of General Psychiatry* **69** 1151–1160.

Mental Health Taskforce and NHS England (2016) *The Five Year Forward View for Mental Health: A report from the independent Mental Health Taskforce to the NHS in England*. London: NHS England. Available at: https://www.england.nhs.uk/wp-content/uploads/2016/02/Mental-Health-Taskforce-FYFV-final.pdf (accessed 26 June 2019).

Minton K, Ogden P, Pain C, Siegel DJ and Van Der Kolk B (2006) *Trauma and the Body: A sensorimotor approach to psychotherapy*. New York: W W Norton and Co.

National Confidential Inquiry (NCI) into Suicide and Homicide by People with Mental Illness (2017) *Suicide by Children and Young People*. Available at: https://www.hqip.org.uk/wp-content/uploads/2018/02/8iQSvI.pdf (accessed 26 June 2019).

Nicholson C, Irwin M and Dwivedi KN (2010) *Children and Adolescents in Trauma: Creative therapeutic approaches*. London: Jessica Kingsley Publishers.

Public Health Wales and Centre for Public Health (2015) *Adverse Childhood Experiences and their impact on health-harming behaviours in the Welsh adult population*. Cardiff: Public Health Wales. Available at: http://www2.nphs.wales.nhs.uk:8080/PRIDDocs.nsf/7c21215d6d0c613e80256f490030c05a/d488a3852491bc1d80257f370038919e/$FILE/ACE%20Report%20FINAL%20(E).pdf (accessed 26 June 2019).

Schilling EA, Aseltine RH and Gore S (2008) The impact of cumulative childhood adversity on young adult mental health: measures, models, and interpretations. *Social Science and Medicine* **66** (5) 1140–1151.

Science and Technology Committee (2018) *Evidence-based Early Years Intervention*. London: House of Commons.

Simpson TL and Miller WR (2002) Concomitance between childhood sexual and physical abuse and substance use problems: a review. *Clinical Psychology Review* **22** (1) 27–77.

Singer MI, Anglin TM, Song LY and Lunghofer L (1995) Adolescents' exposure to violence and associated symptoms of psychological trauma. *Journal of the American Medical Association* **273** 477–482.

Smith M, Williamson AE, Walsh D and McCartney G (2016) Is there a link between childhood adversity, attachment style and Scotland's excess mortality?: evidence, challenges and potential research. *BMC Public Health* **16** 655.

Sweeney A and Taggart D (2018) (Mis)understanding trauma-informed approaches in mental health. *Journal of Mental Health* **27** (5) 383–387.

Van der Kolk B (2005) Developmental Trauma Disorder: toward a rational diagnosis for children with complex trauma histories. *Psychiatric Annals* **35** (5) 401–408.

Varese F (2012) Childhood Adversities Increase the Risk of Psychosis: A meta-analysis of patient-control, prospective- and cross-sectional cohort studies. *Schizophrenia Bulletin* **38** (4) 661–671.

World Health Organization and Calouste Gulbenkian Foundation (2014) *Social Determinants of Mental Health*. Geneva: WHO. Available at: http://apps.who.int/iris/bitstream/10665/112828/1/9789241506809_eng.pdf (accessed 26 June 2019).

World Health Organization (2016) *The International Classification of Diseases (ICD-10)*: Geneva: WHO. Available at: http://apps.who.int/classifications/icd10/browse/2016/en (accessed 26 June 2019).

Websites

YoungMinds: www.youngminds.org.uk

Anna Freud Centre for Children and Families: www.annafreud.org

Body & Soul: www.bodyandsoulcharity.org

Wave Trust: www.wavetrust.org

Chapter 8: Mental Health Promotion in Primary Schools

Adrian Bethune

Key learning points

- Primary schools are well placed to promote positive mental health among their children, as well as identifying those who may need more specialist help with mental health problems.

- Studies show a two-way relationship between good mental health supporting learning, and learning supporting good mental health.

- Positive mental health is best promoted on a whole-school basis where everyone in the school community benefits from an inclusive culture and ethos, that values and prioritises the emotional wellbeing of all.

- The government is placing a greater focus on mental health promotion in schools with more support being offered in the form of mental health support teams and trained designated mental health leads in schools.

- More schools are using evidence-based programmes to support their children's mental health but they must also ensure that their staff's mental health is supported too, especially in a climate of hyper-accountability.

Keywords
Primary school; mental health; emotional wellbeing; whole school approach; evidence-based programmes

Introduction

The promotion of children's mental health in primary schools is of fundamental importance for many reasons. Many teachers will tell you that the happiest children in their classrooms learn best. They are able to focus, get on well with their peers, and engage in learning better than those children struggling with emotional and mental health concerns. And there is good evidence that shows that children's emotional development is essential in the process of learning (Greenhalgh, 1994; Weare, 2004) and that low wellbeing is linked with poor academic performance at school (Parry-Langdon, 2008). Indeed, children with emotional and behavioural difficulties are more likely to be excluded from school, or leave without any qualifications. But let's not forget that learning is also a crucial part of developing good mental health – one of the 'five ways to wellbeing' according to the New Economics Foundation (Government Office for Science, 2008). So, there is a two-way relationship between good mental health supporting children's ability to learn and learning new things being an important part in developing good mental health.

But promoting children's mental health at school is more than just helping push their grades and attainment up. When schools invest in developing the emotional health and psychological wellbeing of their pupils, they set them up for life. Longitudinal studies show that the emotional health of children at the age of 16 is the strongest predictor of adult life satisfaction. Incidentally, the weakest predictor of adult happiness is a child's 'intellectual development' (Layard *et al*, 2013). But can schools really have a big impact on the emotional health of children? Surely nature and parental upbringing hold all of the cards? Recent evidence suggests otherwise and that schools can actually have major effects on the emotional wellbeing of children, with the effects of primary schools and teachers lasting five years and longer (Clark *et al*, 2018).

The simple fact is that primary schools play a pivotal role in children's (and their family's) lives. They are often central to the local community and provide more than just an academic curriculum. It's not uncommon for primary schools to provide wrap-around care and support for children in the form of breakfast clubs, after-school clubs, providing uniforms and sometimes even financial and emotional support for vulnerable families. The smaller and more intimate nature of primary schools means they are often better able to play a more supportive role than their secondary counterparts. They have almost daily face-to-face interaction with the children's main carers and are able to pick up and act upon those initial signs that things may not be going well for certain pupils and their families.

The primary schools that are often most effective at promoting children's mental health are those that act as extended families to their pupils. Teachers and support staff, *in locos parentis*, act as the children's parents in school and, with the right atmosphere and culture, the classmates become supportive siblings for one another. Some experts argue that tapping into children's primitive social instincts in this way, by fostering attachment-based relationships in schools, not only aids learning but also develops their wellbeing (Cozolino, 2013). As well as providing a safe, secure learning environment for their children, many schools also provide extra specialist provision to support those children that have poor mental health or are suffering with a mental illness. School counsellors, educational psychologists and mentors are just a few of the roles that now feature in many primary schools.

With so much flux in the educational landscape, it's important to review what the current evidence tells us about the state of primary school children's mental health, how current government policy supports the promotion of mental health, what works, what schools can do, and which organisations exist to support them in this endeavour.

Children's mental health today

The term 'mental health' has become an umbrella term within education. Are we talking about happiness? Does mental health mean the same thing as mental wellbeing? Are mental health and mental illness the same thing? These and many other questions can arise for people working with children.

Mental health is about how children handle and relate to the feelings, thoughts, moods and emotions that affect their lives. Child mental health is about the capacity for the child's mind to grow, develop and learn with confidence and enjoyment. It is about developing resilience and learning how to cope with life's inevitable difficulties. It is built on foundations of physical and emotional wellbeing, with children gradually understanding more about themselves and the people around them, allowing them to develop secure and healthy relationships. A child with good mental health is able to make the most of their abilities and live a full and happy life.

Conversely, a child with poor mental health may find it difficult to access and take part in the everyday activities that many children enjoy. They may become overwhelmed by anxieties, thoughts and feelings, or continuous low mood may make it hard for them to find the motivation to engage in what life has to offer. Friendships may prove harder to establish and maintain. Sometimes children with poor mental health exhibit erratic behaviour – appearing lively and engaged on some days, and aggressive or isolating on others.

But poor mental health does not mean the same thing has having a mental illness or mental health condition. We all have times when we feel down, low or anxious and, quite often, these feelings are temporary and pass naturally. A child could have a diagnosable mental illness such as obsessive compulsive disorder (OCD) but display good levels of mental health (in the same way that someone with diabetes can manage their illness and lead a full and healthy life). For someone to be diagnosed with a mental health condition (for example, emotional, behavioural, hyperactivity), their symptoms have to be sufficiently severe to cause distress to the child or impair their functioning (World Health Organization, 1993).

Turning our attention towards the statistics on children's mental health in the UK, what do we know about the current situation? The fact that it has been well over a decade since children's mental health has been surveyed on a large scale and in a systematic way (Green *et al*, 2005) gives an indication of how children's welfare is viewed in the UK. The latest report from NHS Digital certainly suggests that the mental health of young people is getting worse (NHS Digital, 2018). There has been a slight increase in the prevalence of mental health conditions in 5 to 15-year-olds, rising from 9.7% in 1999, to 10.1% in 2004, and 11.2% in 2017. More children in this group are experiencing clinically impairing anxiety or depression. One in eight 5 to 19-year-olds has at least one mental health problem now. And we know that children are experiencing more mental health issues as they get older. The research shows a prevalence rate of one in ten (9.5%) five to 10-year-olds. This increases to one in seven (14.4%) for secondary school aged children (11 to 16-year-olds) and rates of mental health issues were highest in 17 to 19-year-olds, with one in six (16.9%) experiencing at least one.

This trend is deeply concerning, especially when you consider that many children with mental health conditions are still not getting timely access to the specialist help they could benefit from (Office of the Children's Commissioner for England, 2018). What the data doesn't tell us are the reasons why more children appear to be suffering from poor mental health. Is it due to the effects of social media, or austerity, or school and exam pressure? We just don't know. It is certainly true that the research shows that children with mental health needs spend more time on social media and have more concerns about it than those children without a mental health condition, but we have no idea which way the causality runs. What this does mean, however, is that there is a greater need to measure children's mental health over time to get a better feel for what may be behind the causes of mental health conditions and, just as importantly, what promotes good mental health in children.

National policy

Given this concerning trend of worsening mental health among children, what is the government doing in response? At the end of 2017, the government published a mental health Green Paper, detailing proposals to create a network of support for children and young people, and their educational settings (Department of Health, 2017). The Green Paper made three main proposals:

1. That every school and college will have a designated lead in mental health by 2025

Their remit will be to:

- oversee the help the school gives to pupils with mental health problems
- help staff to spot pupils who show signs of mental health problems
- offer advice to staff about mental health
- refer children to specialist services if they need to.

2. Mental health support teams should work with schools and colleges

These support teams will offer individual and group help to young people with mild to moderate mental health issues including anxiety, low mood and behavioural difficulties. The idea is that the support teams will work closely with the designated mental health leads and provide a link with more specialist mental health services.

3. To pilot a four-week waiting time for access to specialist NHS children and young people's mental health services

This would dramatically reduce current waiting times for children who desperately need access to child and adolescent mental health services (CAMHS).

However, these proposals were not without criticism. The Education and Health and Social Care Committee criticised the Green Paper, saying it lacked ambition and would fail to help the majority of children who really needed help (Education and Health and Social Care Committee, 2018). They argued that the plans would put more pressure on schools, that funding for the proposals was not guaranteed, that pilot schemes would only cover up to a quarter of the country by 2022/23, and that not enough focus was being put on promoting positive mental health and preventing mental health problems.

Other developments include the new Ofsted inspection framework, which has gone out for consultation and places a greater emphasis on children's 'personal development' (Ofsted, 2019). Inspectors will want to see what schools are doing to develop children's 'character and resilience'. Additionally, plans have been published by the DfE, to make 'health education' compulsory by 2020, which would see schools having to teach children about the benefits of a healthier lifestyle, what determines their physical health and how to build mental resilience and wellbeing.

All of these proposals are certainly welcome, placing a greater emphasis on schools promoting good mental health, with greater access to services and additional support. Whether schools, who are already under great financial and political pressure, will be able to take advantage of these initiatives, only time will tell.

Whole school approaches to good mental health and the school environment

There is no doubt that promoting good mental health in primary schools needs a whole school approach to be most effective. An 'emotionally literate school' (Weare, 2006) looks at the whole school context. It regards the total experience of school life as contributing to the emotional wellbeing of everyone who learns and works there. Without a supportive whole school culture and ethos, any mental health interventions are likely to be severely limited in their impact.

Emotionally literate schools are typically strong in four key areas (Weare, 2000):

- Firstly, relationships are at the heart of them and there is a strong sense of belonging. Everyone feels listened to and respected, and that they can contribute to their school community.

- Secondly, there is a strong sense of engagement and all members of the school community are working cohesively, guided by strong values and common goals.

- Thirdly, these schools promote autonomy and independence. Rather than being rigidly hierarchical, schools that promote good mental health allow staff and children to feel like they are in control of important aspects of their lives and are given a voice.

- Lastly, mental health in schools is promoted by having high expectations of all children and clear boundaries and rules. Everyone knows what is expected of them and what the rewards and consequences are of certain behaviours and choices.

It is important to bear in mind, however, the intense pressure many primary schools face at present. Financial pressures, accountability measures, performance targets, league tables – all of these factors can undermine the wellbeing of staff which, in turn, has been shown to have a negative effect on children's wellbeing and attainment (Black, 2001). So, emotionally literate schools must be aware of the pressures they are under and consciously work to ameliorate the effects of this pressure by prioritising staff and pupil wellbeing.

Oldham Council

Oldham Council have developed a framework called The Whole School and College Approach to Emotional Health and Mental Wellbeing. The framework offers practical guidance to schools and colleges to develop the knowledge and skills needed to promote mental health, and to prevent minor problems from escalating into more serious long-term issues.

As part of the framework, Oldham Council have set up a Mental Wellbeing Team, with co-ordinators allocated to a number of schools and colleges, assisting head teachers and college principles to embed a whole school approach to emotional health and mental wellbeing.

For more information visit: www.oldham.gov.uk/info/200807/mental_health/1795/the_ whole_school_and_college_approach_to_emotional_health_and_mental_wellbeing

What schools can do to promote good mental health

As well as the school environment being important, schools can enhance their offering by adopting specific programmes to promote good mental health among their learners and staff. Well-designed programmes teach children about mental health, tackle risk factors often associated with mental health problems, and promote protective factors such as happiness, resilience and optimism, relationship skills, and stress management. The research shows that children with mental health problems benefit the most from universal approaches targeted at everyone, rather than those focused just on them (Weare, 2006). This doesn't mean that schools cannot offer targeted interventions for groups of children struggling with mental health, but what these children need most is what is good for all children.

Overleaf are some suggestions of programmes and interventions that have a good and growing evidence-base and may provide a useful starting point for thinking about promoting mental health in school settings.

Social and Emotional Aspects of Learning (SEAL)

The primary SEAL programme (ages 4–11) was very popular in primary schools in the mid-2000s. Studies showed it was having a clear impact on social and emotional learning, on behaviour, and even on pupils' reading and science test scores (Hallam *et al*, 2005). It has lost favour in recent years (especially after resources were archived in 2011) but the programme is well-designed and many schools still use it as a staple part of their Personal, Social and Health Education (PSHE) lessons. The archived resources can be found at: https://webarchive. nationalarchives.gov.uk/20110812101121/http://nsonline.org.uk/node/87009

Mindfulness in schools

Mindfulness is a type of mind training that helps develop children's present-moment awareness of their thoughts, feelings, body sensations and what's happening in their external environment, with an attitude of kindness and curiosity. There is a growing body of evidence that shows that teaching children the skills of mindfulness can really benefit their mental health. One recent meta-analysis of mindfulness-based interventions with young people showed significant positive effects, relative to controls, for the outcome categories of mindfulness, executive functioning, attention, depression, anxiety/stress and negative behaviours (Dunning, *et al*, 2018).

The leading providers of mindfulness interventions in schools are the Mindfulness in Schools Project (www.mindfulnessinschools.org), MindUp (www.mindup. org/u-k) and Youth Mindfulness (www.youthmindfulness.org). Importantly, these providers all request that teachers have an established personal mindfulness practice before they begin learning how to bring mindfulness into the classroom.

Lessness Heath Primary School

Lessness Heath Primary school is the first school nationally to be awarded the 'Wellbeing Award for Schools', an award created by the National Children's Bureau and Optimus Education.

The school had identified that staff wellbeing was being adversely affected by the demands of the job. As a result, they introduced measures to protect the mental health of their staff, such as termly CPD with a focus on wellbeing, regular supervision for staff, and creating a wellbeing team with members from the whole school community.

Workshops were held for pupils, staff and parents on the importance of developing good mental health. A family-empowerment programme was created to support families with introducing wellbeing practices at home. Children were selected as 'wellbeing ambassadors' to champion the school's vision to incorporate the 'Five Ways To Wellbeing' into daily life.

Promoting positive mental health has been given centre stage at Lessness Heath. To find out more visit https://lessnessheath-bexley.co.uk/wellbeing/

Resilience training

Organisations such as Bounce Forward (formerly How to Thrive) are training teachers to deliver programmes in schools that develop children's (and teachers') levels of psychological wellbeing by teaching them the skills of resilience and accurate thinking. Their programme for primary schools is aimed at 9 to 11-year-olds and is based on the Penn Resilience Programme, an evidence-based intervention originating from the University of Pennsylvania in America. An impact review of the programme showed significant improvements in children's anxiety and depressive symptoms, along with improvements in behaviour (Challen *et al*, 2011). The evidence showed that the benefits of the programme only lasted in the short term, which highlights the needs for programmes like this to be delivered on a rolling basis, with children being taught the material more than once. For more information see www.bounceforward.com

Physical activity

Regular physical exercise is a fundamental part of the jigsaw of developing and maintaining good physical and mental health. It is a deep concern, therefore, that the vast majority of young people in England do not meet the minimum daily requirements of 60 minutes of moderate to vigorous exercise (Townsend *et al*, 2015). But an increasingly popular physical activity intervention called 'The Daily Mile' (www.thedailymile.co.uk) is taking root in primary schools across Britain. Children simply walk, jog or run for 15 minutes every day at school. They do not need to get changed, and teachers can decide when to fit it into the school day. It is a low-cost, high autonomy intervention. Studies show it can improve children's mood, attention and memory (BBC Learning, 2018) as well as increasing children's fitness and body composition (Chesham *et al*, 2018).

Lessons in mental health

The Anna Freud National Centre for Children and Families (ANCCF) has created 'Schools In Mind' (www.annafreud.org/what-we-do/schools-in-mind), a free network for school staff and allied professionals which shares practical, academic and clinical expertise regarding the wellbeing and mental health issues that affect schools. Similarly, the mental health charity, Heads Together, has also created a website to support schools – www.mentallyhealthyschools.org.uk. Both websites contain a bank of resources with lesson plans and animations that help teachers and children talk about mental health, understand what it is and what contributes to it. There are resources for parents and staff so they can look after their own mental health, and even a wellbeing directory for young people so they can access additional help they may need. The resources are comprehensive and well-designed and will really support school leaders in prioritising the mental health of the whole school community.

Measure children's mental wellbeing

Schools have a strong tradition in gathering academic data and measuring progress in attainment but not so much when it comes to measuring the emotional and mental wellbeing of their children. Many schools simply wouldn't know where to begin. The ANCCF has created a 'Mental Health Toolkit' for schools which includes an online tutorial in how to measure and monitor pupil wellbeing effectively, along with a summary of validated wellbeing measures schools could use. The toolkit is easy to use and should provide schools with the right tools to begin to systematically measure and review their pupils' wellbeing. Not only can this help identify children who may need additional support but it will also help schools evaluate their own 'emotional literacy' and identify areas for improvement. To access the toolkit go to www.annafreud.org/what-we-do/schools-in-mind/resources-for-schools/mental-health-toolkit-for-schools/.

Trained mental health workers in schools

Organisations such as the mental health charity Place 2 Be (www.place2be.org.uk), place highly trained clinical staff and counsellors in schools. They work one-to-one with children offering them counselling, including drop-in sessions at lunchtime for children who wish to talk. They work with groups and whole classes delivering lessons on topics like friendship, self-esteem and bullying. They also provide support for parents too. Research into the impact of these interventions show large improvements in friendships, learning and home life (Place 2 Be, 2018).

The NHS is also currently training Education Health Practitioners (EHPs) to go into schools to support children with mental ill health. The intention is that these practitioners will deliver high-quality, evidence-based early interventions for children and young people experiencing mental health problems within their educational setting, referring them to specialist support as necessary. To find out more about EHPs visit www.healthcareers.nhs.uk/news/could-you-be-education-mental-health-practitioner.

Conclusion

Primary schools are in a pivotal position to promote good mental health among their children and help support those with mental health difficulties. But they face their own intense pressures which are certainly affecting the mental health of teaching staff. Government policy is slowly catching up with the growing mental health problems that an increasing number of young people face today and more focus is being placed on what we can all do to support children's mental health from an early age. An increasing number of organisations are offering evidence-based interventions that schools can employ to promote positive mental health at school and there are more support services placing trained mental health workers in schools. Arguably though, the most important way that primary schools can support the mental health of everyone in the school community is by being an extended loving and supportive family. When relationships are at the heart of schools, when expectations are high and boundaries are clear, and when the mental health of everyone is talked about and prioritised, schools can do a lot to ensure that their children grow up to be happy and healthy.

References

BBC Teach (2018) *Exercise Map* [online]. Available at: https://www.bbc.com/teach/terrific-scientific/KS2/zf7qscw (accessed 26 June 2019).

Black S (2001) Morale matters: when teachers feel good about their work, research shows, student achievement rises. *American School Board Journal* **188** (1) 40–3.

Challen A, Noden P, West A and Machin S (2011) *UK Resilience Programme Evaluation: Final report.* London: Department for Education. Available at: https://assets.publishing.service.gov.uk/government/uploads/system/uploads/attachment_data/file/182419/DFE-RR097.pdf (accessed 26 June 2019).

Chesham RA, Booth JN, Sweeney EL, Ryde GC, Gorely T, Brooks NE and Moran CN (2018) The daily mile makes primary school children more active, less sedentary and improves their fitness and body composition: a quasi-experimental pilot study. *BMC Medicine* **16** (64). Available at: https://doi.org/10.1186/s12916-018-1049-z (accessed 26 June 2019.

Clark AE, Flèche S, Layard R, Powdthavee N and Ward G (2018) *The Origins of Happiness: The Science of Well-being Over the Life Course.* Princeton: Princeton University Press.

Cozolino L (2013) *The Social Neuroscience of Education: Optimizing Attachment and Learning in the Classroom.* New York: WW Norton & Company.

Department of Health (2017) *Transforming Children and Young People's Mental Health Provision: A green paper* [online]. Available at: https://assets.publishing.service.gov.uk/government/uploads/system/uploads/attachment_data/file/728892/government-response-to-consultation-on-transforming-children-and-young-peoples-mental-health.pdf (accessed 26 June 2019).

Dunning DL, Griffiths K, Kuyken W, Crane C, Foulkes L, Parker J and Dalgleish T (2018) The effects of mindfulness-based interventions on cognition and mental health in children and adolescents – a meta-analysis of randomised control trials. *Journal of Child Psychology and Psychiatry*. Available at: https://doi.org/10.1111/jcpp.12980 (accessed 26 June 2019).

Education and Health and Social Care Select Committees (2015) *Thousands of Children to Miss out on Mental Health* [online]. Available at: supporthttps://social.shorthand.com/CommonsHealth/3CYE7IOL7n/thousands-of-children-to-miss-out-on-mental-health-support (accessed 21st October 2019).

Government Office for Science (2008) *Five Ways to Mental Wellbeing.* Available at: https://issuu.com/neweconomicsfoundation/docs/five_ways_to_well-being?viewMode=presentation (accessed 26 June 2019).

Green H *et al* (2005) *Mental Health of Children and Young People in Great Britain, 2004.* Basingstoke: Palgrave MacMillan.

Greenhalgh P (1994) *Emotional Growth and Learning.* London: Routledge.

Hallam S, Rhamie J, Shaw J (2005) *Final Report: Primary behaviour and attendance pilot.* London: Department for Education and Skills.

Health and Social Care Committee (2018) *Thousands of Children to Miss Out on Mental Health Support* [online]. Available at: https://social.shorthand.com/CommonsHealth/3CYE7IOL7n/thousands-of-children-to-miss-out-on-mental-health-support (accessed 26 June 2019).

Layard R, Clark AE, Cornaglia F, Powdthavee N and Vernoit J (2013) 'What predicts a successful life? A life- course model of well-being', Centre for Economic Performance , Discussion Paper No 1245. Available at: http://cep.lse.ac.uk/pubs/download/dp1245.pdf (accessed 26 June 2019).

NHS Digital (2018) *Mental Health of Children and Young People in England.* Available at: https://digital.nhs.uk/data-and-information/publications/statistical/mental-health-of-children-and-young-people-in-england/2017/2017 (accessed 26 June 2019).

Office of the Children's Commissioner for England (2018) *Children's Mental Health Briefing* [online].

Available at: https://www.childrenscommissioner.gov.uk/wp-content/uploads/2019/02/childrens-mental-health-briefing-nov-2018.pdf (accessed 3 July 2019).

Ofsted (2019) *Open Consultation: Education Inspection Framework 2019: Inspecting the Substance of Education* [online]. Available at: https://www.gov.uk/government/consultations/education-inspection-framework-2019-inspecting-the-substance-of-education/education-inspection-framework-2019-inspecting-the-substance-of-education (accessed 26 June 2019).

Parry-Langdon N (Ed) (2008) *Three Years On: Survey of the development and emotional wellbeing of children and young people*. London: Office for National Statistics.

Place 2 Be (2018) *Children and Young People – Impact Evidence* [online]. Available at: https://www.place2be.org.uk/impact-evidence/children-and-young-people.aspx (accessed 26 June 2019).

Townsend N, Wickramasinghe K, Williams J, Bhatnagar P and Rayner M (2015) *Physical Activity Statistics* 2015. London: British Heart Foundation.

Weare K (2000) *Promoting Mental, Emotional and Social Health: A whole school approach*. London: Routledge.

Weare K (2003) *Developing the Emotionally Literate School*. SAGE Publications: London.

World Health Organization (1993) *The ICD-10 Classification of Mental and Behavioural Disorders: Diagnostic criteria for research*. Geneva: World Health Organization.

Chapter 9: The Mental Health Needs of Looked After Children

Kate Bonser and Liz Bailey

Key learning points

- Children can be 'looked after' (ie in the care of the local authority) in a range of places including foster care, residential care or sometimes at home with family members.

- Looked after children experience additional stressors with almost half having a diagnosable mental health condition (Department of Education, 2017), with an increased risk of having neurodevelopmental disorders such as attention deficit hyperactivity disorder and autism spectrum conditions (Green *et al*, 2016).

- Thorough assessments of mental health need to be holistic and include an understanding of the child's life experiences and the long-term impact of early experiences including trauma and neglect.

- Interventions need to support the carers by offering training and consultation; the system needs to work together to support those caring and being cared for.

- Individual therapeutic interventions need to be flexible and timely. Increased attention may need to be given to developing a trusting relationship.

- Key messages from recent policies guiding decision making for the delivery of services are influencing the development of flexible, child focused, specialist services in acknowledgement of the needs for this vulnerable group.

Keywords

Looked after children; mental health; system around the child; adverse childhood experiences; collaboration and participation; multi-agency working

Introduction

Looked after children and young people constitute a vulnerable group of our population, who are at increased risk of developing mental health difficulties. This chapter will focus on the context of being looked after, what makes these young people particularly vulnerable to developing mental ill health and the level of support and intervention that services can offer.

What do we mean by 'looked after' children?

Under the Children Act 1989, a child or young person is **looked after** by a local authority if they fall into one of the following categories:

- The child is provided with accommodation for a continuous period of more than 24 hours. This is a **voluntary** arrangement under **Section 20** of the Act. This requires the consent of the parent if the child is under 16, or the child themselves if over 16.

- The child is subject to a **care order (or an interim care order)**, which involves an order being made by the court (or applied for) where the child is placed in the care of the local authority (LA) or at home under supervision of the LA.

- The child is subject to a **placement order** which is a court order which gives a local authority the legal authority to place a child for adoption. Once a child is adopted, they are no longer classified as looked after and their parent(s) will have full parental responsibility for them.

Most looked after children are placed with foster carers (74%, Department of Education, 2017) but some may be placed in a residential home (which may also provide education); a small number of looked after children may be at home on a care order. The majority of children and young people are looked after due to neglect and abuse (Department of Education, 2017).

Every looked after child will have an allocated **social worker** who will oversee their care plan and their role is to fulfil the council's obligations as a corporate parent. They will work closely with other professionals to ensure that the child receives appropriate care, education and health services. All children who are looked after have regular LAC review meetings which are chaired by an **independent reviewing officer (IRO)**. The IRO has an oversight of the child's care plan and has a role in ensuring the local authority (via the social worker) puts the plans into place for the child.

Any input from mental health workers therefore needs to take into account, and work with, the system around the child.

What makes looked after children vulnerable to increased mental health needs?

Looked after children are known to have a higher rate of exposure to adverse childhood experiences than those not looked after (Ford *et al*, 2007), and this makes them a particularly vulnerable group in terms of their risk of developing mental health problems (Hughes *et al*, 2017). Conduct problems, anxiety, depression and self-harm are particularly common (see Mental Health Foundation, 2002). This group of children and young people are also more likely to have lower educational attainment, a higher level of contact with the criminal justice system and are more vulnerable to becoming homeless (Milich *et al*, 2017). Mental health vulnerability factors include:

1. Pre-natal adversity – drugs and alcohol may have been used during pregnancy, which may have an impact on the developing brain. This may have long term implications for their development e.g. foetal alcohol spectrum disorders and increase the risk of ongoing emotional and behavioural difficulties.

2. Lack of stimulation/poor care due to early neglect – this may lead to developmental delay including delays in physical, emotional, cognitive and social development.

3. A parental learning disability/significant mental health problem which impacts on their ability to care for their children and may increase the chances of their child being more genetically vulnerable to ongoing difficulties.

4. A lack of a consistent caregiver who has provided predictable and responsive care – this may lead to a child developing difficulties trusting caregivers which continues into their new placements.

5. Issues related to being in the care system itself, for example school moves, placement breakdowns, possible sibling separation and maintaining contact with birth family. Contact is often very important for children to maintain their links and identity with their family. However, this can also be an added factor for them to negotiate emotionally.

Adverse childhood experiences – Rosie and Sam

Rosie (aged eight) and Sam (aged five) were brother and sister who came into local authority care following Rosie being hit by her mum. Rosie and Sam had lived with their parents, whose relationship was characterised by significant domestic violence, often fuelled by their drug and alcohol misuse. They had regular parties in their house. Their home was dirty and there was rarely any food in the house. Rosie and Sam often felt like they got in the way, and they never knew when it was safe to ask for a drink or something to eat. If it was the wrong time, they would get shouted at, hit and sent upstairs.

Rosie and Sam were exposed to several adverse childhood experiences, which would increase their risk of developing mental health problems. These experiences included:

- physical abuse
- domestic violence
- parental drug and alcohol misuse
- neglect
- emotional abuse.

How can we support these children and young people?

Everyone involved in the life of a looked after child can help build their resilience, support them and help them reach their potential, and this can range from family and friends, frontline professionals in education, the local authority, youth justice and health, through to voluntary agencies and specialist child and adolescent mental health workers in NHS Child and Adolescent Mental Health Services (CAMHs).

What can CAMHs offer?

Assessment

'Assessments should focus on understanding the individual's mental health and emotional wellbeing in the context of their current situation and past experiences, rather than solely focusing on the presenting symptoms.'
(Milich *et al*, 2017, pp37)

Information will need to be gathered from multiple sources and will need to include:

- family history – from the social worker and their family (where appropriate)
- any psychological assessments conducted for court
- report from the caregiver
- observations in the home and school
- school report
- information from LAC reviews/medicals
- individual assessment of child/young person
- rating scales/questionnaires which look at specific difficulties, such as ADHD.

Ibrahim – assessment

Ibrahim is a six-year-old boy who was presenting with significant behavioural difficulties in his foster home. The carer and social worker requested CAMHs support to understand his emotional and behavioural needs better as they were concerned that he had an intrinsic difficulty, such as ADHD, which was driving his behaviour. Ibrahim had lived at home with his mother until he was five and had witnessed significant domestic violence and neglect before being moved into care.

The psychologist met with the foster carer in the home to gather information and to observe Ibrahim in his home environment. She then met with the designated teacher in school and observed Ibrahim in the playground and in the classroom to inform her assessment. Ibrahim then attended a clinic appointment for a play-based assessment to look at:

- his social interactions
- attention and concentration
- communication skills including language use and emotional literacy
- his understanding of his current living situation
- his attachment style.

The assessment indicted that Ibrahim had difficulties related to the trauma he had experienced whilst living in the family home and this had affected his ability to trust adults. He was often hypervigilant to the environment around him as he had developed a way of coping with the unpredictable outbursts whilst in the family home. There had also been an attempt to return Ibrahim home to live with his mother which had to be terminated due to concerns about his safety. This had increased his anxiety levels and led to a deterioration in his behaviour. The assessment was shared with the social worker and foster carer, and management approaches to supporting his anxiety were discussed.

Intervention

It is essential that any intervention for mental health problems in looked after children is guided by a comprehensive mental health assessment and detailed formulation. This is to avoid the use of inappropriate or ineffective interventions. It must be recognised that a child who has experienced a traumatic early attachment history is likely to find it very difficult to trust adults and feel safe enough to talk about their experiences. Thus, time must be given to developing the collaborative therapeutic alliance, which is recognised as a key component of therapeutic progress (Fonagy *et al*, 2016).

Often, there are many people involved in a looked after child's life, for example, family, foster or residential carers, social worker and school staff; thinking systemically about the child and their network will help to target interventions. Mental health interventions for looked after children can range from psychological to pharmacological; from individual, to care/child dyad interventions, to consultation to the network around the child. Interventions should be driven by evidence-based practice and the National Institute for Clinical Excellence (NICE) guidance (NICE, 2019) provide summaries of the current evidence-base.

Child/young person

Direct interventions with the child/young person need to be collaborative and needs-led. They can target specific here-and-now mental health problems or address past trauma with a view to alleviating some of the difficulties the young person may be having as a result of the trauma. Often, interventions may need to be eclectic to meet the needs of these young people with complex needs.

Interventions include:

- Dialectical Behaviour Therapy (DBT)
- Cognitive Behavioural Therapy (CBT)
- Eye Movement Desensitization and Reprocessing (EMDR) or trauma-focused CBT
- psychotherapy
- compassion-focused therapy
- play therapy
- medication (as an adjunct to psychological intervention).

Child/young person and carer dyad

Interventions focusing on the child/young person and carer dyad can help in facilitating attachment security, improving the child's mental health and reducing the risk of placement breakdown. Such interventions include:

- Dyadic Developmental Psychotherapy
- play therapies eg Theraplay
- family therapy.

Carer

The importance of the carer–child relationship cannot be underestimated in terms of the protective value it adds to the child's emotional wellbeing and mental health. It is therefore essential to ensure that carers and residential childcare workers are skilled and trained in working with children who have often experienced developmental trauma and attachment difficulties. National Institute for Health and Care Excellence (NICE) guidance (NICE, 2015) recommends parental sensitivity and behavioural training. Examples of this include:

- fostering changes (Briskman *et al*, 2012)
- nurturing attachments (Golding, 2013)
- video-interaction guidance
- psychoeducation.

Professionals

Consultation with professionals in the child's network is paramount in ensuring that everyone is working together to meet the mental health needs of the child. Consultation may include:

- psychoeducation around areas such as attachment, developmental trauma and mental health
- sharing a formulation to help ensure consistency and to develop a shared multi-agency understanding of the child's needs
- collaborative reflection and guidance to think about how best to meet the child's needs in whichever environment they are in.

Faith – consultation

Faith (aged 11) presented as being very fearful of her foster Faith. When her foster carer even slightly raised her voice, Faith started shaking. Erin would often run off and had no sense of danger. She would go up to strangers and have no fear. At school Faith was rough with her peers and controlling. She wouldn't let them choose their games and when she didn't get her own way, she would hit out.

The social worker, school staff and foster carer were offered consultation from the mental health CAMHs clinician to link Faith's presenting behavioural concerns to her past experiences. These concerns were:

- being fearful of her foster carer
- having no sense of danger
- being controlling with peers
- hitting out at peers.

Faith had been physically abused and was frightened of adults as they could be very unpredictable and hurt her. Faith was used to raised voices leading to being hit, and as such, her foster carer's raised voice triggered fear in Faith. Faith's past experiences were such that she had been passed around lots of strangers in her parents' house when they were having parties and she had not learned any stranger awareness. She had also grown up in a house where hitting was a way that people managed challenges and confrontations, and this may have become a learned behaviour.

Once her presentation was contextualised in relation to what had happened to her using developmental trauma and attachment theories, the CAMHs clinician advised the carer and professionals on strategies to help Faith experience new ways of seeing the world and to help her when she was displaying these behaviours.

Young person's participation and involvement

Any therapeutic mental health input with a looked after child and/or their carers should be collaborative with them. However, the views and input from young people are also invaluable in all areas of service development and delivery, to ensure that services represent what young people want and need. Young people should be included in:

- working with commissioners
- mental health service staff recruitment
- co-delivery of training

- service design and development

- service reviews.

Remi – collaboration with young person

Remi was referred to CAMHs by his social worker for anger management work. He was living in a children's home and kept losing his temper and damaging property. He had to be restrained on several occasions. Remi wasn't told about the referral for fear that he wouldn't attend. Remi was brought to his first CAMHs appointment by an agency worker, whom he barely knew. They told him in the waiting room that he was seeing a psychologist and needed anger management. Remi ran off on arrival and said he wasn't mental.

What could have been done differently by the professionals involved?

Consider:

- collaboration (i.e. doing 'with', rather than doing 'to'); getting Remi's consent

- Adverse childhood experiences i.e. what has happened to Remi, rather than what is wrong with him?

- Would it be helpful having someone he knows well and trusts to bring him?

Policy

The vulnerability of looked after children to developing mental health problems and the difficulty they have in accessing services is increasingly being recognised in government documents and policies. The statutory guidance on *Promoting the Health and Wellbeing of Looked After Children* (Department of Education and Department of Health, 2015) stresses that the mental health of looked after children deserves equal parity with physical health, and that there should be targeted and dedicated mental health support for looked after children. It also reinforces that need for local authorities to screen the emotional wellbeing of every looked after child using the *Strength and Difficulties Questionnaire* (Goodman, 2001) as routine.

The **Future in Mind** (Department of Health, 2015) document made recommendations about transforming Child and Adolescent Mental Health Services (CAMHS) to meet the needs of this vulnerable group, which included:

- increased multi-agency working between education, health, social care and youth justice, with mental health workers embedded in non-mental health teams

- having bespoke pathways targeting the needs of the child

- having more trauma-informed care and skilling the workforce in this

- having mental health consultation services

- ensuring evidence-based interventions are offered to vulnerable children

- having a lead professional to co-ordinate and integrate services.

A report produced by an expert working group (Milich *et al*, 2017) and commissioned by the Department of Health and Department for Education, made recommendations around improving the emotional and mental health of looked after children and care leavers. This work drew upon research evidence, adults involved in the child's network and young people themselves. It reinforced the need for a virtual mental health lead to ensure that children are getting the right support and that mental health services should be needs-led with different choices of mental health support. There was also an emphasis on local authorities, health and education working together to commission and deliver services jointly and to be informed by local need.

Educational needs

Attainment data for looked after children shows that they do not perform as well at key assessment stages when compared to non-looked after children. Reasons for this may include:

- periods off school due to early neglect which may lead to gaps in their learning

- changes of schools due to placement moves which may make sustaining friendships/developing trusting relationships with teachers difficult

- the emotional impact of their early experiences can make learning difficult as they may experience high levels of anxiety and find transitions more challenging than other children which can lead to disruptive behaviour

- developmental difficulties will impact on learning style.

If a child is having difficulties in school, this is also likely to impact on their placement. Every school should have a **designated teacher** who has a **statutory** role to ensure this vulnerable group's needs are considered and will link into the **virtual head**. All looked-after children should have a Personal Education Plan (PEP) which is part of the child's care plan and this must be reviewed regularly.

Conclusion

Looked after children and young people are a vulnerable group of our population, who may have experienced a high number of adverse childhood experiences that have compromised the caregiving that they received. This will impact on their development and places them at greater risk of developing mental health difficulties. Services targeting mental health for these young people need to work with the child and the network of adults around the child in a needs-led and systemic way.

References

Briskman J, Castle J, Blackeby K *et al* (2012) *Randomised Controlled Trial of the Fostering Changes Programme*. London: Department for Education. Available at: https://assets.publishing.service.gov.uk/government/uploads/system/uploads/attachment_data/file/183398/DFE-RR237.pdf Accessed 26 June 2019.

Department of Education (2017) *Children Looked After in England, Year Ending 31 March* [online]. London: DfE. Available at: https://www.gov.uk/government/uploads/system/uploads/attachment_data/file/647852/SFR50_2017-Children_looked_after_in_England.pdf (accessed 26 June 2019).

Department of Education and Department of Health (2015) *Promoting the Health and Wellbeing of Looked After Children* [online]. London: DfE/DH. Available at: https://www.gov.uk/government/publications/promoting-the-health-and-wellbeing-of-looked-after-children--2 (accessed 26 June 2019).

Department of Health (2015) *Future in Mind. Promoting, Protecting and Improving our Children and Young People's Mental Health and Wellbeing*. London: DH. Available at: https://assets.publishing.service.gov.uk/government/uploads/system/uploads/attachment_data/file/414024/Childrens_Mental_Health.pdf (accessed 26 June 2019).

Fonagy P, Cottrell D, Phillips J, Bevington D, Glaser D and Allison E (2016) *What Works for Whom? A Critical Review of Treatments for Children and Adolescents* (2nd edition). New York: Guilford Press.

Ford T, Vostanis P, Meltzer H and Goodman R (2007) Psychiatric disorder among British children looked after by local authorities: comparison with children living in private households. British Journal of Psychiatry 190 319–325.

Golding K (2013) *Nurturing Attachments Training Resource*. London: Jessica Kingsley.

Goodman R (2001) Psychometric properties of the strengths and difficulties questionnaire. *Journal of the American Academy of Child and Adolescent Psychiatry* **40** (11) 1337–45.

Green J, Leadbitter K, Kay C and Sharma K (2016) Autism spectrum disorder in children adopted after early care breakdown. *Journal of Autism and Developmental Disorders* **46** (4) 1392–1402.

Hughes K, Bellis M, Hardcastle K *et al* (2017) The effect of multiple adverse childhood experiences on health: a systematic review and meta-analysis. *Lancet Public Health* **2** 356–66. Available at: https://www.thelancet.com/action/showPdf?pii=S2468-2667%2817%2930118-4 (accessed 26 June 2019).

Mental Health Foundation (2002) *The Mental Health of Looked-After Children* [online]. London: MHF. Available at: https://www.mentalhealth.org.uk/publications/mental-health-looked-after-children (accessed 26 June 2019).

Milich L, Goulder S, Gibson S and Lindsay-Walters F (2017) *Improving Mental Health Support for Our Children and Young People*. London: SCIE. Available at: https://www.scie.org.uk/files/children/care/mental-health/recommendations/improving-mental-health-support-for-our-children-and-young-people-full-report.pdf (accessed 26 June 2019).

National Institute for Health and Care Excellence (2015) *Children's Attachment: Attachment in children and young people who are adopted from care, in care or at high risk of going into care* (NICE guideline 26) [online]. London: NIHCE. Available at: https://www.nice.org.uk/guidance/ng26 (accessed 26 June 2019).

National Institute for Health and Care Excellence (2019) *Nice Guidance* [online] Available at: https://www.nice.org.uk/guidance (accessed 1 August 2019).

Chapter 10: The Mental Health of Children and Young People with Learning Disabilities

Paula Lavis and Christine-Koulla Burke (with thanks to Professor Richard Hastings)

Key learning points

- Children and young people (CYP) with learning disabilities (LD) are at a higher risk than the general population of developing mental health problems.

- They often have other health and neurodevelopmental problems, which results in them having very complex issues.

- Mental health problems are not necessarily related to LD.

- Early intervention is essential as many problems are preventable or modifiable if picked up early enough.

- As with any CYP, having easy access to appropriate mental health services in their local community is essential.

Keywords

Learning disabilities; mental health; intellectual disability; discrimination; access to services; early intervention; specialist services

What is a learning disability?

The Department of Health, in their report *Valuing People: A new strategy for learning disability for the 21st century* (Department of Health, 2001) uses the term 'learning disabilities' when the following three core criteria are present:

- a significantly reduced ability to understand new or complex information, to learn new skills (impaired intelligence), *with*

- a reduced ability to cope independently (impaired social functioning)

- which started before adulthood, with a lasting effect on development.

There are about 286,000 school age children in England who have a learning disability (Emerson *et al*, 2012). People have learning disabilities from birth or develop them during infancy or childhood. They affect the person's development and are long-lasting. People with learning disabilities need additional support with learning while at school, and often with daily activities all through their life. There are many causes of learning disabilities and the specific cause is often unknown.

People with LD will have varying levels of disability ranging from mild to severe or profound as well as other comorbidities. Whilst all CYP with learning disabilities will meet the same overall definitional requirements for LD, their needs will vary and so the support they need will vary as well.

Other definitions

Many definitions of learning disabilities also specify that the person will have an IQ of less than 70. To put this in context, the average IQ is about 90–110 (eg the World Health Organization International Classification of Diseases (ICD-10) Classification of Mental and Behavioural Disorders (2010). IQ is measured by intelligence tests, which allow a person's scores to be compared with the range of scores achieved by large numbers of people on the same test. However, it must be remembered that an IQ score does not give any information about a person's social, medical, educational and personal needs, nor what help and support the person might need. Therefore, IQ is used as part of the assessment for LD but is not the sole criterion.

Autistic spectrum disorders (ASD) are not the same as a learning disability, but about 50% of people with ASD may also have a learning disability (NICE, 2011), and will probably have quite complex needs.

How many children and young people with a learning disability have a mental health problem?

We know that children and young people with a learning disability are at a much higher risk of developing a mental health problem. The government recently commissioned a national survey of children and young people's mental health to estimate the prevalence of mental health in this group, but unfortunately it doesn't include any specific data on those with learning disabilities (Sadler *et al*, 2018).

- 36% of this group will have an additional mental health need, and they are four to five times more likely to have a diagnosable psychiatric problem than those without a learning disability.
- 14% or one in seven of all CYP with mental health problems in the UK will also have a learning disability.
- CYP with LD were also more likely to have more complex mental health needs as they were more likely to have more than one mental health problem.

(Emerson & Hatton, 2007a)

Listening to children and young people and taking their issues seriously

Young people with LD tell us that they are not listened to, and feel ignored (Lavis *et al*, 2019). They are confused, lonely, angry and being sad, but are not confident that someone will help them if they try to talk to them about their mental health. Parents have told us that they have to battle to try to ensure that their children get some support, often with no one listening to them or taking responsibility for their care.

The importance of early interventions

There is a strong argument for early intervention, given the high prevalence of mental health problems in young people with LD and how it impacts on their quality of life. It is often social and environmental issues that these young people face, such as poverty, loneliness and bullying, that impact on their mental health, rather than the learning disability itself.

Mental health problems can be identified at a very young age and intervening much earlier, even in pre-school children, is important. As with any child or young person, a full range of universal-level services are needed, that are aimed at every child, and include health visitor checks during the very early years, support for families and primary care services; as well as targeted and specialist services – speech and language therapists, mental health services, including school based counselling services.

Early intervention is only possible if CYP, such as Mark in the case study below, are able to tell someone about their problems and appropriate action will be taken. If we want CYP to tell someone about their concerns regarding how they are feeling or if they are having difficult thoughts and behaviours, they need to be able to have the vocabulary necessary to do that. This can be hard for any CYP, but can be even harder for those with LD, because they may have problems expressing themselves.

Mark

Mark was a sensitive young man who always displayed symptoms of anxiety and depression.

He was referred for support many times with little success as he was not seen as presenting with mental health problems. It was not until a training session with the Foundation for People with Learning Disabilities, on the 'Feeling down guide – looking after my mental health' (Burke, 2014) that he was able to describe what was causing his heightened anxiety. He heard voices that made him scared to the extent that he would have to hide and shout to drown the voices in his head. It was the first time that he was able to express his symptoms. He was then referred for support and had a response in three months, but with a three month waiting list.

The importance of listening

In focus groups, young people have said that they have told someone about how they felt, but they did not feel confident that anyone would help them (Lavis *et al*, 2019). These young people also said that they feel ignored and that people spoke over them or for them. These CYP will be in contact with a number of different professionals so there are a number of opportunities to identify problems or issues that give cause for concern. Whilst some may need specialist help, there are a number of things that anyone can do. Children and young people may have problems expressing themselves, or they might even have speech and language problems – it is important that we take time to listen to them and find out what their concerns are. We must also not assume that issues going on in their own lives and communities don't impact on them; they may have relationship problems, family problems, concerns about violence in their communities, or be experiencing bullying and discrimination. As when talking to any child or young person, it is vital we take their concerns seriously.

It might be tempting to conclude from the prevalence research that learning disability itself is somehow the reason for increased mental health problems in this group of CYP. There are undoubtedly some contributing genetic risk factors that are associated with learning disability, such as the heightened risk of psychotic disorders in young people who have Prader Willi syndrome (eg Skokauskas *et al*, 2012). However, the vast majority of the evidence suggests that the group differences in the mental health of CYP with learning disabilities compared to other CYP constitutes a mental health inequality – that is, a group difference in health that does not have to exist. The reason for this conclusion is that the factors found to be associated with increased risk for mental health problems in CYP with learning disability are modifiable. Not only that, but most significant risk variables are the same as those associated with mental health problems in all CYP – although CYP with learning disabilities may be more exposed to these risks, their mental health is determined by similar factors (Emerson & Hatton, 2007b).

Access to services – the need for community-based services

Only 27.9% of CYP with learning disability who also had a diagnosable psychiatric disorder (based on a clinical interview) had any contact with mental health services in the preceding year, similar to the proportion of CYP without learning disability who had mental health problems and had received mental health services support (23.5%) (Toms *et al*, 2015). Waiting times are commonplace for all CYP, but May's case study, below, highlights the implications of what this can mean for the individual.

May

May is a young woman with learning disabilities who has just left special school to go to college. At school she presented with anxiety and depression as well as self-harming behaviours. Her anxiety was heightened when she started college and she refused to leave the house and was self-harming. She also displayed hording behaviours, which were impacting on her family.

May was very distressed and started to be aggressive towards her mother at the suggestion of returning to college.

When she was at school, she was referred several times to CAMHS but with no response; any support she did receive mostly came from the school. When she was a bit older, she was referred by the college to CAMHS – it was eight months before she had a response, with a six month waiting time to be seen.

This impacted on her parent's mental health and forced May to be confined to the house.

These UK population-based data did not suggest an inequality in access to mental health services, but did suggest that only a minority of all CYP with significant mental health problems received mental health support. However, details of treatment offered and delivered were not available and more recent population-based data are not available.

A significant treatment-related inequality does, however, exist when it comes to the availability of evidence for treating mental health problems in CYP with learning disability. The National Institute of Health and Care Excellence (NICE, 2016) clinical guidelines on mental health problems in children and adults with learning disabilities included comprehensive reviews of pharmacological and psychological treatments.

The general stance was taken that evidence for pharmacological treatments could be considered directly from the research literature on CYP generally with mental health problems – although there was also some evidence testing pharmacological treatments for ADHD in CYP with learning disabilities (NICE, 2016). However, psychological treatments require some adaptation to be suitable for CYP with learning disabilities. An analysis of this evidence found that adapted parent-training interventions can have a positive impact on the mental health problems of CYP with learning disabilities, but the quality of the studies was variable (NICE, 2016).

Holstead and Dalton (2013) compared cognitive behavioural therapy with individualised behavioural interventions in the treatment of trauma/PTSD symptoms in adolescents with learning disability. The quality of this research study was graded as Very Low. Therefore, in effect, there is currently no evidence for psychological treatments delivered directly to CYP with learning disabilities – representing an inequality in availability of treatment evidence. Research on psychological treatments for mental health problems in CYP with learning disabilities is needed urgently (NICE, 2016). It is also important to point out that NICE Guidance *is just guidance* and practitioners can bypass any recommendations given based on the limited evidence-base.

Children and young people with severe learning disabilities are an even more marginalised group. They are more likely to be prescribed psycho-active medications in the absence of a diagnosis of mental health problems (Vedi & Bernard, 2012). In addition, there are no assessments or measurement tools for mental health problems in CYP with learning disability with evidence of psychometrically robust properties for those with severe learning disability (see systematic review by Flynn *et al*, 2017). In a further systematic review of pharmacological or psychological treatments for mental health problems, there was only one intervention study (on vocal and motor tics in an adolescent with Tourette's syndrome), with evidence reported specifically for CYP with severe learning disabilities (Vereenooghe *et al*, 2017). Thus, research and clinical evidence on the assessment and psychological treatment, in particular for mental health problems in CYP with severe learning disabilities, is a priority for the immediate future.

Policy context

The NHS Long Term Plan, which sets out priorities for the NHS over the next 10 years, has a focus on CYP's mental health, but this section of the document makes no specific reference to learning disabilities (NHS England, 2019). Children and young people with a learning disability are still children, and you would expect them to be covered by this policy agenda, but we know that in practice this is not always the case.

There is a specific section on learning disabilities which includes some specific proposals. Some of these are very specific, with a timeframe, and others are quite vague.

The NHS Long Term Plan sets the following priorities:

- Commitment that the whole NHS will improve its understanding of the needs of people with learning disabilities and autism and to work together to improve their health and wellbeing.

- Provide NHS staff with information and training on supporting people with learning disabilities and autism.

- New national learning disabilities improvement standards will be implemented and apply to all NHS funded services.

- Increase the number of people with a learning disability aged over 14 having an annual health check.

- By 2023/24, CYP with a learning disability, autism or both with the most complex needs will have a designated keyworker, implementing the recommendation made by Dame Christine Lenehan (2017).

- By March 2023/24, inpatient provision will have been reduced to less than half of 2015 levels (on a like-for-like basis and taking into account population growth). For CYP, no more than 12 to 15 CYP with a learning disability, autism or both per million, will be cared for in an inpatient facility.

■ By 2023/24, all care commissioned by the NHS will need to meet the Learning Disability Improvement Standards. NHS England will work with the Care Quality Commission to implement recommendations on restricting the use of seclusion, long-term segregation and restraint for all patients in inpatient settings, particularly for CYP.

■ NHS England will review and look to strengthen the existing Care, Education and Treatment Review (CETR) and Care and Treatment Review (CTR) policies, in partnership with people with a learning disability, autism or both, and families and clinicians, to assess their effectiveness in preventing and supporting discharge planning.

Older policy documents, such as *Future in Mind* (DH & NHS England, 2015), recommended strengthening the links between children's mental health and learning disabilities services and services for CYP with special educational needs and disabilities (SEND) (Department for Health & NHS England, 2015). The *Five Year Forward View for Mental Health* (Mental Health Taskforce, 2016) says very little about learning disabilities, and defers to *Transforming Care* (NHS England, 2015), but this doesn't have a great focus on young people apart from a very specific cohort (ie those who are in inpatient settings).

There is a drive to prevent admissions to hospitals, but in March 2019 there were still about 240 under 18s, and 430 young people between the ages of 18–24 with a learning disability on inpatient units (NHS Digital, 2019); many of them will stay there for prolonged periods of time, often miles from their homes. Care, Education and Treatment reviews/Care and Treatment Reviews have been developed to help prevent admission if possible and find alternatives, and agree discharge plans (ADASS *et al*, 2015). There is concern about how well this is being implemented, as even young people with these plans are apparently not getting the help they need. It would be useful to find out whether this is an effective process as there is no independent evaluation.

The reforms to special educational needs (SEN) provision now includes social, emotional and mental health as an area of need (Code of practice) (Department for Education, 2014), which is a breakthrough as the policy framework now enables schools to talk about mental health in a way that they couldn't previously. The change in the age range is also significant in that it now covers 0–25 years – theoretically, this provides an opportunity for early intervention, and to help young people make the transition to adult life. It also encourages joint working by placing a duty on local authorities and their partner commissioning bodies to improve services for 0–25-year-old CYP who have SEN or disabilities, and including those who have an Education, Health and Care

Plan (EHCP). There is, however, discrepancy on the quality of EHCP and how they involve CYP and their families.

Conclusion

Children and young people with LD are at higher risk of developing mental health problems. This is not necessarily because of their LD, but often due to wider social factors that can be identified at a young age and are often preventable. Anyone working with CYP with LD should be mindful of that person's specific LD and the difficulties that this brings, but must be careful not to assume that all of their problems are connected to this.

There are a number of things that anyone working with CYP with LD can do. For instance, listening and giving time to both them and their parents to ensure that they are able to indicate the things that are of concern. Early intervention and prevention are paramount in supporting young people and their families and should not be excluded from policy and guidance. Commissioners need to be aware of the needs of all CYP, including those with LD. They should also be aware of the steps that can be put in place to ensure that CYP with LD are able to lead healthy lives in the community, and that early intervention will undoubtedly avoid exclusions. It is also important that they implement a 'no out-of-borough placements' policy for those needing extra support. This should at all times be offered locally with the best practitioners available at the point of referral to ensure that they stand the best chance of having a good life.

References

ADASS, Care Quality Commission, Department of Health, Health Education England, Local Government Association and NHS England (2015) *Transforming Care for People with Learning Disabilities: Next steps* [online]. Available at: https://www.england.nhs.uk/wp-content/uploads/2015/01/transform-care-nxt-stps.pdf (accessed 26 June 2019).

Burke C (2014) Feeling Down: Looking after my mental health. London: Foundation for People with Learning Disabilities. Available at: https://www.mentalhealth.org.uk/learning-disabilities/publications/feeling-down-looking-after-my-mental-health (accessed 26 June 2019).

Department for Education (2014) *Special Educational Needs Code of Practice*. London: Department for Education. Available at: https://www.gov.uk/topic/schools-colleges-childrens-services/special-educational-needs-disabilities (accessed 26 June 2019).

Department of Health and NHS England (2015) *Future in Mind: Promoting, protecting and improving our children and young people's mental health and wellbeing*. London: DH/NHS England. Available at: https://www.gov.uk/government/uploads/system/uploads/attachment_data/file/414024/Childrens_Mental_Health.pdf (accessed 26 June 2019).

Department of Health (2001) *Valuing People: A New Strategy for Learning Disability for the 21st Century*. London: Department of Health. Available at: https://www.gov.uk/government/uploads/system/uploads/attachment_data/file/250877/5086.pdf (accessed 26 June 2019).

Emerson C and Hatton C (2007a) *The Mental Health of Children and Adolescents with Learning Disabilities in Britain*. Lancaster, Lancaster University. Available at: https://www.lancaster.ac.uk/staff/emersone/FASSWeb/Emerson_07_FPLD_MentalHealth.pdf (accessed 26 June 2019).

Emerson C and Hatton C (2007b) Mental health of children and adolescents with intellectual disabilities in Britain. *British Journal of Psychiatry* **191** 439–499.

Emerson C, Hatton C, Robertson J, Roberts H, Baines S, Evison F and Glover G (2012) People with learning disabilities in England 2011. London: Learning Disabilities Observatory. Available at: https://webarchive.nationalarchives.gov.uk/20160704171409/http://www.improvinghealthandlives.org.uk/publications/1063/People_with_Learning_Disabilities_in_England_2011 (accessed 29 July 2019).

Flynn S, Vereenooghe L, Hastings RP, Adams D, Cooper S-A, Gore N, Hatton C, Hood K, Jahoda A, Langdon PE, McNamara R, Oliver C, Roy A, Totsika V and Waite J (2017) Measurement tools for mental health problems and mental wellbeing in people with severe or profound intellectual disabilities: A systematic review. *Clinical Psychology Review* **57** 32-44.

Holstead J and Dalton J (2013) Utilization of Trauma-Focused Cognitive Behavioral Therapy (TF-CBT) for Children with Cognitive Disabilities. *Journal of Child Welfare* **7** 536–548.

Lavis P, Burke C and Hastings R (2019) *Overshadowed: The mental health needs of children and young people with learning disabilities*. London: Children and Young People's Mental Health Coalition. Available at: http://www.cypmhc.org.uk/resources/overshadowed (accessed 29 July 2019).

Lenehan C (2017) *These are our Children*. London: Council for Disabled Children. Available at: https://www.ncb.org.uk/sites/default/files/field/attachment/These%20are%20Our%20CHildren_Lenehan_Review_Report.pdf (accessed 29 July 2019).

Mental Health Taskforce (2016) *The Five Year Forward View for Mental Health*. London: NHS England. Available at: https://www.england.nhs.uk/publication/the-five-year-forward-view-for-mental-health/ (accessed 29 July 2019).

NHS Digital (2019) *Learning Disability Services Monthly Statistics Data from the Assuring Transformation Collection* Available at: https://files.digital.nhs.uk/4B/9EB138/ldsm-Mar-19-Main-Report.pdf (accessed 26 June 2019).

NHS England (2015) *Transforming Care*. London: NHS England. Available at: https://www.england.nhs.uk/learning-disabilities/care/ (accessed 26 June 2019).

NHS England (2019) *NHS Long Term Plan*. London: NHS England. Available at: https://www.longtermplan.nhs.uk/ (accessed 26 June 2019).

NICE (2011) *Autism Spectrum Disorder in Under 19s*. London: NICE. Available at: https://www.nice.org.uk/guidance/cg128/resources/autism-spectrum-disorder-in-under-19s-recognition-referral-and-diagnosis-pdf-35109456621253 (accessed 26 June 2019).

NICE (2016) *Mental health problems in people with learning disabilities: prevention, assessment, and management*. NICE Guideline NG54. Available at: https://www.nice.org.uk/guidance/ng54/evidence/full-guideline-pdf-2612227933 (accessed 26 June 2019).

Sadler K, Vizard T, Ford T, Marcheselli F, Pearce N, Mandalia D, Davis J, Brodie E, Forbes N, Goodman A, Goodman R, McManus S, and Collinson, D (2018) *Mental Health of Children and Young People in England, 2017*. London: NHS Digital https://digital.nhs.uk/data-and-information/publications/statistical/mental-health-of-children-and-young-people-in-england/2017/2017 (accessed 29 July 2019)

Skokauskas N, Sweeny E, Meehan J and Gallagher L (2012) Mental health problems in children with Prader-Willi Syndrome. *Journal of the Canadian Academy of Child and Adolescent Psychiatry* **21** 194–203.

Toms G, Totsika V, Hastings RP and Healy H (2015) Access to services by children with intellectual disability and mental health problems: population-based evidence from the UK. *Journal of Intellectual and Developmental Disabilities* **40** 239–247.

Vedi K and Bernard S (2012) The mental health needs of children and adolescents with learning disabilities. *Current Opinion in Psychiatry* **25** 353–358.

Verennooghe L, Flynn S, Hastings R, Adams D, Chauhan U, Cooper S-A, Gore N, Hatton C, Hood K, Jahoda A, Langdon PE, McNamara R, Oliver C, Roy A, Totsika V, and Waite J (2017) *Interventions for mental health problems in children and adults with severe intellectual disabilities: A systematic review.* BMJ Open 8 e021911. Available at: https://bmjopen.bmj.com/content/bmjopen/8/6/e021911.full.pdf (accessed 26 June 2019).

World Health Organization (WHO) *2010 International Statistical Classification of Diseases and Related Health Problems 10th revision.* Geneva: WHO. Available at: http://apps.who.int/classifications/icd10/browse/2010/en (accessed 26 June 2019).

Useful resources

Foundation for People with Learning Disabilities: https://www.mentalhealth.org.uk/learning-disabilities

Mencap – What is a learning disability?: https://www.mencap.org.uk/learning-disability-explained (accessed 26 June 2019).

Chapter 11: Transition from Child to Adult Mental Health Services

Cathy Street and Louise Theodosiou

Key learning points

- Transition refers to the process of moving someone from one service to another and should involve the co-ordination, planning and continued care and support throughout.

- Poor and disjointed care at the point of young people leaving Child and Adolescent Mental Health Services (CAMHS), results in many failing to move successfully to Adult Mental Health Services (AMHS), when ongoing mental health needs indicate this is required, is an area of longstanding concern.

- We have good research evidence that the transition from adolescence to adulthood is a key life stage with regard to the emergence of mental health disorders, making the need for access for mental health care at this point even more critical.

- Over the last decade at least, improving transitional care between CAMHS and AMHS has been a national policy imperative.

- Although much progress has been made, there is more work to be done to enable young people to transition into the adult mental health services that they need.

- Young people should play a central role in the planning, development, implementation and review of transition services and their own transition journey.

- Clinicians, commissioners and wider stakeholders from child and adult services must work with young people to develop transition services and enhance transition pathways.

- More research is needed to understand the barriers that impact on the delivery of co-ordinated care at the point of transition and to disseminate learning as to what works..

Keywords
Transition; young people's involvement; gaps; developmentally appropriate services; coordination; continuity of care

Introduction

Improving transition between different services is of critical importance for young people with mental health needs if we are to avoid the risks of young people falling into service gaps; being subject to inconsistent referral processes which can leave them unsupported at critical points in their lives and which may lead to them disengaging from services altogether. Concerns about transition are not new and have been the subject of a variety of national inquiries, policy initiatives and research studies. In this chapter, we provide an overview of some of the key findings of these activities, noting that many of the difficulties that beset good transitional care reflect the legacy of different service histories and the impact of this on treatment approaches.

In exploring why it important that we improve this aspect of mental health care, we outline some of the pointers from the research evidence base as to the things that may make a difference, identify those groups of young people most likely to need to transition to adult services and also the barriers they may face. We also briefly touch on some of research data about new service models that have emerged to try and address these issues.

A key running throughout is that it is essential to fully involve young people in the transition process – and where appropriate, their parents and carers – not least because one of the concerns most frequently raised by young people in transition is that their views are ignored, they are given little or no information and are excluded from decision-making about this crucial service move.

What is transition?

Transition describes the process of moving someone from one service to another. It differs from transfer in that, as opposed to the termination of care by a children's provider and then a re-starting of care with a new service, transition should be co-ordinated, planned, prepared for, and the person should be supported throughout leaving one service and engaging with another. With regard to mental health services for young people, transition to adult services typically happens at the age of 18, although this age boundary can vary.

Poor and disjointed care offered to young people at transition is a longstanding concern, with research highlighting that many young people experience poor planning, little information, limited choice and a sense of the whole process being left to the last minute and then rushed, often with no one person taking responsibility to ensure that decisions are followed through. These circumstances crucially can leave young people unsupported, with some falling through the gap of inconsistent referral criteria or being left to navigate their way through complicated service arrangements (Hall *et al*, 2013; Islam *et al*, 2016; Street *et al*, 2018a; Street *et al*, 2018b). Concerns about the differences between services, including high service thresholds, have also been identified as leading to hesitance among CYPMHS clinicians about trying to transition young people to AMHS (Paul *et al*, 2015).

There have been many government policy initiatives aimed at improving young people's transitions. In 2017 NHS England introduced a new CQUIN (Commissioning for Quality and Innovation) focused on young people and transition. CQUINs are contractual levers intended to improve services, in this case to incentivise services to support young people as they transition from child and young people's mental health services (CYPMHS). This requires services to audit their case notes and survey young people's transition experience before and after moving services, and illustrates the current high level of policy interest and the determination to improve this aspect of mental health care.

The legacy of different service histories

The way services have developed has an important bearing in understanding why mental health transitional care seems to be so challenging to deliver. Services for children and adults have evolved from separate places, with developmentally-focused and family-based models being used with children and young people, whilst in adult services a recovery-focused autonomy-enhancing structure predominates. While the principles of both provide many people with effective care, they complicate moving between services. A range of other factors also play a role: different terminology; different approaches to diagnosis; different treatment modalities; and the limited incorporation of developmental principles in adult care. When services are under pressure, it also appears that these differences become more marked.

Signorini and colleagues (2018) mapped mental health services across Europe in 2017 and reported that the historical development of separate facilities for children and adolescents and those for adults, is a significant bottleneck to transitional care. At a practical level, different service configurations can impede joined up care – for example, some children's services are based within acute trusts providing physical and mental health care while others are based within mental health trusts serving both children and adults. This can mean that young people will transition into adult services in a different trust covering the same area, which complicates information-sharing and the development of shared protocols.

Furthermore, some services offered in CYPMHS, for example for young people with attention deficit hyperactivity disorder (ADHD), are limited in adult mental health services (AMHS) (Hall *et al*, 2013). There is also a widespread lack of transition protocols, variations in referral criteria and, often, a practical barrier in that child and adult services used different sets of clinical notes and electronic data systems.

Why improving young people's transition is a critical issue

Research identifies the transition from adolescence to adulthood as an important life stage in terms of social and emotional development and also with regard to psychopathology. Good practice guidance from the Child and Adolescent Faculty of the Royal College of Psychiatrists (Lamb *et al*, 2008) notes that transition 'coincides with the emergence of personality disorders and a steep rise in the rates of mental disorder'. Research by Reef *et al* (2010) and Kessler *et al* (2007) makes similar points and Kessler's earlier work (2005) highlights the link between mental health conditions in adolescence and in adults, noting that 75% of all disorders in adults had started by the age of 24, and 50% before the age of 14.

Jones (2013) reports that most mental health problems have their origins in adolescence and describes the years 16–18 as a 'particularly critical period of vulnerability'. Other data suggest young people who fail to transition often present to adult services later on, either in crisis or when more serious and chronic problems have developed (Singh, 2009: Signorini *et al*, 2018). The potentially devastating consequences of this are illustrated by data presented by the Care Quality Commission that around 60% of young people under the age of 20 who die by suicide were found to have previous CYPMHS contact (CQC, 2017).

A general conclusion reached by a number of researchers is that mental health service delivery appears to be especially weak at a time of pressing need (Birchwood & Singh, 2013) and collectively, these data illustrate how vital it is that there is continuity of care across the transition boundary.

Michael

Michael is approaching his 18th birthday. He has complex needs; he is a looked after child living in his own accommodation, he uses alcohol and cannabis with older peers and has involvement with youth justice services. Michael has mild learning difficulties. He also has ADHD but is not currently taking medication as he does not feel that the medication helps. Michael struggles to attend appointments, he has been visited at home by the nurse who is the link between youth justice and CAMHS. This has been helpful at times when he is distressed or anxious. Michael is not perceived as meeting the threshold of need for adult mental health services, and instead is offered a referral to the voluntary sector counselling service that works with young adults, which he declines. Michael is discharged to his general practice without an ongoing mental health service.

The national policy context

Addressing the problem of transition has been a recurrent theme in national policy and guidance. Key examples include the *National Service Framework for Children and Maternity Services* (Department of Health & Department for Education and Skills, 2004) which identified the need to address the mental health needs of 16 and 17-year-olds and the CAMHS National Review *Children and Young People in Mind* (Department of Health and Department for Children, Schools and Families, 2008), which noted, 'during our practice visits, it was transition from CAMHS to adult services that causes children, their families and service providers most concern'. Guidance for commissioners issued by the Joint Commissioning Panel for Mental Health (2012) emphasised the need for:

- developmentally appropriate services for 16–17-year-olds

- robust multi-agency working

- supporting young people in out of area placements

- meeting the needs of vulnerable young people and ensuring that these are identified in Joint Strategic Needs Assessments (JSNAs)

- ensuring that there were formal transition arrangements and protocols between CYPMHS and AMHS to address structural and procedural difficulties at this interface and also difficulties arising from the cultural differences between these services.

Future in Mind (Department of Health and NHS England, 2015), the final report of the Children and Young People's Mental Health and Wellbeing Taskforce, set out the vision for mental health services for children and young people and a substantial section is focused on transition. It is noted: 'the Taskforce does not wish to be prescriptive about the age of transition, but does recognise that transition at 18 will often not be appropriate. We recommend flexibility around age boundaries, in which transition is based on individual circumstances rather than absolute age, with joint working and shared practice between services'.

The *Five Year Forward View for Mental Health* (Mental Health Taskforce, 2016) notes that the strategy it puts forward builds on *Future in Mind*, including the emphasis on improving transitional care.

Encouragingly, this high-level interest in improving transition has continued with the *NHS Long Term Plan* (NHS England, 2019), which not only commits to extra funding for children and young people's mental health services, but also creates a comprehensive service model for 0–25-year-olds, as a part of the wider 'Long Term Plan' implementation. Furthermore, there is mention of the expansion of services through schools and colleges, and work with Universities UK via the Mental Health in Higher Education programme, to deliver an integrated approach across health, social care, education and the voluntary sector, to improve provision and build capacity in services for the 0–25 age range.

Research findings and other key reports

The *Transition from CAMHS to Adult Mental Health Service (TRACK)* study (Singh *et al*, 2005; 2010) described the difficulties faced by young people in transition from CYPMHS into AMHS. TRACK identified four optimal markers of transition:

1. Good information transfer

2. A period of parallel care (when CYPMHS and AMHS work together)

3. Planning (including the holding of a meeting involving the young person)

4. Continuity of care.

TRACK followed 154 young people in transition over a one-year period and, unfortunately, found that less than 5% experienced all four markers. The study reported that young people with illnesses defined as 'major mental illness' were more likely to transition into adult care and those with neurodevelopmental conditions such as ADHD were less likely to transition successfully. Singh *et al*'s research additionally highlighted the value of transition protocols but also their very limited implementation.

New research from a five-year study of young people's transitions from children's mental health services – the MILESTONE Project – led by Singh and colleagues from seven other European countries, will be available late summer 2019. Funded by the EU's Seventh Framework Programme for research, technological development and demonstration, the study has involved over 1,000 young people. For further information see https://warwick.ac.uk/fac/sci/med/research/hscience/mhwellbeing/mh/transition/milestone.

The Young Minds *Stressed Out and Struggling* project (Pugh, 2006) emphasised the importance of involving young people and families in the preparation for transition. The project identified major barriers for young people aged 16 and 17 in accessing mental health services including: their hours of operation; the age appropriateness of the service environment; the availability of services for young people in crisis and their ability to work with the many diverse needs presented by this age group. It was highlighted that services need to know about agencies that can work with young people who do not meet the threshold for AMHS but who require support.

In *Good Mental Health Services for Young People* (Royal College of Psychiatrists, 2017) a range of relevant research findings on the CYPMHS/AMHS divide and transition are presented. It identifies four groups of young people who may transition from CAMHS:

1. Those with severe or enduring mental health conditions who clearly meet the eligibility criteria for AMHS – e.g. young people with psychosis or eating disorders.

2. Young people with severe or enduring mental health conditions who do not meet the eligibility criteria of most AMHS – e.g. those with neurodevelopmental disorders.

3. Vulnerable young people with pronounced needs that may not be clearly expressed as mental health problems but who have risk factors for poor outcomes – e.g. those with a history of severe trauma, severe repetitive self-harm, those in care or in the youth justice system.

4. Those with chronic physical illness comorbid with mental illness.

Barriers to transition include:

- different thresholds and concepts of what constitutes a mental health condition

- different models of care and expectations (for young people, families and service providers)

- a different level of intensity of care in adult services (compared to children's services)

- diverse pathways from children's to adult services and a lack of training and expertise in AMHS regarding working with young people.

The report identifies particular groups of young people who are at much higher risk of developing a mental health condition and argues that they should be prioritised when developing mental health services for young people. The groups include:

- looked after children

- young people with an intellectual disability

- those with special educational needs

- those with a physical illness

- homeless young people

- young offenders

- young people who self-harm

- teenage parents

- young carers

- young people with a family history of psychosis, major mood disorder or prodromal symptoms.

In terms of transition models, the report notes the value of transition clinics, condition specific clinics, multi-agency 'one-stop-shop' models, clinics based in primary care and virtual teams between child and adult services. Such models can enable young people to avoid the challenge of multiple simultaneous transitions and ensure that they have professionals who they know to support them in times of crisis.

In 2016, the National Institute of Health and Care Excellence produced *Transition from children's to adults' services for young people using health or social care services*. This guideline suggests that transition planning needs to start at least six months before a young person's 18th birthday; it recommends that a young person has a named worker who will act as a link between services and provide continuity of support for a minimum of six month before and after transition. There should be a senior executive accountable for transition strategies and an operational-level champion with responsibility for reviewing effectiveness of the local transition strategy. Five quality standards are proposed:

1. Services should start planning transition with health and social care by school year 9.

2. There should be annual meetings to review transition progress.

3. There should be a named worker co-ordinating transition.

4. The young person should meet with an adult worker prior to transition.

5. If people do not attend an appointment they are contacted by adult services.

Are We Listening? A review of children and young people's mental health services (CQC, 2018) presents the findings of the CQC 2017 independent review. It notes:

'...we found that confusion about the point at which transition should take place posed a barrier to high-quality care.'

It highlighted concerns about services rigidly transitioning young people when they turn 18 (noted to be contrary to good practice and official guidance) and poor transition planning, alongside providing examples of practice seen as enabling transition to take place. These included:

- moves taking place gradually over time

- good communication and information sharing (including about possible options)

- support workers who stayed with the young person as they moved between services

- psychiatrists who usually worked with adults being deployed to work with teenagers during and after transition in order to maintain a consistent relationship during a period of change.

In 2018 the Healthcare Safety Investigation Branch (HSIB) investigated transition from CYPMHS to AMHS. The HSIB was contacted following the suicide of a young man shortly after his transition to AMHS. The findings emphasised the importance of flexible, carefully planned transitions which incorporate a period of shared care, provide continuity of care and follow up. Furthermore, HSIB notes:

'...flexible services are especially important for young people with emotional problems, complex needs, mild learning disability, ADHD and ASD, for whom services in adult mental health services are limited.'

HSIB makes six safety recommendations for NHS England and NHS Improvement. These include:

- work within the *NHS Long-Term Plan* (NHS England, 2019) to identify and meet the needs of young adults who do not meet the criteria for AMHS

- that transition guidance, pathways and performance measures require that structured conversations take place with young people in transition to assess their readiness for this move, and their understanding of their condition, and to empower them to ask questions

- that NHS England, within the NHS Long-Term Plan, requires services to move from age-based transition criteria towards more flexible criteria based on an individual's needs.

The following case study provides an illustration of how a young person's transition might be supported if some of HSIB's recommendations were implemented.

Yasmin

Yasmin is a young person with post-traumatic symptoms, anxiety, low mood and thoughts of suicide. Yasmin is using the drug 'spice', and worries about her physical health, but she does not want a referral to a substance use service. She is living in independent accommodation where she struggles with bills and feels unsafe. Yasmin has just started an apprenticeship in mechanics which she is enjoying. She has struggled to engage in therapy work, however there are times when she struggles to regulate her emotions and does benefit from supportive work with the nurse in CAMHS. Jane and the nurse jointly develop a formulation to identify her areas of strength, her sources of support and her unmet needs. The nurse contacts the community adult mental health team and they agree to meet with her and to undertake ongoing reviews of her mental health and social care needs. Yasmin is able to transition into the adult service after a joint meeting with child and adult services.

Young people's experiences

In the UK, 18 is the age that a young person legally becomes an adult. At 18 a person can vote in government elections, get married without parental consent, buy property and join the army. They can no longer be adopted and they would be tried for an alleged crime in adult court. The Care Act (2014) offers safeguards to adults who are deemed as vulnerable, but regardless of a person's developmental age at 18, they are perceived as an adult.

Within the health system, this means that many young people will be referred into adult services, although some transitions begin before a young person turns 16. At the age of 17 a young person may access emergency healthcare from adult services, and this can cause challenges if they are still accessing other aspects of care from children's services.

Young people have fed back that they do not always feel ready to transition at age 18. Others have reported concerns about their transition from CYPMHS which provide a vivid illustration of some of the barriers affecting continuity of care at this time point. These suggest that all too often there is a disconnect between national policy and guidance and practice down on the ground and highlight some of the more subtle cultural differences between services that can impede transition.

Examples of some of the difficulties encountered by young people when transitioning from CAMHS include:

- little planning and inadequate information about possible service options
- professionals who took a 'they know best' approach and failed to involve young people in discussions, or who followed guidance about holding a transition planning meeting but failed to explain to the young person who the different professionals were.

As reported in Street *et al* (2018a), one young person commented:

'*I would have liked to have known the full meeting agenda, who the people were, what services they came from and what help they could offer me. Instead I felt put on the spot to talk to a room full of strangers about deeply personal issues... this made me feel marginalised, hopeless and helpless...*'

This young person's poor experience of a transition meeting was further compounded when they were asked to leave the meeting at the point of decisions being made.

Other problems at transition related to young people's transitions coinciding with them moving area to go to university. This move seemed to make it impossible for services to work collaboratively across different geographic areas. Various reports of young people's experiences have also documented them being told they were 'not ill enough' to meet the referral criteria for AMHS or being left on long waiting lists for AMHS with no support in the interim and then finally arriving at the first appointment in AMHS only to find that the service knew nothing about their mental health care history or needs. In this situation, not only did young people have to re-tell their story, something many found upsetting, some felt that they were having to prove their need for care (Street *et al*, 2018).

The situation can be further complicated for children with additional needs such as learning difficulties, limited family support, physical and mental health problems, young people who have been supported within specialist placements and those in contact with the youth justice system. And crucially, young people have talked of these experiences making them feel guilty (of putting pressure on their families or on over-stretched services), scared (of the unknown and of being left without support) and disempowered. Hardly surprising, therefore, that various research data indicate that a sizeable number of young people disengage from mental health services at transition, or report finding themselves in services that do not appear to fit with their needs.

Conclusion

Young adult's mental health care should be seamless and their health should not be allowed to deteriorate during the process of transition, nor should they be allowed to fall into a 'care gap' between services, only to later access help when in crisis or with more entrenched difficulties. Clearly, there is pressure on all mental health services, and transition initiatives cannot address service pressures. However, as briefly reviewed in this chapter, there is a wealth of data about what does or does not work to support young people in transition, clear pointers about what is needed to improve transitional care, information about groups of young people who may need to be prioritised and examples of service models and ways of working that have been found valuable. Drawing together young people's experiences, findings from research studies that have explored transition and good practice guidance, there is clearly much that could be done, at the very least to improve information sharing, planning and the involvement of young people and their families and carers.

References

Birchwood M and Singh SP (2013) Mental health services for young people: matching the service to the need. *British Journal of Psychiatry* **202** (suppl 54) s1–2.

Care Quality Commission (2017) *Review of Children and Young People's Mental Health Services: Phase one report* [online]. London: CQC. Available at: www.cqc.org.uk

Care Quality Commission (2018) *Are We Listening? Review of Children and Young People's Mental Health Services*. London: CQC. Available at: www.cqc.org.uk

Department of Health and NHS England (2015) *Future in Mind: Promoting, Protecting and Improving our Children and Young People's Mental Health and Wellbeing*. London: DH/NHS England.

Department of Health and Department for Children, Schools and Families (2008) *Children and Young People in Mind: Final report of the CAMHS national review*. London: DH/DCSF. Available at: https://webarchive.nationalarchives.gov.uk/20090615071556/http://publications.dcsf.gov.uk/eOrderingDownload/CAMHS-Review.pdf (accessed 26 June 2019).

Department of Health and Department for Education and Skills (2004) *National Service Framework for children, young people and maternity services*. London: DH/DfES. Available at: https://www.gov.uk/government/publications/national-service-framework-children-young-people-and-maternity-services (accessed 26 June 2019).

Hall C, Newell K and Taylor J (2013) Mind the gap – mapping services for young people with ADHD transitioning from child to adult services. *BMC Psychiatry* **10** (13) 186..

Healthcare Safety Investigation Branch (HSIB) (2018) *Investigation into the transition from child and adolescent mental health services to adult mental health services* [online]. London: HSIB. Available at: https://www.hsib.org.uk/investigations-cases/transition-from-child-and-adolescent-mental-health-services-to-adult-mental-health-services/ (accessed 26 June 2019).

Islam Z, Ford T, Kramer T and Paul M (2016) Mind how you cross the gap! Outcomes for young people who failed to make the transition from child to adult services: the TRACK study. *British Journal of Psychology Bulletin* **40** (3) 142–148.

Joint Commissioning Panel for Mental Health (2012) *Guidance for Commissioners of Mental Health Services for Young People Making the Transition from Child to Adult Mental Health Services*. London: JCPMH. Available at: https://www.jcpmh.info/wp-content/uploads/jcpmh-camhstransitions-guide.pdf (accessed 26 June 2019).

Jones PB (2013) Adult mental health disorders and their age of onset. *British Journal of Psychiatry* **202** (54) s5–10.

Kessler RC, Chiu WT, Demler O, Merikangas KR and Walters EE (2005) Prevalence, severity and comorbidity of 12-month DSM-IV disorders in the National Comorbidity Survey Replication. *Archives of General Psychiatry* **62** 617–627.

Kessler RC Amminger GP, Aguilar-Gaxiola S, Alonso J, Lee S and Ustün TB (2007) Age of onset of mental disorders: a review of recent literature. *Current Opinion in Psychiatry* **20** 359–264.

Lamb C, Hall D, Kelvin R and Van Beinum M (2008) *Working at the CAMHS/Adult Interface: Good practice guidance for the provision of psychiatric services to adolescents/young adults*. Paper from the Interfaculty working group of the Child and Adolescent Faculty and the General and Community Faculty of the Royal College of Psychiatrists.

Mental Health Taskforce (2016) *The Five Year Forward View for Mental Health*. London: Mental Health Taskforce. Available at: https://www.england.nhs.uk/wp-content/uploads/2016/02/Mental-Health-Taskforce-FYFV-final.pdf (accessed 26 June 2019).

NHS England (2019) *The NHS Long Term Plan*. London: NHS England. Available at: www.longtermplan.nhs.uk (accessed 26 June 2019).

National Institute for Health and Care Excellence (2016) *Transition from Children's to Adults Services for Young People Using Health or Social Care Services*. London: NIHCE. Available at: https://www.nice.org.uk/guidance/ng43/resources/transition-from-childrens-to-adults-services-for-young-people-using-health-or-social-care-services-pdf-1837451149765 (accessed 26 June 2019).

NHS England CQUIN (2017) *Transitions Out of Children and Young People's Mental Health Services*. London: NHS England. Available at: https://www.england.nhs.uk/wp-content/uploads/2016/11/cquin-2017-19-guidance.pdf (accessed 26 June 2019).

Paul M, Street C, Wheeler N and Singh S (2015) Transition to adult services for young people with mental health needs: a systematic review. *Clinical child psychology and psychiatry* **20** 436–457.

Pugh K (2006) *Stressed Out and Struggling: Commissioning Mental Health Services for 16-25 Year-olds*. London: YoungMinds.

Reef J, Hall D, Kelvin R and Van Beinum M (2010) Predicting adult emotional and behavioural problems from externalizing trajectories in a 24-year longitudinal study. *European Child and Adolescent Psychiatry* **19** 932–942.

Royal College of Psychiatrists (2017) *Good Mental Health Services for Young People*. Faculty Report FR/CAP/GAP/. London: RCP.

Signorini G, Singh S, Boricevic Marsanic V, Dielman G, Dogic-Curkovic K, Franic T, Gerritsen S, Griffin J, Maras A, McNicholas F, O'Hara L, Purper-Ouakil D, Paul M, Russet F, Santosh P, Schulze U, Street C, Tremmery S, Tuomainen H, Verhulst F, Warwick J and de Girolamo G for the MILESTONE Consortium (2018) The interface between child/adolescent and adult mental health services: results from a European 28-country survey. *European Child & Adolescent Psychiatry* **27** (4) 501–511.

Singh S (2009) Transition of care from child to adult mental health services: the great divide. *Current Opinion in Psychiatry* **22** (4) 386–390.

Singh S, Evans N, Sireling L and Stuart H (2005) Mind the gap: the interface between child and adult mental health services. *Psychiatric Bulletin* **29** (8) 292–294.

Singh S, Paul M, Ford T, Kramer T, Weaver T, McLaren S, Hovish K, Islam Z, Belling R and White S (2010) Process, outcome and experience of transition from child to adult mental healthcare: multiperspective study. *British Journal of Psychiatry* **197** (4) 305–312.

Street C, Walker L, Tuffrey A and Wilson A (2018a) Transition between different UK mental health services – young people's experiences on what makes a difference. *Journal of Clinical Psychiatry and Cognitive Psychology* **2** (1) 1–5.

Street C, Walker L and Tuffrey A (2018b) Young people's experiences of transition in mental health services – a key perspective to consider. *EC Psychology and Psychiatry* **7** (11).

Chapter 12: Valuing Youth Involvement in Mental Health Service Design and Delivery

Sarah-Jane Fenton, Sarah Carr, Layne Boyden, James Molloy, Holly Moyse, Imaan Rathore, Bethany Skinner, Charlie Tresadern, Hope Virgo, Beckye Williams and Niyah Campbell

Key learning points

■ Health service goals (often linked to change and quality improvement) are not irreconcilable with the motivations of young people, however, understanding young people's motivations for involvement and setting clear expectations and goals are critical to successful engagement and involvement.

■ A key motivation for young people is to affect change and make a difference. It is therefore vital to have transparency and clarity about their scope of influence, what is possible and to evidence change where it has happened as a result of involvement.

■ When young people become involved in health service design and delivery or research, there is a need to be mindful of the power dynamics and assumptions that often exist.

■ When involving young people, thinking about representation and accessibility are important. If involvement is done poorly and young people do not feel listened to during participation, not only will young people disengage from the process but there is a risk that they disengage from services themselves due to their negative experience of involvement.

Keywords
Involvement; young people; co-production; mental health; health policy

Introduction

One of the challenges when people talk about 'involving young people' is that it is unclear what that involvement looks like: *who* gets to be involved? *How much* are young people involved? To what extent does the involvement of young people have *any effect* on the thing that they are involved in? These are all challenges that we will discuss in this chapter.

Initially, we will examine some definitions of involvement and different types of involvement. We will explore where both the definition and the practice of involvement of young people with lived experience of mental distress and mental ill health come from. We will then discuss the wider context for youth involvement, the evidence-base around this work, and the reasons why you would involve young people in mental health service design or delivery.

The main body of the chapter frames the debate about different understandings of how to use expertise through examining the experiences of young people. We explore how services might engage young people in meaningful interactions that lead to co-produced outcomes. We use personal case studies to explain what meaningful involvement looks and feels like, and what poor quality involvement feels like and results in. Instead of giving you a shopping list of what to do, or not to do, we felt explaining some of the logic behind why processes may fail or succeed may be more useful. Finally, we offer some thoughts on future directions for research and practice through asking how we could all work together to support participatory approaches with young people being adopted in service design and delivery.

It would be very odd to write a chapter about young people's involvement without involving young people themselves as a starting point. However, we have decided that if we mean it when we say young people's involvement should be valued, we should 'practise what we preach'. For that reason, this chapter has been co-authored by the Institute for Mental Health's Youth Advisory Group (IMH YAG) at the University of Birmingham (YAG Institute for Mental Health, 2018). The IMH YAG decided the questions that needed to be asked, the answers to which were used to frame each of the sections of this chapter. They sent the researchers away to find out information, but equal weight was given to the IMH YAG's lived experiences of being involved in the design and delivery of mental health services, such as being lay members sitting on health boards. Each of the young people (and the academic staff) who have contributed to this chapter is therefore listed as an author. We hope that you enjoy the chapter and find it useful when you are thinking about your own experience, your care, your role, your work, your service, or your setting.

What do we mean when we say 'involvement'?

Very often, when involvement is talked about in mental health, it is either through agreed principles for involvement or ways of working. The emphasis is often placed on engaging people with lived experience in the first place, in ways that are mutually acceptable, rather than on what should happen as a result of that engagement.

Service-user involvement began when disabled people and people with mental health problems started to campaign for a say in decisions about the health and social care services and support that ultimately affected their lives. In the 1970s they formed campaigning groups and organisations to change the way services were provided and designed, and moved from having to live in institutions and group homes to living independently, with the right support, in their own homes and communities (Campbell & Oliver, 1996). From then until now, disabled people, people with learning disabilities and those with mental health problems continue to campaign for involvement and co-production in designing, delivering and researching services and support (Carr & Beresford, 2012). They do so collectively though user-led organisations (ULOs) or as individuals, both locally and nationally. Those from black, Asian and minority ethnic (BAME) communities and lesbian, gay, bisexual and transgender (LGBT) people, among others, also campaign for services and support that better meets their needs (Beresford, 2013). Children and young people's involvement was influenced by the 1989 *UN Convention on the Rights of the Child* which says that the views of the child should be respected (UN General Assembly, 1990). Voluntary organisations have been supporting and campaigning for the involvement of children and young people, particularly those who are disabled, over the past 20 years and NHS England has emphasised the importance of the involvement of young people in mental health (Reeve, 2018).

The language to describe the activity of involvement is varied, with people also using the terms 'participation' and 'co-production', and it's important to note the co-production is different to involvement and participation. Involvement and participation may mean consultation or engagement. An example of consultation is people who use services filling in surveys but having no power to effect change. Engagement means people expressing their views and possibly being able to influence decisions if professionals or policy makers allow. Co-production is 'an equal (and long-term) relationship between people who use services and people responsible for services. They work together from design to delivery, sharing strategic decision-making as well as decisions about the best way to deliver services' (TLAP, 2016). Co-production means that those who use services are equal partners in achieving change.

Principles for involvement and co-production

Many groups have worked on principles for involvement and co-production in adult health and social care which are transferable for young people. Early work in Australia has highlighted some basic principles for youth participation in mental health services themselves (James, 2007). Whilst work in the UK has highlighted the contribution that involving young people can make to services, and showcases some different models for doing this (National Children's Bureau, 2016; Street & Herts, 2005; Young Minds, 2011). The Council for Disabled Children has produced several factsheets about the involvement of children and young people, highlighting methods and levels of participation; the participation process; barriers; and developing a supportive environment (CDC, no date).

The most relevant principles for this chapter are ones for mental health, however these are not youth specific. The main guides in use in the UK at present are by a national mental health ULO called the National Survivor User Network (NSUN) (NSUN, 2015; Ormerod *et al*, 2018), The New Economics Foundation (NEF) (NEF, 2013) and the National Development Team for Inclusion (NDTi) (Carr & Patel, 2016), which are social policy and practice organisations. The Social Care Institute for Excellence (SCIE), which is a social care research and development organisation, also has helpful guidance on how to do co-production (SCIE, 2015).

NSUN has the evidence-based '4Pi' framework, which stands for 'Principles, Purpose, Presence, Process, Impact':

1. 'Principles – How do we relate to each other?

2. Purpose – Why are we involving people? Why are we becoming involved?

3. Presence – Who is involved? Are the right people involved in the right places?

4. Process – How are people involved? How do people feel about the involvement process?

5. Impact – What difference does involvement make? How can we tell that we have made a difference?'

(NSUN, 2015)

NSUN emphasises the importance of impact, as the evidence shows that service users who engage with involvement and co-production do so because they want to make positive changes, especially if they've had bad experiences with services in the past (Carr & Beresford, 2012). NDTi's guidelines for co-production in mental health emphasize the importance of setting up, coming together and working together in collaboration to achieve genuine co-productive change:

'Step 1. Setting the scene: Understanding the context and environment in which co-production is going to take place
Step 2. Coming together: Creating the right conditions for co-production to work
Step 3. Working together: Achieving parity and genuine collaboration'
(Carr & Patel, 2016)

So, the guidelines on co-production in mental health stress the importance of both *the process* and *the impact*.

When we looked at existing definitions of youth involvement, we decided that whilst there were some excellent qualities listed in principles of involvement, there was something specific about involving young people that was perhaps not captured in many of these lists. When working with young people to design and deliver mental health services, we decided that what we meant by *meaningful* youth involvement was:

'*A mutually beneficial exchange, whereby young people are equally valued as members of a group that facilitates change and receives feedback as part of that exchange.*'

The emphasis different groups of young people may place on what are the key and most important principles for involvement may differ. Not everyone is going to be starting from the same place or understanding, and so agreeing principles for involvement and what is most important is a useful starting point. This is important when understanding the need for everyone to get something out of involvement (mutual benefit), which links to our later exploration in this chapter about young people's motivations for becoming involved.

When we talk about equal value, what is often missing from principles that may be related to more adult-oriented service involvement, is the idea that just because you are young in years it does not mean that you do not have a wealth of your own experience that is as valuable as another person's. There is a need to be mindful of the power dynamics and assumptions that often exist when young people are asked to become involved.

An example of what power dynamics feel like (YAG member 1)

As a young person, I think it's easy to sit back and listen to others who are older and who I always assume have more experience and expertise. Since becoming involved [on the Board], it's become clear that this isn't the case.

I can imagine that with youth participation it would be easy to fall into the tried and tested method of the adult leading a session or workshop and the young person following their lead. After all, an adult is likely to have qualifications and hold a position of power through their job. They undoubtedly have plenty of experience and expertise, but then again so do young people. We have lived experience as the young people using the mental health services that the adults have created or work with. I believe that for youth involvement to succeed the dynamic between adults and young people needs to be balanced. There should be an understanding that there is expertise and experience on both sides that will be different but of equal importance.

It can be difficult for young people to share their experiences at the best of times, let alone in an environment where they feel undervalued or intimidated. Creating an environment where we feel equal and respected is key to allowing us to share our opinions and experiences openly and honestly. From my experience there are many young people who want to make a difference in the area of mental health and we need people not just to listen and respect our ideas, but to help us actually create the change.

A final key attribute of involving young people is that they need to feel that they are being genuinely asked with the intention to use their feedback. So, rather than just writing it down and discounting it later, organisations need to return feedback on what has changed or why change was not possible, to reinforce both that everyone's opinion is of equal value and the principal of mutuality in the design or delivery of a service.

How do we do things differently when setting up and running involvement?

There are several stages in the process where participation can go wrong, and when this occurs it needs to be put right. A crucial stage is at the very beginning, when the participation is being set up and the goals and strategies are discussed and agreed. Then the group needs to be run properly, sustained, and members need to feel valued and to know their contributions are making an impact.

Commonly cited reasons for young people wanting to become involved in health service design and delivery in guidelines or on documents about involving young people include things such as:

- for young people to have a voice

- because it is good for their skills development

- because they are paid to participate (reward reasoning)

- because involving people in their care is something that you should do (clinical reasoning)

- because it is the 'right thing to do' (altruistic reasoning) (Barrett *et al*, 2016; Day, 2008).

What is less well evidenced in the guidance available or wider academic literature are the *actual* rather than the *perceived* motivations for young people taking part in health service design or delivery activities.

When we looked at cited motivations for involvement in the literature, whilst there was nothing wrong with young people becoming involved for career building/career aspiration purposes or to develop skills per se, this was not the chief reason that we felt ourselves, our peers, or our colleagues, would become involved in mental health service design or delivery. What instead motivated us, and we feel is a key motivating factor for young people, is *our lived experience of mental health and mental distress*, either through our own experience or through supporting someone else with their experience. As a direct result of our experience, the logic for our involvement was linked to far more personal reasoning such as wanting to improve quality of services for others, or to be useful through supporting change or making a difference (experience of care reasoning).

When you are thinking about youth involvement, *motivation matters*. If you think that the reason a young person is happy to be involved in your service redesign or thinking about delivery is that they want to gain skills and receive a contributory payment, you are likely to recruit and work with young people based on those messages and those underpinning assumptions about motivations. This plays out for young people in their involvement being solely about being present and 'having a voice', so focusing on the importance of *listening* to young people. Whilst this is vitally important, if it is not the young person's main motivation then just being listened to will not fulfil their main goal, which may be to witness and be part of driving change or quality improvement. Health service goals (often linked to change and quality improvement) are not irreconcilable with the motivations of young people, but it is important to be honest about everyone's motivations and intentions and think about the ways of working together from the outset.

What disingenuous co-production feels like (YAG member 1)

When a person has been through mental health services they are perfectly positioned to give insight into service delivery and understanding around what does and doesn't work. The problem arises when people with mental health problems are not treated like they are valued parts of the process. Too often it feels like a tick box exercise or tokenistic when we are asked to help. What we need is communication in a positive way: we need to be brought in right from the start and be seen as experts. We need our opinions to be taken seriously and not treated in a patronising way.

From my experience, even at times when I have been brought in to represent service users on panels or at conferences, people don't always take what you are saying as a valued part of the contribution. This is hard for the individual because they then feel like that added extra. When this happens, I find it slightly embarrassing.

Transparency is a huge issue when working with individuals on mental health services and support. There are huge concerns for us around making sure that things are right – we know what it is like to be through services and whilst I understand that there are problems around funding and that things happen very slowly within so many areas, it is hard being promised false timelines and not being kept in the loop with where things are at.

Think about power dynamics

Participating in places like health boards where there's a lot of formality and powerful professionals can be challenging, especially if there's an imbalance in the ratio of professionals to young people. Things can go wrong at the start when it feels as though all the power is with the professionals around the table, and when the practitioners use their professional titles and introduce themselves using their academic qualifications. This can be off-putting and intimidating and sets up the situation to divide the group between 'doctors' and 'patients', which makes it very hard to work on an equal footing.

In the medium-to-long term, power inequalities can cause issues. The formation of strong ties and hierarchies within groups is a completely natural occurrence as humans are social beings. The development of strong ties is largely a positive outcome in group settings but occasionally this can prove to become problematic if cliques form within the group. The issue with cliques is that those outside of the clique tend to feel marginalised and become disengaged. They can feel that their presence and/or actions aren't as valued as those within the clique. As a result, members outside the clique stop attending, prospective members are put off and ultimately the numbers participating in the activity stagnates or declines, as does its quality.

For these reasons, strong but equitable and facilitative leadership is needed within youth participation groups to ensure that there is equal opportunity for all involved and responsibility for the resolution of issues within the group belongs to one person. Equally, it is important that this leader appreciate that power is shared within the group and that ownership of their position should not be used to undermine or devalue another person's position or dictate the actions of group members. Things can start to feel wrong when the leader stops feeling like a liaison between the young people and the organisation and starts to feel like they are dictating to the young people on behalf of the organisation.

Set clear expectations and shared goals

As we have outlined, involvement does not stop at listening; it should instead be a reciprocal exchange of feedback that should produce meaningful interactions, resulting in change. Nobody likes discussing things repeatedly when nothing happens as a result of the discussions, and this especially applies to young people's involvement. When expectations and goals aren't properly discussed and agreed at the beginning, the young people involved won't know the reality of what's possible and if or how their influence will be restricted. Young people need to know what they're getting into and how much difference they can make at the very start. If there is an organisational mission statement on involvement and what it can influence don't disregard it – the message from the IMH YAG is 'be transparent and practice what you preach'. Ignoring the negatives and only wanting to listen to the positives isn't a fair or helpful way of involving young people.

An example of what poor involvement feels like (YAG member 2)

Nature of involvement: I was part of an NHS Mental Health Board for two years – I then became a 'remote' member and participated via answering emails. I was one of the only members that consistently attended meetings, and I was also the youngest member of the Board.

My experience: There was a consistent lack of accessibility for me, it was two hours away and meetings were at 6–8pm. It was very difficult for me to get there on time as it was rush hour and I was too young to drive myself and had to get transport from my parent. It was a very stressful experience to me, as it was a 'formal' type of meeting, it was very distressing being late as they would have to halt the meeting to catch me up – it made me feel like an inconvenience. It was also clear that the meetings were at 6–8pm as it was directly after they finished working. Additionally, the doors were only accessible with a work pass. When arriving late or even on time you could spend a significant amount of time locked out of the building. In terms of making me feel welcome and that they wanted my opinion it actually achieved the opposite, it felt like we were actually just there so they could state that they had consulted young people. Sometimes due to being locked out I was actually unable to attend the meeting altogether, as I had no phone number to contact the adults, just an email. It was honestly a very excluding process and led to me eventually being unmotivated to attend meetings or respond to them at all.

There was a large power inequality between the young people and the adults who were part of the NHS, each meeting had about three regular adults in attendance plus guest adults. There were always more adults than young people.

The guest adults would also use NHS jargon that was not really understandable, they would also state their full title at the start of meetings and it made it really intimidating to ask questions or critique the services as I was not qualified with a PhD.

Service-related outcomes or changes as a result of your involvement: the advertisement I had seen for this youth board has suggested that I would be 'providing a voice for young people, ensuring that their services meet their needs'. However, I really don't feel like I successfully achieved any service redesign for young people. As they knew I had a background in their services they would consistently call on me to give my opinion of the services that I used. I felt I was only useful for this one area of expertise, and advice that I gave about the service, I never actually saw anything come from it. It genuinely felt like my opinion had been written down in front of me to look like they had taken it on board and then it was thrown in the bin. →

The only outcome that I was aware of through feedback in meetings was when we were consulted to redecorate a reception room to make it more appealing to younger people instead of stark white and depressing. We never physically went there, but we saw that they had ordered from the catalogues we had been provided. It honestly felt that we (the youth board) were only trusted and had valid opinions when it came to decorating and our opinions about how to change services so young people would be more likely to access them (the main point of the board) was invalid.

As illustrated by the case study above, young people getting no feedback and only having tokenistic discussions at meetings is one of the biggest mistakes, and it is all too common. Professionals or organisations not listening to or remembering requests for feedback on what happened as a result of participation can affect young people badly. When there's a lack of feedback and impact, when young people aren't listened to and change doesn't happen, they can disengage and groups can slowly disband. Sometimes participation projects stop and young people can get blamed for the lack of change, when they had no power to make change in the first place.

When nothing meaningful happens to policy and services as a result of young people's involvement, it's seen by many young people as a waste of time and money for them and for the service. They will then disengage from participation. Some places rebrand their participation when nothing happens but young people know that the reputation is damaged, and may be unlikely to take part, particularly if they've discussed participation experiences with their peers or friends. Most worryingly, if young people aren't listened to or responded to in mental health participation, there could even be a risk that they start to disengage from services themselves as they may lose faith in them because of their negative experience of participation.

Consider recruitment to your group, accessibility, and group dynamics

It shouldn't be assumed that young people will get along with each other just because they're young people. If the young people who are participating don't have the opportunity or time to get to know each other (for example, if the only time they're together is in formal meetings) and build up trust, then when new young people join things can go wrong if efforts are not made to introduce them and support them to participate, and to keep the group working together.

It is important to ensure that there is diversity in the group so that the group reflects the population that it is being said to represent. Equally, once a group has been assembled, it's important not to solely direct queries or actions to people based on their personal characteristics. For example, although you might appreciate the insight that a member of the LGBT or BAME community might bring to matters related to those communities, it's unfair to treat them as the 'expert representative'.

Not considering accessibility and making reasonable adjustments excludes young people whose access needs aren't met. Ask the young person why they have the access need – if they say they need something to be in place so they can participate, don't ask why, just work with them and get it right. For example, in the case study on the previous page, if timings and venues of meetings are only designed for the professionals involved, this can exclude young people. Similarly, think about the way you communicate information to young people.

An example of why accessible communication matters (YAG member 3)

It is important that facilitators contact young people in a manner that they are comfortable with. For example, in my case, I much prefer that I am contacted via e-mail as I only have to check my e-mail once a day which is much less anxiety-inducing than knowing that I might receive a phone call or text at any moment and face the pressure of having to respond.

It is also important to acknowledge personal differences and cater to these when possible. For example, some people prefer to be addressed using a different name to their birth name or would always choose to meet face-to-face rather than have a discussion via phone. There is often a very good reason behind such requests and taking the time to understand them will help acknowledge the importance of catering to them.

Sharing work and approaching it from various perspectives leads to changes in understanding

When young people become involved in projects or organisations, they can offer a unique perspective. Sharing work to produce outcomes happens in many ways. For example, young people may wish to share their experience to benefit others; similarly, some young people find it very useful to hear other people's experiences. Sharing involves feeling part of something, or that you can contribute to something, and when done well means that young people will want to remain involved in working on projects or with people.

An example of what good involvement feels like (YAG member 5)

Nature of involvement: Monthly co-production steering group (NHS) working with a group of 7–10 people with experience of mental health and illness alongside professionals (i.e. clinicians, managers). Once the group got together we focused on one piece of work – opening up a crisis café.

My experience: We [the group] decided to focus on the crisis café because the staff saw it as a clinical need and there were other examples locally of this model/concept. We each brought our own experience in terms of mental health crisis and what that looked like and then talked about how we would want someone to approach us.

It was a safe environment with ground rules of confidentiality established. The clinical workers were very mindful in terms of making sure everybody's voice got heard. The group was modelled around an image of what we would like rather than what the clinical workers would like. We had a broad group with people from different BAME backgrounds. I was one of the only young people but I never felt belittled. It didn't really matter about age, it was more to do with my experience. Me being young and my experience, it matters, because by being that young person in the group they may not know about anything current about services for young people let's say, and so it gives a generational perspective.

I found the clinical workers have always been quite encouraging in wanting us to take ownership of the group. They are there in the background to support us, but want us to bring in our own ideas and chair our own meetings. We were given a training day to build our group skills. Before it used to be the clinical workers chairing, but now someone wanted to chair from within the group. In the last couple of months they started asking group members to attend and add our voice to NHS Board meetings.

I think this is valuable because you get to find out what is going on in current mental health systems, but it is daunting to be with all these fancy people in suits and whatnot. They acknowledge that you are there rather than pretend that you are not. They will ask your opinion about things and paraphrase your opinion back to show they are listening or broaden conversation a bit more after I have brought my opinion/perspective. My being there means we are all able to see it from a totally different perspective that they weren't able to see it from before. →

> **Service-related outcomes or changes as a result of your involvement:** I worked on the crisis café development for 3–4 months of last year and it was implemented then independently evaluated and found to be good so is still running. I am still involved in the steering group and now go to board meetings; I've been working with the Trust for about 18 months. I felt really valued by people in the group, I'm still part of the group, and I still feel valued by clinical workers as well as other members of the group.

It is essential to ensure that the group is made up of individuals from diverse backgrounds (mindful of all the protected characteristics, not just one). Power, group recruitment, and group dynamics come together and need to be managed to ensure genuine sharing of ideas and solutions takes place. In groups that work well, intergenerational as well as intersectional perspectives can be taken into account, which supports more meaningful exchanges of ideas. The unique perspectives are what helps to reason out or work on a problem, to find a shared solution. This will be beneficial in the long term as the young people will witness and benefit from the diversity in the group to understand that everyone can have a different opinion on the topic, and that diversity enables the group to bring forward different opinions and ideas to tackle mental health issues.

Conclusions and future directions

In writing this chapter, we have provided some of the rationale behind youth involvement work – how it works best; when it doesn't work; what it can achieve and why. The chapter has drawn on the involvement of young people with lived experiences of mental ill health in service design and delivery, who have worked in partnership with academics in order to produce a useful reference tool for people working in health services.

Whilst researching this chapter, there were questions that the academics could not answer due to a lack of research evidence. We do not know how much policy or service development (what percentage) involves young people with lived experience, either nationally or more locally. We think this would be helpful for organisations to make clear. Whilst there are many models for doing youth involvement work (Barrett *et al*, 2016; Flanagan & Warwick, 2018; HQIP, 2015; James, 2007), at present there is no research *evaluating* the different approaches to youth involvement. This supports other research findings that suggests there is relatively little robust evidence about the impact of Patient and Public Involvement on health and social care research (Brett *et al*, 2014). We don't know what works, for whom, in what circumstances and why, and we think comparing different models is an important area for future research.

Acknowledgements: We would like to acknowledge and thank the Health Services Management Centre Library & Information Service at the University of Birmingham (https://www.birmingham.ac.uk/facilities/hsmc-library/index.aspx) who ran some literature searches to help us to understand how young people have been involved in mental health service design and delivery.

References

Barrett C, Miles H and Pacquette-Simpson R (2016) *Setting Up an Involvement Group*. London and South East CYP-IAPT Learning Collaborative.

Beresford P (2013) *Beyond the Usual Suspects*. London: Shaping Our Lives.

Brett J, Staniszewska S, Mockford C, Herron-Marx S, Hughes J, Tysall C and Suleman R (2014) Mapping the impact of patient and public involvement on health and social care research: a systematic review. *Health Expectations* **17** 637–650. Available at: https://doi.org/10.1111/j.1369-7625.2012.00795.x (accessed 26 June 2019).

Campbell J and Oliver M (1996) *Disability Politics: Understanding our past, changing our future*. London: Routledge.

Carr S and Beresford P (2012) *Social Care, Service Users and User Involvement*. London/Philadelphia: Jessica Kingsley Publishers.

Carr S and Patel M (2016) *Practical Guide: Progressing transformative co-production in mental health*. London: National Development Team for Inclusion.

Day C (2008) Children's and young people's involvement and participation in mental health care. *Child and Adolescent Mental Health* **13** 2–8. Available at: https://doi.org/10.1111/j.1475-3588.2007.00462.x (accessed 26 June 2019).

Flanagan P and Warwick P (2018) "What does a fantastic CAMHS inpatient unit look and feel like for you?" - Co-designing a new inpatient service with young people in Humber | i-THRIVE [WWW Document]. Available at: http://www.implementingthrive.org/case-studies-2/service-design-case-studies/what-does-a-fantastic-camhs-inpatient-unit-look-and-feel-like-for-you-co-designing-a-new-inpatient-service-with-young-people-in-humber/ (accessed 26 June 2019).

HQIP (2015) *Case study: involving children and young people for QI* [online]. Available at: https://www.hqip.org.uk/resource/case-study-involving-children-and-young-people-for-qi/ (accessed 26 June 2019).

Institute for Mental Health (2019) Institute for Mental Health – University of Birmingham [online]. Available at: https://www.birmingham.ac.uk/research/activity/mental-health/index.aspx (accessed 26 June 2019).

James A (2007) Principles of youth participation in mental health services. *Medical Journal of Australia* **187** (S7) s57–60. Available at: https://doi.org/10.5694/j.1326-5377.2007.tb01339.x (accessed 26 June 2019).

National Children's Bureau (2016) *Ready to Listen – Why, when and how to involve young children and their families in local decisions about health and wellbeing*. London: NCB.

The New Economics Foundation (2013) *Co-production in Mental Health: Literature review* [online]. Mind. Available at: https://neweconomics.org/2013/11/co-production-mental-health/ (accessed 05 August 2019).

National Survivor User Network (NSUN) (2015) *Involvement for Influence: 4PI Standards for Involvement* [online]. Available at: https://www.nsun.org.uk/faqs/4pi-national-involvement-standards (accessed 05 August 2019).

Ormerod E, Beresford P, Carr S, Gould D, Jeffreys S, Machin K, Poursanidou D, Thompson S and Yiannoullou S (2018) *Survivor Researcher Network Manifesto: mental health knowledge built by service users and survivors.* Available at: https://www.nsun.org.uk/news/survivor-researcher-network-launch-manifesto (accessed 26 June 2019).

Reeve L (2018) Why participation in children and young people's mental health is key. London: NHS England. Available at: https://www.england.nhs.uk/blog/why-participation-in-children-and-young-peoples-mental-health-is-key/ (accessed 26 June 2019).

SCIE (2015) *Co-Production in Social Care: What it is and how to do it – at a glance.* London: SCIE.

Slay J and Stephens L (2013) *Co-production in Mental Health.* London: New Economics Foundation (NEF).

Street C and Herts B (2005) *Putting Participation Into Practice: A guide for practitioners working in services to promote the mental health and wellbeing of children and young people.* London: YoungMinds.

UN General Assembly (1990) *UN Convention on the Rights of the Child.* Geneva: United Nations.

TLAP (2016) *Co-Production: It's a long-term relationship.* London: TLAP.

YAG Institute for Mental Health (2018) Youth Advisory Group - University of Birmingham (online document). Available at: https://www.birmingham.ac.uk/research/activity/mental-health/youth-advisory-group.aspx (accessed 26 June 2019).

Young Minds (2011) *What is Participation in Children and Young People's Mental Health?* Amplified power pack. London: YoungMinds.

Chapter 13: A Whole School Approach to Mental Health

Jonathan Glazzard and Rachel Bostwick

Key learning points

- The role of school climate in creating mentally healthy schools.

- The importance of a mental health curriculum.

- Ways of working in partnership with children and young people.

- Strategies for identifying mental health needs.

- Ways of working in partnership with parents.

Keywords
Mental health; schools; whole school approach; parents

Introduction

In December 2017 the Department for Education (DfE) and Department of Health (DoE) in England jointly published a green paper, *Transforming Children and Young People's Mental Health Provision* (DfE/DoH, 2017), in which mental ill health in children and young people was described as a 'historic injustice' (p2). The green paper demonstrated a political determination to address this problem and emphasised the role of schools and colleges in supporting children and young people with mental health conditions. This chapter outlines the elements of whole school approach to mental health. Whilst schools and colleges do play an important reactive role in identifying needs early and providing rapid and targeted interventions, a proactive approach ensures that all members of the school or college community can thrive and stay mentally healthy, thus reducing the likelihood of members of that community developing mental health issues. This chapter outlines elements of the whole school or college approach identified by Public Health England (2015). These include:

- the role of the school climate
- the curriculum
- student voice
- staff development
- approaches for identifying needs
- working with parents and carers
- targeted support and referral
- leadership and management.

Practical approaches are identified to support schools and colleges with the implementation of this model. Throughout this chapter, 'schools' is used to refer to schools and colleges of further education.

School climate

A positive school climate enables all members of the school community to thrive. It supports individuals to experience a sense of belonging and contributes significantly to people's overall wellbeing.

School and college leaders should develop a positive ethos. Diversity should be valued and celebrated so that people experience a sense of inclusion. Positive relationships between staff, between staff and students, and between students underpin a positive school ethos. All members of the school community have a right to be treated with respect, to be valued, listened to and to have a voice. There is no place for a climate of fear in a mentally healthy school.

Students and staff are able to thrive if they feel that they are trusted and are able to experience a sense of agency. A positive school culture is underpinned by a commitment to values such as trust, kindness, courage, determination, fairness, honesty, care, respect, compassion, equality and democracy. The school values should be visible and consistently applied in practice by all members of the school community. When the values are not upheld, members of the school community have a responsibility to challenge those individuals who undermine them.

Effective school and college leaders recognise that the wellbeing of staff is critical. If staff are not mentally healthy, they are less likely to perform their roles effectively and this can have a detrimental impact on student wellbeing, teaching, student progress and attainment. Leaders have a duty of care to staff and consequently they should be proactive in reducing unnecessary workload. Staff cannot thrive if they experience burn-out. In addition, leaders should ensure that staff and students do not experience bullying, harassment or discrimination. All members of the community have a right to feel safe. Effective leaders recognise that staff perform better if they are trusted to do their jobs and if they are afforded professional autonomy. Levels of monitoring staff performance should be reasonable and excessive micro-management and autocratic styles of leadership lead to staff feeling resentful. Leaders should ensure that assessments of staff capabilities are objective and fair and not influenced by personal feelings towards specific members of staff. Effective leaders develop policies to support staff wellbeing and provide support when members of staff experience mental ill health. They promote a positive attitude towards mental health by making it a focus of discussions in meetings and by being a good role model to staff and students. Examples of effective approaches which leaders may adopt include:

- being honest and open about their own mental health

- establishing clear policies in relation to the use of email outside of normal working hours

- applying flexibility when staff have personal or family commitments to attend to

- establishing clear expectations about the time that staff spend in school

- allowing home working where this is possible

- developing policies which reduce unnecessary workload

- developing systems for monitoring staff wellbeing on a regular basis.

Curriculum

Young people should be provided with an age-appropriate mental health curriculum. This should be designed to help them to understand their feelings and to develop their knowledge of strategies to improve wellbeing, including the role of physical activity and social connections in staying mentally healthy. Young people should learn about what mental health is, the signs of mental health issues and strategies for managing common mental health conditions. They should be introduced to the concept of resilience and to strategies to improve their resilience. They should also be taught how to seek help if they experience mental health issues and how to listen to others who need support. A discrete mental health curriculum can improve young people's mental health literacy and reduce stigma. The stigma associated with mental health problems becomes apparent to people at an early age (Campos *et al*, 2018). However, research suggests that the attitudes of young people can be changed more easily than those of adults (Corrigan & Watson, 2007) and therefore a mental health curriculum can play a powerful role in eradicating stigma.

Young people should also be taught to develop the skills of digital literacy so that they can keep themselves safe online. Through a well-planned mental health curriculum young people can learn about the myths and facts associated with mental health and stereotypes associated with mental illness can be challenged.

In addition, the digital curriculum should introduce young people to the concept of digital citizenship so that they conduct themselves responsibly online. The concept of digital resilience also needs to be addressed so that young people can learn how to respond to distressing online content. They should be taught about the link between social media and mental health and they should learn to critically engage with online content.

A mental health curriculum should provide young people with strategies to manage their own mental health. Evidence-based approaches include mindfulness and physical activity. Young people need to be provided with a wide range of strategies to manage stress and anxiety, particularly during times when these may be heightened, such as during exams or when they have heavy coursework demands. They also need to be taught how to manage heavy workloads to reduce the build-up of stress.

A discrete mental health curriculum for all young people will support them in developing help-seeking behaviours should they experience mental health problems. In addition, the theme of mental health can be integrated throughout the curriculum as well as being taught discretely. Through history lessons, young people can learn about how views on mental health have changed over time, as part of the curriculum. In art, students can use a range of media to represent mental health. In English a range of texts, including poetry, explore the theme of mental health. These are illustrative examples; through a carefully planned curriculum mental health awareness can be integrated into a wider range of subject areas.

Student voice

A commitment to the student voice reflects Article 12 of the *United Nations Convention of the Rights of the Child* (1989), which states that children have a right to express their views, and the views of the child should be given due weight in accordance with their age and maturity. Giving young people a voice empowers them, particularly if they are given opportunities to influence school policies and practices.

One approach is to develop student mental health champions or ambassadors. The roles and responsibilities of these individuals can be determined locally but may include:

- reviewing school policies to assess the likely impact on student mental health
- researching the school factors which contribute to student mental health issues and disseminating the outcomes of their research to senior leaders
- auditing the physical and emotional environment across the school
- reviewing and co-producing the school mental health curriculum
- commenting on processes for identifying mental health problems
- evaluating the effectiveness of interventions through consulting other students
- leading workshops on mental health for staff and students
- reviewing the library resources on mental health
- undertaking training to become 'peer mentors'.

Peer mentoring is an evidence-based strategy which can be highly effective. Student mentors could be trained to provide support for children and young people who need support. The training might include aspects such as how to be an effective listener and when to refer cases on to a designated member of staff. The case study overleaf illustrates how peer mentoring helps both the mentor and the mentee. According to Public Health England (2015, p14):

'Involving students in decisions that impact on them can benefit their emotional health and wellbeing by helping them to feel part of the school and wider community and to have some control over their lives'.

> ### Alex
>
> Alex was a mental health lead in a large secondary school in the south of England. He wanted to empower his students to become leaders in mental health. He introduced a peer mentoring scheme which trained students to become peer listeners. These students provided a friendly, non-judgemental 'listening ear' to younger students who needed support. The peer listeners were recruited from Years 10 and 11. They were required to apply for the role and they were interviewed for it. Once recruited, they were required to complete a six-session course. This included sessions on what mental health is, types of mental ill health, strategies for supporting students with specific needs, strategies for effective listening, the need for confidentiality and when to refer cases on to an adult. The mentors were then matched to younger students who needed support. The mentors developed empathy, leadership skills and confidence. The younger students who received support enjoyed speaking about their mental health to other students rather than talking to staff.

Staff development

Mental health is everyone's responsibility. It is therefore critical that all staff who work in schools and colleges have access to basic professional development which supports them in identifying the signs of mental health problems. Staff also need training in how to manage a disclosure from a child or young person. This may include learning how to structure a conversation if a student discloses that they are self-harming, are depressed or have attempted suicide. It is very easy to make an inappropriate comment in response to student disclosures and this could make the situation worse for the child or young person. Staff also may need training in how to support other colleagues who are experiencing mental ill health, for example, how to support a colleague who is experiencing grief, loss or family illness.

Identifying needs

Identifying mental health needs at the earliest opportunity is critical to prevent problems from escalating. However, whilst some young people demonstrate visible signs of mental health issues, some do not. It is relatively easy to identify common warning signs, including changes in mood, behaviour, attendance and declining academic progress. These signs may indicate that the young person has mental health problems. However, some young people will go to extraordinary lengths to hide the fact that they are unwell. Therefore, if schools only focus on identifying children and young people with visible signs of mental health conditions this is a reactive rather than proactive approach. It will result in some young people with mental health needs not being identified and therefore not gaining access to intervention and support.

A proactive approach to the identification of needs involves universal screening for all children and young people. Self-assessment tools such as standardised wellbeing or life satisfaction surveys are a quick and economical way of identifying needs, particularly for adolescents. However, they depend on young people being honest when they complete them. Another approach to needs identification is to provide training for dedicated members of staff to conduct 'wellbeing conversations' with all children and young people on a regular basis throughout the academic year. Whilst this process may be time-consuming, it does provide a richer insight into young people's mental health than a self-assessment tool can provide.

No approach to needs identification is perfect because young people's mental health can change rapidly in response to life experiences. Schools should therefore ensure that young people are aware of who they can contact if they need to talk to someone. Providing them with access to a dedicated member of staff or team is essential, especially in times of crisis. Additionally, schools should be vigilant to sudden changes in mood or behaviour which may indicate that a child or young person has a problem.

Some young people may not be comfortable approaching a named member of staff to discuss their feelings. Developing systems of online support, such as instant anonymous chat systems, may be a useful alternative so that young people can gain access to online help. For younger children, the use of a feelings board or feelings box in each classroom provides an opportunity for children to express to an adult how they feel each day. Adults can then provide immediate support for children who have negative feelings, and this can prevent problems from escalating.

Working with parents and carers

Developing effective relationships with parents and carers is important. Parents, carers and the wider family play an important role in influencing children and young people's emotional health and wellbeing (Stewart-Brown, 2006). Parents' views should be sought during the processes of identifying needs and when establishing goals for the child or young person. In addition, parents should be fully included in the process of reviewing the child or young person's progress.

Some parents will require support in relation to managing their child's mood and behaviour at home and the school can provide useful direction in relation to this. In addition, schools can support parents to understand the inter-relationship between physical, social, emotional and mental wellbeing by suggesting practical strategies to improve their child's wellbeing outside of school. Some parents may also need support from schools to manage their child's use of social media.

Children and young people with mental health issues may also have parents who have mental health conditions. Schools and colleges play an important role in signposting parents to appropriate services in the community to help them get support. If parents are not mentally healthy, they may find it more difficult to support their child to be mentally healthy; therefore, increasing parents' awareness of services they themselves can access can be beneficial in supporting the child. Some schools may consider developing workshops for parents on managing behaviour, stress, anxiety and depression and some may wish to offer mindfulness sessions to parents.

Targeted support and referral

Universal support for all children and young people is through the development of a mental health curriculum which is taught to everyone. This can increase young people's mental health literacy and increase help-seeking behaviours. However, some children will need access to small-group interventions or highly personalised individual interventions if they have additional, complex and enduring needs which cannot be met through the mental health curriculum.

Schools should ensure that a range of evidence-based interventions are available to support children and young people's mental health needs. These interventions may include:

- school counselling services

- psychological interventions such as cognitive behaviour therapy

- peer mentoring

- sand, art or Lego therapies

- grief counselling

- managing stress, anxiety and depression

- resilience interventions

- social and emotional interventions, for example teaching young people about feelings.

Some children and young people with particularly complex needs are likely to require additional support. This is because their mental health needs are related to a wider range of issues such as speech problems or a disability. Therefore, school staff will benefit from liaising with a multi-agency team, which is likely to include professionals such as speech and language therapists, and occupational therapists, as well as mental health professionals.

Schools need to develop approaches for monitoring the impact of interventions. Interventions should be time-limited, and the assessment of impact should be focused. Pre-and post-intervention assessments can support practitioners in measuring the impact of interventions, for example the use of a resilience self-assessment scale before and after a resilience intervention. If the intervention does not result in a positive impact on the attribute that it seeks to change, schools should consider implementing alternative interventions. Seeking the perspectives of children and young people in relation to interventions is also an effective strategy for assessing impact.

Schools should develop a clear policy on when to refer children and young people on to external services. Child and adolescent mental health services (CAMHS) in England will usually only work with children and young people who have serious, complex and enduring needs so it is important to take account of the referral criteria for the local service. Some schools are able to consult with local CAMHS and health professionals when they are concerned about a particular child. This can help schools think through what the concern is as CAMHS may not be the support required. Some children and young people may have mental ill health needs which have been caused by family factors, including abuse, neglect, parental conflict or parental substance abuse. In these cases, the Designated Safeguarding Lead may need to refer the case to social care services. Again, it is critical that schools have a clear policy which outlines when a referral is necessary and when a referral is not required. In these cases, children and young people need to know why a referral is necessary, what information will be shared and what will happen next.

For those children and young people who receive individual or small-group intervention in school, it is essential that teachers are aware of the skills and knowledge that are being developed through these interventions. This will enable them to make explicit connections with the interventions when the students are in class. They can then build on what children are learning in the interventions in the context of the classroom.

Leadership and management

A whole-school approach to mental health can only work if the leadership team actively champions mental health. Leadership teams play a critical role in developing a mentally healthy culture in the school or college. There should be no culture of bullying, harassment, fear or discrimination for staff or students. Leaders also play a crucial role in de-stigmatising mental health. Staff, children and young people need to know that they can talk openly and frankly about their mental health without fear of consequences. Effective leadership teams promote a culture of openness. The mental health of all members of the school community is viewed as a strategic priority and is an essential part of the school strategic plan. Effective leaders recognise that there are no tensions between promoting a culture of positive wellbeing and raising academic standards. When teachers are mentally healthy, they teach well and when young people are mentally healthy, they thrive academically.

The leadership team need to invest in school-based interventions so that children and young people can receive swift, bespoke support. They should invest in staff training and deploy a dedicated member of staff who is responsible for mental health. Effective leadership teams also dedicate investment in external services so that children and young people can gain support from suitably qualified individuals. They should ensure that policies and practices are reviewed regularly through the lens of mental health, and unnecessary workload for staff should be eradicated.

Conclusion

The whole school approach to mental health which has been outlined in this chapter is a proactive universal approach to mental health which should reduce the number of children and young people needing support. It is not sufficient for schools to provide support for children and young people who demonstrate visible signs of mental health problems. Many will go to great lengths to hide their needs and thus an identification process which only picks up young people with visible signs is not sufficient. Schools need to develop universal approaches to identification so that children and young people do not fall under the radar. A universal mental health curriculum which is progressive and provided to all children and young people will help to develop students' mental health literacy and increase help-seeking behaviours. If this is implemented over a long period of time it might also improve students' wellbeing. Schools need to ascertain what interventions are effective and evidence-based so that financial investment is based on sound research evidence. Developing a whole-school culture which destigmatises mental health for staff, children and young people will help to create a climate of openness in which members of the school community feel able to talk about their own mental health. Developing a school climate which promotes inclusion helps to foster a sense of belonging. This will ensure that members of the school community become connected to the school and this will promote their investment in it. Through developing physical, social, emotional and mental wellbeing in staff and students, schools and colleges are in the best position to be able to thrive.

References

Campos L, Dias P, Duarte A, Veiga E, Camila Dias C and Palh F (2013) Is it possible to 'find space for mental health' in young people? Effectiveness of a school-based mental health literacy promotion program. *International Journal of Environmental Research and Public Health* 15 (1426) 1–12.

Corrigan P and Watson A (2007) How children stigmatize people with mental illness. *International Journal of Social Psychiatry* **53** 526–546.

DfE/DoH (2017) *Transforming Children and Young People's Mental Health Provision: A green paper*. [online] London: The Stationery Office. Available at: https://www.gov.uk/government/consultations/transforming-children-and-young-peoples-mental-health-provision-a-green-paper (accessed 26 June 2019).

Public Health England (PHE) (2015) *Promoting Children and Young People's Emotional Health and Wellbeing: A Whole School and College Approach*. London: PHE.

Stewart-Brown S (2006) *What is the Evidence on School Health Promotion in Improving Health or Preventing Disease and, Specifically, What is the Effectiveness of the Health Promoting Schools Approach?* Copenhagen: WHO Regional Office for Europe.

United Nations (1989) *United Nations Convention on the Rights of the Child*. Geneva: United Nations. Available at: https://downloads.unicef.org.uk/wp-content/uploads/2010/05/UNCRC_united_nations_convention_on_the_rights_of_the_child.pdf?_ga=2.53685805.400542381.1548530851-2107065727.1548530851 (accessed 26 June 2019).

Chapter 14: The Mental Health of Young People in Contact with the Criminal Justice System

Prathiba Chitsabesan

Key learning points

- The development of antisocial behaviour involves a complex interaction of intrinsic and psychosocial risk and protective factors.

- Young people in contact with the criminal justice system have multiple levels of needs across domains (health, education and social).

- They have disproportionately high levels of mental health needs and neurodisability which increases their vulnerability.

- Assessing and addressing unmet health needs can inform individual care plans including addressing mental health needs.

- Early co-ordinated care and multi-agency approaches are essential in meeting the needs of this complex group of young people.

Keywords

Young offender, mental health, neurodevelopmental impairment, developmental pathways, assessment, evidence-based interventions, youth justice services, legal framework

Introduction

Over the last decade, studies have highlighted that young people with high and multiple needs have clustered in the criminal justice system. These young people experience higher levels of mental health problems and neurodisability than the general population. This chapter provides a developmental approach to understanding the needs of young people in contact with the criminal justice system. It reviews the prevalence of a range of mental health and neurodevelopmental needs in young offenders and describes the key principles of assessment and intervention approaches. The policy and legal framework have been illustrated by reference to the system in England, but will have relevance to readers from further afield.

Developmental pathways to antisocial behaviour

Adolescence is a transitional stage of development between childhood and adulthood; the developmental tasks of adolescence centre on autonomy and connection with others, rebellion and the development of independence and identity. Delinquency, conduct problems and aggression all refer to antisocial behaviours that reflect a failure of the individual to conform his or her behaviour to the expectations of some authority figure, to societal norms, or to respect the rights of other people. Neuroscience suggests that there is a lack of synchrony in late childhood and adolescence in the development of two of the critical brain systems that enable the development of adaptive behaviour. The mesolimbic system develops more quickly than the frontal system resulting in the adolescent brain, which has a heightened need for basic reward but a lower capacity to manage short term rewards for greater long-term gains.

Epidemiological studies suggest that the development of antisocial behaviour involves a complex interaction of intrinsic and psychosocial risk and protective factors (Murray & Farrington, 2010). Antisocial behaviour also shows strong associations with adverse childhood experiences (ACE). Parental mental illness, family breakdown, parenting style and association with other antisocial peers influence outcomes. Detachment from school through truancy and exclusion may increase the risk of offending through reduced supervision, loss of any positive socialisation effects of school and by creating delinquent groups of young people. Heritable influences contribute towards a gene-environment interaction suggesting pathways are complex.

However, it is important to bear in mind that protective or resilience factors for the young person or within the system around them can also modify outcomes. This is particularly relevant for interventions and an important underpinning principle of the risk and resilience approach which focuses on building important 'assets' in the child's health and emotional wellbeing.

Prevalence of mental health needs and neurodevelopmental needs

Mental health needs

Many young people within the criminal justice system who present with pervasive and complex presentations often have an extensive history of repeated interpersonal traumatic experiences. Rates of mental health needs are significantly greater in young offenders in comparison with the general population. In the UK, 9% of 13–18-year-old young offenders in secure care were found to have a diagnosis of PTSD (Lennox & Khan, 2013).

Disruption to the early attachment process through interpersonal trauma has a direct impact on the development of a child's brain, attachment style and emotional regulation systems. A review of 25 studies of children and young people in custody found that around 11% of boys and 29% of girls suffered from major depression (Fazel *et al*, 2008). An association between antisocial behaviour and suicidal behaviour has also been demonstrated with concerns regarding higher rates of self-harm and suicide.

Substance misuse issues are defined by sustained maladaptive behaviours related to or caused by substance misuse. Young people's substance misuse differs from that of adult substance misusing offenders. Cannabis and alcohol are the main substances of use reported by adolescents, and polydrug use is common (Theodosiou, 2017).

Neurodevelopmental needs

The neurocognitive profiles of young offenders include deficits in language skills, attention and impulse control as well as low IQ scores. Deficits in executive function can affect the young person's ability to regulate their behaviours, plan and generate alternative strategies. A report for the Office of the Children's Commissioner highlighted high rates of neurodisability in young people in contact with the criminal justice system (Hughes *et al*, 2012).

ADHD

Rates of ADHD were found to be significantly greater for young offenders (12% for young male offenders and 19% for females) than for the general population (Fazel *et al*, 2008).

Autism

Autism is a neurodevelopmental condition characterised by a triad of impairments in social communication. Certain features of autism may predispose young people to offend, including social naïvete, misinterpretation of social cues and poor empathy.

The majority of young offenders with a learning disability frequently have an IQ in the 'mild range' (between 50 and 69) and may therefore be less likely to have had their learning needs identified in mainstream schools, where those needs are often overshadowed by their challenging behaviour. Communication issues relate to problems with speech, language and communication that significantly impact day-to-day functioning. Studies have found communication difficulties, including expressive and receptive language difficulties are common and frequently missed.

Traumatic brain injury (TBI)

A traumatic brain injury (TBI) is any injury to the brain caused by an impact, and the severity is typically measured by the depth of loss of consciousness (LOC). The majority of TBIs appear to be mild, although long-term effects on academic performance, behaviour, emotional control and social interactions have been reported in young offenders.

Gender and ethnicity

Whilst studies of mental health needs have predominantly focused on male offenders, gender differences have been reported. Female offenders are significantly more likely to experience mental health needs including depression, PTSD and self-harm. There are also concerns that there is an over-representation of some minority ethnic groups within the criminal justice system and that these groups of young people have poorer access to services.

Screening and assessment

One of the most common reasons for unmet need is lack of appropriate and timely assessment. Lack of identification hampers opportunities for early intervention and promotion of healthy development and resilience in young people.

Initial assessment is a key factor in the successful treatment of mental health needs for young offenders. Early identification of mental health needs may also reduce the later risk of developing mental health issues. However, assessment can be complicated by a number of factors, including the non-clear nature of emerging mental health symptoms in children and young people in comparison to presentations in adults, the minimisation of symptoms by young offenders and the disinclination of young people to engage with mental health services due to fear of stigma.

Historically, screening and assessment tools have been developed focusing on single problem areas such as mental health or substance misuse; however, young people who offend often have multiple areas of need. In recognition of these difficulties, the Comprehensive Health Assessment Tool (CHAT) was introduced for young offenders in custody across England and Wales supported by the development of *Healthcare Standards for Children and Young People in Secure Settings* (Royal College of Paediatrics and Child Health, 2013). The Comprehensive Health Assessment Tool (CHAT) is a semi-structured assessment developed to provide a standardised approach to health screening for all young offenders admitted to the secure estate and includes assessment of mental health needs, physical health, substance misuse and neurodevelopmental impairment. Assessing and managing unmet health needs can inform individual care plans, help to address offending behaviour and provide a valuable opportunity to re-engage young people with health and educational services to address unmet needs.

Principles of risk assessment

Risk assessment combines clinical information in a way that integrates historical variables, individual/clinical factors in the context of social/environmental and protective factors. Risk assessments can vary in the type of risk they assess, for example some assess general offending, while others assess the risk of interpersonal violence.

The aim of a risk formulation is to provide a better understanding of the origins of violence and how it has developed, is maintained and changes including predisposing factors, precipitating factors, perpetuating factors, and protective factors (Millington & Lennox, 2017).

Interventions

A large number of different treatments have been developed to reduce antisocial behaviour. Meta-analyses of treatment approaches to juvenile delinquency have produced reasonably consistent findings (Kazdin, 2007). The best results were obtained from cognitive behavioural, skills-orientated, and multi-modal methods. Specifically, treatment approaches that were participatory, collaborative and problem-solving were particularly likely to be beneficial. Family and parenting interventions also seem to reduce the risk of subsequent delinquency among older children and adolescents.

CBT is an effective psychological intervention for a number of mental health difficulties in childhood and adolescence including depression, social anxiety and post-traumatic stress. Studies that have been conducted with young people engaging in high risk behaviours indicate that CBT may be useful for young offenders with a range of mental health needs. However, the format and delivery of CBT may require adaptation taking into account the young person's level of cognitive, social and emotional development including neurodevelopmental impairment. Adaptations include the use of visual cues, encouraging verbal learning through games, reducing distractions and using simplified language.

NICE (2013) recommend multimodal interventions which address family-based factors as well, such as functional family therapy and multisystemic therapy for the treatment of conduct disorder in children and young people aged between 11 and 17 years.

Leon

Background

Leon is a 13-year-old boy who lives with his mother and two younger siblings. The home environment was described as chaotic. Social care children services had been involved in the past.

Leon had a history of behavioural difficulties at nursery and primary school, where he was described by teachers as being 'always on the go, fidgety, unable to focus on specific tasks', requiring additional support in class. Difficulties continued at secondary school, where he received a number of short-term exclusions and had poor educational attainment.

Leon was charged with assault following a fight with a peer outside of school. He was due to appear at youth court.

Assessment

Concern regarding Leon's mental health was raised by the police due to his apparent difficulties in concentrating during the police interview. The CAMHS Liaison and Diversion Team undertook a brief assessment in police custody, and significant difficulties regarding impulsivity and inattention were noted. Discussion with the Community Forensic CAMHS team resulted in an urgent assessment by the local CAMHS. Information gathered from his mother and school, including the SNAP-IV Rating Scales, supplemented a clinical assessment including clinical observation. Leon also completed a QbTest assessment at CAMHS. The collation of the assessment information resulted in Leon being diagnosed with ADHD. ➔

Formulation

Leon's ADHD resulted in various difficulties throughout his childhood, including a number of minor accidents due to him impulsively and hyperactively climbing trees. Leon's ADHD had contributed to him exhibiting challenging behaviour in the home, in the form of fighting with his siblings, and at school, by disrupting class when he would impulsively shout out. His poor concentration during lessons resulted in educational underachievement. His impulsivity contributed to him being involved in frequent conflict with peers.

Treatment

Following his ADHD assessment, Leon was prescribed long-acting methylphenidate medication. His blood pressure and weight were monitored and his response to medication was assessed via further standardised assessments. This resulted in a significant reduction in his impulsivity and an improvement in his ability to concentrate and focus on individual tasks.

Leon pleaded guilty to the offence and received a community sentence. This resulted in input from the Youth Offending Team (YOT), which included specific sessions related to anger management. His mother was encouraged to attend some of these sessions so that Leon could be supported in utilising techniques learnt in the home environment. CAMHS and YOT also liaised with Leon's school and a behavioural management plan was agreed, which included Leon being able to request 'time out' from lessons and a consistent approach to negative behaviours.

Youth justice services and legal framework

The Youth Justice Board for England and Wales is a non-departmental public body responsible for the youth justice system; its primary aim is to reduce offending. Youth offending teams are community-based teams working with young people on prevention, out-of-court interventions and community sentences. Young people may be given a custodial sentence by courts for more serious offences and placed within a secure custody estate (secure children's home, secure training centres and young offenders' institution). Liaison and diversion teams work within police custody suites and courts to assess and divert young people into alternative community-based services where possible, away from the criminal justice system. More recently, there has been investment in community-based forensic CAMHS teams (FCAMHS) providing consultation, advice and assessment for young people with complex needs and a range of risk-taking behaviours.

A 'child' is defined by the Children Act and the United Nations Convention on the Rights of the Child as 'any person under the age of 18'. In England, Wales and Northern Ireland, criminal responsibility is set at the age of 10. However, there is evidence that brain development continues into the early 20s with frontal lobes developing later.

The principle of 'effective participation' is very important to children and young people. It examines the ability of the young person to engage with the trial. A child's age, level of maturity and intellectual and emotional capacities must be taken into account when they are charged with a criminal offence and appropriate steps should be taken in order to promote their ability to understand and participate in the court proceedings. It is therefore important to be aware of the possibility that a young person may not be able to participate effectively in the trial process, particularly if they are under 14 years old or have learning problems, or a history of absence from school.

Conclusion

Politicians and professionals have begun to acknowledge the importance of meeting the needs of offenders, as long-term costs to society become increasingly apparent.

This chapter has evidenced the high prevalence of mental health needs and neurodisability in young people who offend and outlined the implications for policy and practice, including recent developments. It demonstrates the increasing importance of providing a standardised and evidence-based approach to screening and intervention for a variety of health needs. Early coordinated care is essential in meeting the complex needs of this group of young people, highlighting the important role of a multi-agency public health strategy (Delmage, 2017).

References

Delmage E (2017) Children and the Law. In S Bailey, P Chitsabesan and P Tarbuck (eds) *Forensic Child and Adolescent Mental Health: Meeting the Needs of Young Offenders*, pp289–299. Cambridge: Cambridge University Press.

Fazel S, Doll H and Langstrom N (2008) Mental disorders among adolescents in juvenile detention and correctional facilities: a systematic review and metaregression analysis of 25 surveys. *Journal of the American Academy of Child and Adolescent Psychiatry* **47** (9) 1010–1019.

Hughes N, Williams HW, Chitsabesan P *et al* (2012) *Nobody Made the Connection: The prevalence of neurodisability in young people who offend*. London: Office for the Children's Commissioner.

Kazdin A (2007) Psychosocial Treatments for Conduct Disorder in Children and Adolescents. In P Nathan and J Gorman (eds) *A Guide to Treatments that Work* (3rd edition), pp71–104. New York: Oxford University Press.

Lennox C and Khan L (2013) *Youth Justice*. In: Annual Report of the Chief Medical Officer 2012 'Our children deserve better: prevention pays', pp200–214. London: Chief Medical Officer's Report.

Millington J and Lennox C (2017) Risk Assessment and Management Approaches with Young Offenders. In S Bailey, P Chitsabesan and P Tarbuck (eds) *Forensic Child and Adolescent Mental Health: Meeting the Needs of Young Offenders*, pp55–67. Cambridge: Cambridge University Press.

Murray J and Farrington DP (2010) Risk factors for conduct disorder and delinquency: key findings from longitudinal studies. *Canadian Journal of Psychiatry* **55** 633–42.

National Institute for Health and Clinical Excellence (2013) *Antisocial Behaviour and Conduct Disorder in Children and Young People: Recognition, intervention and management*. London: NICE.

Royal College of Paediatrics and Child Health (2013) *Healthcare Standards for Children and Young People in Secure Settings*. London: RCPCH.

Theodosiou L (2017) Substance misuse in young people with antisocial behaviour. In S Bailey, P Chitsabesan and P Tarbuck (eds) *Forensic Child and Adolescent Mental Health: Meeting the Needs of Young Offenders*, pp177–189. Cambridge: Cambridge University Press.

Chapter 15: Depression and Bipolar Disorder in Children and Young People

Eunice Ayodeji and Bernadka Dubicka

Key learning points

- If not managed effectively, depression and bipolar disorder can lead to complications and have a profound impact on the young person and their families.

- Children and adolescents who have had one episode of depression are at risk of further episodes.

- Depression in childhood and adolescence is rarely uncomplicated and often presents with other mental health conditions such as anxiety or conduct disorders.

- The core symptoms of depression in children and adolescents are similar to those seen in adulthood. However, there can be notable differences.

- Young people who experience depression and bipolar disorder face a number of negative outcomes, including impaired family and peer relationships, in addition to interference with academic functioning.

Keywords
Depression; bipolar disorder; adolescents; children; young people; assessment; treatment

Introduction

Depression and bipolar disorders in children and young people are serious mental health conditions which require timely evidence-based treatments to ensure the best possible outcome. Both conditions can cause considerable distress, and can have a profound impact on the child and their families/carers. Children who experience depression and bipolar disorder face a number of potential negative outcomes including school refusal, academic failure, impaired family functioning and physical and mental health problems in adulthood (Thaper *et al*, 2012).

This chapter covers factors that can lead to the development of depression and bipolar disorder, prevalence, and outlines current evidence-based treatments.

Depression

Signs and symptoms

Depression is one of the most common mental health conditions in children and young people (Whiteford *et al*, 2013). It may often present with other mental health conditions such as disruptive or other emotional disorders in younger children and anxiety or conduct disorders in adolescence. Although it is uncommon in prepubertal children, the prevalence rate is between 1–2%, rising to 20% for adolescents (Costello *et al*, 2006; Avenevoli *et al*, 2015). The presence of other mental health conditions often indicates a poorer outcome in relation to suicidality, duration, impairment and risk of recurrence.

Assessment and detection

It can be difficult to identify depression in this age group as it is common for many young people to experience periods of sadness and despondency. However, for a diagnosis of clinical depression there should be evidence of significant symptoms of depression and impairment in social, educational and other areas of functioning. The core symptoms of childhood and adolescent onset depression are similar to those seen in adults; however, depression in children and young people is associated with a greater number of psychosocial difficulties than in adult onset depression (McLeod *et al*, 2016). In addition, there are significant developmental differences; symptom presentation and the clinical picture is dependent on the developmental stage of the young person (see Table 15.1). For example, younger children may present with somatic symptoms such as tummy aches and headaches, as well as behavioural changes like refusing to go to school and separation anxiety (Yorbik *et al*, 2004). Older children may present as being 'bored', irritable and oversleeping, as well as presenting with more typical symptoms such as hopelessness, lack of energy, weight loss and suicidality.

Table 15.1: Red flags for depression across childhood

Symptom	6 years	6–12 years	Adolescents
Somatic	Failure to thrive sleep/eating problems	Headaches, tummy aches sleep/appetite changes	Headaches, tummy aches sleep and appetite changes
Behavioural	Disruptive behaviour social withdrawal reduced enjoyment (observed)	Irritability, boredom, apathy fatigue, decreased enjoyment (observed or self-reported)	Apathy, boredom, social isolation increased sexual activity, aggression, self-injurious behaviours
Developmental	Developmental delay or regression	Decreased ability to concentrate at school	Decreased ability to concentrate at school, decreased academic performance

(Chung & Soares, 2012)

Due to the differences in presentations, it can be difficult to recognise depression and the symptoms of depression may be overlooked (NICE, 2019). Therefore, a detailed biopsychosocial assessment is essential, including enquiring about all possible symptoms. In order to receive a diagnosis of depression, at least five of nine symptoms (see Table 15.2) need to be present during the same two-week period in addition to impairment in functioning. One of the core symptoms must be present at all times, either depressed mood, irritability, or marked diminished interest or pleasure in almost all activities.

A number of screening rating scales such as the Revised Children's Anxiety Scale (Chorpita *et al*, 2000) and Mood and Feelings Questionnaire (Angold *et al*, 1995) are available. However, there is limited consensus regarding their use (Simmons *et al*, 2015). The scales are not generally used to diagnose depression, but to assess and monitor symptom severity.

Table 15.2: DSM-5 criteria for depression

Major depressive episode (adult)*	Provision for children and adolescents
Depressed mood	Persistent sad or irritable mood, increased
	Irritability, anger or hostility
Loss of interest or pleasure	
Significant weight loss or reduction in appetite	More than 5% of body weight or failure to make expected weight gain
	Frequent vague, non-specific physical complaints
Insomnia or hypersomnia	
Psychomotor agitation or retardation	
Fatigue or lack of energy	Frequent absences from school or poor School performance
Feelings of worthlessness or guilt	
Decreased concentration	Being bored
Recurrent thoughts of suicide or death	Reckless behaviour, alcohol or substance misuse
*Diagnosis requires five or more symptoms, including either depressed mood or decreased interest/pleasure in activities during the past two weeks.	

Risk and protective factors

There are a number of psychosocial risk factors associated with depression (see Table 15.3) as well as resilience factors (see Table 15.4) which can protect against the development of depression in children and adolescents. Parental depression is associated with higher rates of depression in offspring, hence the treatment of parental depression should be considered. Studies have demonstrated that remission of maternal depression is associated with significant improvement in the child's depression (Brent *et al*, 2016).

Table 15.3: Examples of psychosocial risk factors for depression

- Being female
- Parental depression
- Past history of depression
- Life events
- Family discord
- Authoritarian parenting
- Adversity and trauma
- Drug and alcohol misuse
- Smoking
- Medical problems
- Poor sleep
- Bullying
- Deprivation
- LGBT youth
- Academic demands
- Symptoms of borderline personality disorder
- Refugee status
- Homelessness
- Living in institutional settings
- Deprivation

Table 15.4: Mental health resilience in adolescent offspring of parents with depression

- Main parent positive expressed emotion
- Co-parent support
- Good-quality social relationships
- Self-efficacy
- Frequent exercise

(Collishaw, 2015)

Treatment and management

Depression in children and young people is an important public health problem and associated with increased suicidality (Avenevoli *et al*, 2015), therefore early intervention is paramount in order to reduce risks and ensure the best possible outcomes. Findings from a British longitudinal study have highlighted the importance of early referral to child and adolescent mental health services (CAMHS). In this study, adolescents at age 14 with depression who have had no contact with CAMHS were seven times more likely to report depressive symptoms by age 17, when compared to those who had contact (Neufield *et al*, 2017).

There are a number of available evidence-based treatments for depression. For mild depression NICE recommends 'watchful waiting' for a period of up to two weeks as a first line approach. If there is little or no improvement in symptoms, digital CBT, group CBT, non-directive supportive therapy, group interpersonal psychotherapy, attachment-based family therapy and individual CBT should be offered. The evidence base for psychological intervention in 5–11-year-olds with moderate to severe depression is very limited, however for this age group family-based interpersonal psychotherapy, family therapy (family-focused treatment for childhood depression and systematic integrative family therapy), and psychodynamic psychotherapy, individual CBT are recommended. For young people aged 12–18, the evidence base suggests that there is little indication one type of psychological therapy is more effective than other types. For the treatment of moderate to severe depression NICE recommends interpersonal therapy for adolescents, family therapy (attachment-based or systemic), brief psychosocial intervention, psychodynamic psychotherapy (NICE, 2019). For further review of evidence-based treatments see (Hussain *et al*, 2018).

The use of medication for this age group remains controversial, nevertheless medication remains an important therapeutic option for moderate to severe depression (Brent *et al*, 2018). NICE currently recommends the antidepressant fluoxetine in combination with a psychological intervention. It is important that both the risks and benefits are discussed in a collaborative way between the child, family and the mental health professional (Dubicka & Wilkinson, 2018), and consideration is given to what outcomes matter most for the child or young person (www.minded.org.uk; *What Really Matters in Children and Young People's Mental Health*, Royal College of Psychiatrists, 2016). Clear information in relation to common side effects such as tiredness, headache or nausea and less common side effects, such as potential interactions with other medications, should be discussed in a transparent manner. In particular, the short term reported increased suicidal thoughts and behaviours should be stated. Clinicians should contextualise this information by explaining the risk factors and complications associated with untreated depression, including suicidal behaviour. The decision to prescribe medication will depend on the severity of the depression, whilst the risks and benefits should be assessed on an individual basis. It is essential the monitoring of any adverse reactions and general progress takes place on a regular basis. For the majority of children and adolescents, depression is often best treated in the community, and hospital admission is unwarranted and, in some circumstances, counterproductive, for example if the young person is self-harming (Royal College of Psychiatrists, 2019, in press). Nevertheless, there are circumstances when admission should be considered, for example when it is not possible to safely manage the level of risk, and if the severity of symptoms is increasing and not responding to treatment. In severe cases where the young person makes choices that are against their best interests or safety, compulsory admission under the appropriate legal framework may be necessary.

Amelia

Amelia, aged 12, has been treated with medication for ADHD since she was 7 years old. Her behaviour has always been challenging in the school and home environment and she has been permanently excluded from school on a number of occasions. With support from a variety of agencies and CAMHS, Amelia remains in mainstream provision. Over the past six months her behaviour has become increasingly more challenging and defiant. School has made a referral to a specialist provision for children with challenging behaviour. During a recent medication review at CAMHS, Amelia's parents reported that Amelia is increasingly irritable and has been complaining of headaches and tummy aches on a daily basis. Additionally, she regularly refuses to go to school, stating that school is 'boring, teachers are always giving me hassle and getting on my nerves, even my friends are giving me hassle'. Parents are wondering if these are side effects of the medication and if it would be possible to prescribe an alternative. Amelia's mother has recently noticed some weight loss and does not top up Amelia's lunchtime account as often as before since Amelia does not appear to be eating at lunchtimes, eating very little in the evenings too. Both parents have observed decreased enjoyment in activities that she previously enjoyed. Amelia has also been spending long periods of time in her bedroom alone and is reluctant to socialise with friends.

Comment: This is an example of depression in the context of comorbidity, behaviour problems, physical symptoms and school refusal. Depression can often be missed in these situations and requires careful history taking.

Bipolar disorder

Signs and symptoms

Bipolar disorder is a serious, remitting and relapsing mental illness which is characterised by episodes of depression and periods of mania or hypomania. Bipolar disorder is uncommon in children, and controversy exists over the diagnosis and prevalence of bipolar disorder prior to the onset of puberty. Longitudinal studies of the children of bipolar parents have consistently shown that cases of diagnosed manic or hypomanic episodes are rare or completely absent prior to puberty (Duffy *et al*, 2017). However, there are apparent variations in prevalence rates, in particular data from the United States suggests admission rates for bipolar is higher than in the UK (James *et al*, 2014). This may be a reflection of different prevalence rates or differing thresholds for admission.

The diagnosis of bipolar disorder in younger children remains controversial as there is considerable overlap between the symptoms of mania and other childhood problems, such as attention deficit disorder (ADHD) and consideration of developmental factors which can make the interpretation of symptoms difficult (Carlson & Dubicka, 2019). In addition, co-occurring conditions such as ADHD, and substance misuse in adolescents are common and need to be identified and treated. However, these more complex comorbid presentations can also lead to difficulties and delay in making the diagnosis. Anxiety is common, occurring in approximately half of young people with bipolar disorder and can have a negative impact on recovery if not treated (Sala *et al*, 2014). In older adolescents, bipolar disorder can also co-occur with emerging borderline personality disorder with overlapping symptoms resulting in diagnostic delay. The presence of accompanying mental health problems complicates treatment and can indicate a poorer outcome if not treated. It is essential that bipolar disorder is treated in a timely manner as the symptoms of mania can result in risky behaviours and difficulties in functioning if left untreated. There are a number of complications associated with untreated bipolar disorder but the most worrying complication is suicide. Adolescents with bipolar disorder have a nine times greater risk of suicide when compared with adolescents without a mental illness (Brent *et al*, 1993).

The core symptom of mania is an elated, expansive or irritable mood, different from a patient's usual self which must be present for a minimum of seven consecutive days; less if hospital admission is required. In hypomania, irritability and related symptoms or abnormally elevated mood must also be present for at least four days (see Table 15.5).

Table 15.5: DSM-5 Bipolar I disorder

Characterised by the occurrence of one or more manic or mixed episodes.

Criteria for manic episode:

- A distinct period (at least one week) of abnormally and persistently elevated, expansive or irritable mood, during which at least three (four if mood is only irritable) of the following symptoms have persisted and have been present to a significant degree:
  - inflated self-esteem or grandiosity
  - decreased need for sleep
  - more talkative than usual, or pressure to keep talking
  - flight of ideas or subjective racing of thoughts
  - distractibility
  - increase in goal-directed activity
  - excessive involvement in high risk activities.

In addition:

- The episode is associated with an unequivocal change in functioning.
- The mood disturbance and change in functioning are observable by others.
- The episode is not severe enough to cause impairment in functioning, or hospitalisation and psychotic features are absent.
- Symptoms are not due to substance abuse, a general medical condition, or somatic antidepressant therapy.

Bipolar II disorder is characterised by the occurrence of one or more major depressive episodes and at least one hypomanic episode. In hypomania, irritability and related symptoms or abnormally elevated mood must also be present for at least four days.

Due to the complex presentation of this condition, NICE recommends that assessment should be undertaken by a professional who has experience of the condition. In addition, it is essential that a physical health assessment is undertaken to exclude physical causes of mania/hypomania, e.g. effects of substance misuse, medication and head injury. A careful and thorough assessment of the young person's development and previous levels of functioning is essential to determine whether there is an episodic change from the child's usual behaviour. An understanding of the family context is important, including a family history of mood disorders and any previous history of mood symptoms within the young person.

There are a number of known psychosocial risk factors associated with bipolar disorder. When compared to other groups, there is a significantly higher rate of physical and sexual abuse histories (Leverich *et al*, 2002). A number of studies have shown a family history of bipolar is a significant risk factor. This risk is eight to ten times higher for children who have a parent with bipolar disorder compared to those with no family history (Birmaher *et al*, 2009); there is also a two-fold increased risk of developing depression when compared to the general population (Duffy *et al*, 2017).

Bipolar disorder is a serious mental health condition which may affect academic, social and family functioning. For this reason, psychosocial interventions in the form of individual psychological and family interventions should be considered and offered throughout the course of the illness.

Management and treatment

First line treatment is medication; second generation anti-psychotics are recommended by NICE and the National Collaborating Centre for Mental Health (2014). However, NICE states that the illness should be significantly affecting the young person and the diagnosis has been established before considering medication. The role of medication is to normalise mood, energy levels, impulsivity and consequently reduce illness-related risks to the young person. The risks and benefits of medication need to be discussed and carefully assessed on an individual basis (Dubicka *et al*, 2010). In particular, clear information should be communicated to the young person and family about the significant side effects of medication used to treat bipolar disorder (Dubicka *et al*, 2010). Common side effects include drowsiness, weight gain and gastrointestinal disturbances. Metabolic and cardiovascular effects can also occur and need careful monitoring.

To maximise adherence to treatment and engagement with their care plan, it is important that treatment decisions are made in collaboration with the young person and their family (MindEd, 2018). Depending on the young person's presentation, it can be difficult for the young person to understand information and remain focused, therefore clear, open communication is essential. Clinicians should pay careful attention to actively engaging the young person and family throughout the assessment and treatment period. They should adopt a balanced approach, demonstrate empathy and respect and avoid challenging the young person's beliefs, at the same time not reinforcing or adding credibility to the belief. This will build trust and maintain positive relationships, particularly in the acute stages of the illness when the young person may not believe they are unwell. During the acute stages of the illness, particularly if the young person is experiencing psychotic or manic symptoms, parents and carers may feel overwhelmed and may struggle to understand the extreme changes in the young person's behaviour. Psychoeducation in relation to symptoms, treatment and management, in addition to honest communication about how the condition can impact on family and peer relationships as well as academic functioning, will enable parents to feel supported and contribute to their understanding of the condition. Clinicians should always consider the individual circumstances of the family and adapt communication to ensure that both the young person and parents understand the information.

Hospital admission should be considered if the young person presents with high risk behaviours such as suicidal, impulsive or disinhibited behaviours, including sexualised behaviour, aggression or a psychotic presentation. If the young person's level of understanding is compromised by the symptoms of the illness, treatment decisions will need to be made in collaboration with parents. In some instances, mental health legislation may need to be used and treatment will be carried out against the young person's wishes. In some cases, parents may also not agree with treatment decisions and it is important that they are given as much information as possible to gain a clear understanding of why certain treatment decisions are made, ensuring that information is communicated in a timely and sensitive way. If this is unsuccessful, the legal framework will need to be reviewed. These situations are stressful to all parties, and it is important that clinicians continue to engage both parents and the young person.

Regular reviews by a child and adolescent psychiatrist are essential to monitor treatment, in particular mood monitoring and risk, as rapidly changing moods are more common in young people than adults. Antidepressant medication should be stopped during a manic or hypomanic episode. Caution should be exerted if considering such medication during a depressed phase, or to treat anxiety, and consultation with an expert is advised (British Association of Psychopharmacology, 2016).

Psychoeducation in relation to the core presenting symptoms, severity, risk of relapse and developmental course of the illness need to be clearly communicated to the young person and their family. This needs to be carefully balanced with the positive outcomes following treatment.

Kwame

Kwame, aged 14, has been brought to the hospital's emergency department by his mother following a paracetamol overdose. Kwame lives with his maternal grandparents. Kwame's mother has been treated for depression and anxiety on several occasions and is currently on medication. In the interview, Kwame was monosyllabic and extremely tearful throughout. He sat very close to his mum and refused to be interviewed separately, saying he was afraid of leaving her because the 'voices' had told him she would be harmed. His mother reports Kwame generally enjoys school and, apart from one occasion when he was bullied by some older boys, there have been no difficulties within the school environment. However, Kwame's behaviour at home has always been problematic, and is often oppositional and defiant to his mother and grandparents. In recent months his behaviour has significantly deteriorated, with aggressive and defiant behaviour both within school and at home. His mother reports that money has gone missing from his grandparents, and when asked about this, he flew into a rage and verbally and physically attacked his mum. The paracetamol overdose occurred immediately after this incident. Kwame's mother is understandably concerned about her son's behaviour and reported that his personality had changed significantly during the past few months, with times when he is extremely talkative and follows his grandparents around the house, seemingly unable to focus on any activity for more than a few minutes. These episodes can last for days at a time. At other times he is isolative, spending long periods alone in his bedroom. Kwame has always been a poor sleeper, however, recently he told his grandmother he had so much energy he no longer requires sleep; consequently, he was staying up all night playing on his Xbox and eating large quantities of ice cream. As a result, Kwame, often sleeps until mid-afternoon and is irritable and tired during the day. This has had a negative impact on his school attendance and academic performance.

Conclusion

Although bipolar disorder is uncommon in children and young people, it is a serious, complex and high-risk condition which requires careful specialist management. Early detection, intervention and monitoring by a professional who has experience of the condition, is essential to help to prevent some of the serious long-term consequences.

References

Angold A, Costello EJ, Messer SC, Pickles A, Winder F and Silver D (1995) The development of a short questionnaire for use in epidemiological studies of depression in children and adolescents. *International Journal of Methods in Psychiatric Research* **5** 237–249.

American Psychiatric Association (2013) *Diagnostic and Statistical Manual of Mental Disorders* (5th edition) (DSM 5). Washington DC: American Psychiatric Publishing.

Avenevoli S, Swendsen J, He J-P, Burstein M and Merikangas K, (2015) Depression in the national comorbidity survey – adolescent supplement: prevalence, correlates, and treatment. *Journal of the American Academy of Child and Adolescent Psychiatry* **54** (1) 37–44. Available at: doi:10.1016/j.jaac.2014.10.010 (accessed 26 June 2019).

Birmaher B, Axelson D, Monk K, Kalas C, Goldstein B and Hickey MB (2009) Lifetime psychiatric disorders in school-aged offspring of parents with bipolar disorder: the Pittsburgh bipolar offspring study. *Archives of General Psychiatry* **66** (3) 287–296.

BMJ Best practice (2019) *Bipolar Disorder in Children*. London: BMJ Publishing Group.

Brent D, Perper J and Moritz G (1993) Psychiatric risk factors for adolescent suicide: a case-control study. *Journal of the American Academy Child and Adolescent Psychiatry* **32** (3) 521–529

Brent DA, Brunwasser SM and Hollon SD (2016) Effect of cognitive-behaviour prevention program on depression 6 years after implementation among at-risk adolescents: a randomized clinical trial. *Journal American Medical Association Psychiatry* **72** 1110–18.

Brent D, Gibbons R, Wilkinson P and Dubicka B (2018) Antidepressants in paediatric depression: do not look back in anger but around in awareness. *British Journal of Psychiatry Bulletin* **42** 1–4.

British Association of Psychopharmacology (2016) Evidence-based guidelines for treating bipolar disorder: revised third edition. *Journal of Psychopharmacology* **30** (6) 495–553.

Carlson G and Dubicka B (2018) Debate editorial: Very early onset bipolar disorder -international differences in prevalence, practice or language? *Child and Adolescent Mental Health* **24** (1) 86–87.

Chorpita BF, Yim L, Moffitt C, Umemoto LA and Francis SE (2000) Assessment of symptoms of DSM-IV anxiety and depression in children: a revised child anxiety and depression scale. *Behaviour Research and Therapy* **38** (8) 835–855.

Chung P and Soares NS (2012) Childhood depression: recognition and management. *Consultant for Paediatricians* **11** 259–267.

Collishaw S (2015) Annual research review: secular trends in child and adolescent mental health. *Journal of Child Psychology and Psychiatry* **56** 370–93.

Costello EJ, Erkanli A and Angold A (2006) Is there an epidemic of child or adolescent depression? *Journal of Child Psychology and Psychiatry* **47** 1263–1271.

Dubicka B, Wilkinson P, Kelvin RG and Goodyer IM (2010) Pharmacological treatment of depression and bipolar disorder in children and adolescents. *Advances in Psychiatric Treatment* **16** 402–412.

Dubicka B and Wilkinson PO (2018) Latest thinking on antidepressants in children and young people. *Archives of Disease in Childhood* **103** (8) 720–721.

Duffy A, Vandeleur C, Heffer N and Preisig M (2017) The clinical trajectory of emerging bipolar disorder among the high-risk offspring of bipolar parents: current understanding and future considerations. *International Journal of Bipolar Disorders* **5** (37).

Hussain H, Dubicka B and Wilkinson P (2018) Recent developments in the treatment of major depressive disorder in children and adolescents. *Evidence Based Mental Health* **21** (3).

James, A, Hoang, U, Seagroatt V, Clacey J, Goldacre M and Leibenluft E (2014) A comparison of American and English hospital discharge rates for pediatric bipolar disorder, 2000–2010. *Journal American Academy Child Adolescent Psychiatry* 53 614–624.

Leverich G, McElroy S, Suppes T, Keck P, Denicoff K, Nolen A, Altshuler LL, Rush AJ, Kupka R, Frye MA, Autio KA and Post RM (2002) Early physical and sexual abuse associated with adverse cause of bipolar illness. *Biological Psychiatry* 51 (4).

McLeod G, Horwood L and Fergusson D (2016) Adolescent depression, adult mental health and psychosocial outcomes at 30 and 35 years. *Psychological Medicine* 46 (7) 1401–12.

National Collaborating Centre for Mental Health (2014) *Bipolar Disorder: The Management of Bipolar Disorder in Adults, Children and Adolescents, in Primary and Secondary Care*. London: National Institute for Health and Clinical Excellence.

National Institute for Health and Care Excellence (2019) *Depression in Children and Young People: Identification and management in primary, community and secondary care*. London: NICE.

Neufeld S and Dunn Jones B (2017) Reduction in adolescent depression after contact with mental health services: a longitudinal cohort study in the UK [online]. *Lancet* 4 (3) 120–127. Available at: dx.doi.org/10.1016/S2215-0366 (17)30002-0 (accessed 26 June 2019).

MindEd (2018) *What Matters to Child and Young People: A values-based approach*. London: Royal College of Psychiatrists.

Royal College of Psychiatrists (2019) *Repeat Self-harm in Adolescence 'Everybody's Business? Nobody's Business?' Review of admissions to inpatient services*. London: Royal College of Psychiatrists.

Sala R, Strober MA and Axelson DA (2014) Effects of comorbid anxiety disorders on the longitudinal course of pediatric bipolar disorders. Journal of the American Academy of Child and Adolescent Psychiatry 53 72–81.

Simmons M, Wilkinson P and Dubicka B (2015) Measurement issues: depression measures in children and adolescents. *Child and Adolescent Mental Health* 20 230–41.

Thaper A, Collishaw S, Pine DS and Thaper AK (2012) Depression in adolescence. *Lancet* 379 1056–1067.

Whiteford HA, Degenhardt L, Rehm J, Baxter A, Ferrari A, Erskine HE, Charlson FJ, Norman RE, Flaxman AD, Johns N, Burstein R and Murray CJL (2013) Global burden of disease attributable to mental and substance use disorders: findings from the Global Burden of Disease Study 2010. *Lancet* 382 1575– 1586.

Yorkbik O, Birmaher B and Axelson D (2004) Clinical characteristics of depressive symptoms in children and adolescents with major depressive disorder. *Journal of Clinical Psychiatry* 65 1654– 1659.

Web resources

MindEd: https://www.minded.org.uk/

YoungMinds: http://www.youngminds.org.uk/

Royal College of Psychiatrists: http://www.rcpsych.ac.uk/

Young Minds Medication resource: http://www.headmeds.org.uk/

Chapter 16: Early Intervention in Psychosis for Children and Young People

Peter Sweeney, Fiona Donnelly, Richard J Drake and Louise Theodosiou

Key learning points

- There are effective treatments for psychosis in children and young people (CYP).

- Early intervention is key; reduced duration of untreated psychosis enhances outcomes for CYP.

- It is important for treatment to address all domains of a child's life; psychological, social, occupational and medical interventions.

- Where hospital treatment is needed, it should be the minimum period of time and delivered in a non-stigmatising way.

Keywords
Psychosis; early intervention; effective treatment

Introduction

While psychosis is not a common phenomenon in children and young people, it is important that all staff working with children and young people are aware of this condition. When psychosis is recognised early, it can be treated effectively. A key element of this treatment involves educating the person with psychosis and their family in the early warning signs of a future episode. Schizophrenia is a form of psychosis, bipolar affective disorder is another form of psychosis.

Psychosis is characterised by symptoms that can affect a child or young person's (CYP) mood, thoughts, perception and behaviour (NICE, 2013a). However, it is important to remember that every CYP is unique and their experience of psychosis will reflect their developmental level and experiences. Typically, the presentation of schizophrenia is divided into:

'Positive symptoms', such as:

- disorganised speech (ideas are at best loosely linked)
- disorganised behaviour, often with repeated purposeless gestures (catatonic symptoms)
- delusions (beliefs which are fixed and false)
- hallucinations (perceptions which not caused by stimulus), and

'Negative symptoms', such as:

- reduced motivation and speech
- blunting of emotions
- reduced self-care
- social withdrawal.

While psychosis can be transient and may only be experienced by a young person once in their lifetime, it also forms part of a wider range of mental health conditions, including schizophrenia and severe mood disorders. NICE (2013b) notes that this is a very frightening condition. It is often associated with substance misuse.

How common is it?

Schizophrenia in childhood is very rare, it is estimated to be between 1.6 to 1.9 per 100,000 of the child population (Burd & Kerbeshian, 1987; Gillberg, 1984; 2001; Hellgren *et al*, 1987).

How is it diagnosed?

Diagnostic criteria for psychoses can be found in the *International Classification of Diseases (ICD) Version 10* (ICD-10) (World Health Organization, 1992) and ICD-11 (World Health Organization, 2018) and in DSM-5 (American Psychiatric Association, 2013). Relevant diagnoses include schizophrenia, acute psychotic disorders, organic delusional disorders, substance induced psychoses, mania or severe depression with psychosis.

At-risk mental state

There are times when the symptoms are not severe enough to meet diagnostic criteria, and such CYP may be perceived as having an 'at-risk mental state' (NICE, 2013a). NHS England (2016) notes that an 'at-risk mental state' can be defined as a period of time during which young people experience less severe symptoms of psychosis, a period of psychosis which lasts for less than a week or a process of deteriorating cognitive and social functioning with a family history of psychosis.

What causes psychosis?

The cause of psychosis is not clearly understood, but an interaction of genetic, biological, social and psychological factors appears likely (NICE, 2013b). As with adults, the stress-vulnerability model (Zubin & Spring, 1977) can be applied to CYP. This proposes that some people are particularly vulnerable to later stresses for genetic or early environmental reasons. Such stressors include life events; drug use, for example, cannabis consumption; and physical health problems. Psychosis is believed to be linked to abnormal striatal dopamine function amongst many other abnormalities.

What might look like psychosis?

CYP with physical health problems, such as specific forms of epilepsy or rare problems with metabolism, may display symptoms of psychosis. Additionally, young people with developmental conditions, such as autistic spectrum conditions, may, during times of intense distress, appear to have psychosis and will require assessment by clinicians with appropriate training.

What is the importance of duration of untreated psychosis?

The time that a CYP experiences symptoms of psychosis without treatment is referred to as the 'duration of untreated psychosis'. NICE (2013b) notes that the longer that psychosis is untreated, the harder it is to treat. Long duration can reduce the degree of recovery and increase risk of suicide, and delays more often occur in CAMHS services (Birchwood, 2013).

How do we assess for psychosis?

Assessment should be undertaken by a full multidisciplinary team with specialist training. In addition to assessing for the symptoms described, the CYP will have physical investigations including a medical history, physical examination, blood tests and a brain scan. A holistic assessment should also include substance misuse, social, educational and family circumstances. There should be a thorough assessment of risk of self-harm (including suicide), self neglect, vulnerability and risk to others.

What is the role of early intervention services?

Generally speaking, young people are treated in early intervention services (EIS) (NICE, 2013a). Such services were introduced in 2000 (Department of Health, 2000). Typically, they work with people aged between 14 and 35 years. EIS will work with CYP with at-risk mental states or psychosis for an average of three years. An early intervention service has a number of key functions:

1. To reduce stigma.
2. To reduce the length of time young people remain undiagnosed and untreated.
3. To develop meaningful engagement, to provide evidence-based interventions and promote recovery during the early phase of illness.
4. To increase stability in the lives of service users, facilitate development and provide opportunities for personal fulfilment.
5. To provide a user-centred service i.e. a seamless service available for those from age 14 to 65 that effectively integrates child, adolescent and adult mental health services and works in partnership with primary care, education, social services, youth and other services.
6. To ensure that the care is transferred thoughtfully and effectively at the end of the treatment period.

What are the key principles to treating psychosis?

As noted previously, it is important to treat psychosis as soon as possible. As the symptoms can be frightening, it is critical that professionals establish trust with the child or young person, and explain that their symptoms can be understood and treated. NICE (2013a) provides clear principles for treatment:

1. CYP and their families should be provided with information and enabled to participate as fully as possible, consistent with the team's duty of care to the CYP.

2. Clinicians should explain the principles of confidentiality and explain when information will need to be shared.

3. The young person's ability to believe, understand, retain and process information (capacity) will need to be assessed and understood.

4. CYP and families should be provided with information about local and national support groups.

5. It is important to address the issue of stigma and to consider the cultural context of the individual child and family.

6. Cognitive behavioural therapy and antipsychotic medication are essential elements of treatment. There is a range of dopamine antagonist antipsychotic medications available, some in the form of tablets and others in the form of long-acting injections. They all work to reduce the 'positive' symptoms of psychosis. Sometimes, young people will require hospital admission, and once again this will need to be explained to CYP and their families.

Prognosis

Childhood onset of psychosis is associated with poorer outcomes than adult onset. Psychosis more frequently manifests in late adolescence and early adulthood. More often than adult schizophrenia, childhood schizophrenia is slow to manifest rather than being an abrupt departure from the person's usual self. Deteriorating school performance, loss of friendships, and withdrawn and odd/eccentric behaviour can characterise some of the subtle signs of at-risk mental states and early illness changes. Children and adolescents tend to present with more negative symptoms, disorganisation and poor social and interpersonal function, which all signal a poor prognosis.

Joseph

Joseph is a 16-year-old male, referred to the early intervention service due to concerns with regards to a change in his behaviour. At initial assessment, he reported over the previous few weeks he had discovered that the CIA were spying on him. Joseph stated that he had heard several people talk about him, when no one was there. These voices claimed that the US government believed that he had found out information which could pose a national security threat, and as a result he needed to be monitored. Joseph was unsure what this meant, and felt confused and scared by the situation.

At assessment, there was evidence of thought disorder, and Joseph flitted between various different topics. He was concerned that his thoughts were being broadcast to the CIA, and as a result had lined the windows with aluminium foil, in an attempt to stop this. A significant decline had been noted in his functioning over the previous few weeks, with Joseph self-isolating himself in his room, and disposing of all electronic devices. He was not washing at all, and had stopped attending college.

Premorbidly, Joseph was academically doing well, however was noted to suffer from anxiety symptoms. He had never misused any illicit substances, and had no contact with mental health services prior to this. There was a family history of psychosis, with Joseph's older brother and paternal uncle both having inpatient admissions to mental health units due to acute psychotic episodes.

Following initial assessment, it was formulated that Joseph was presenting with a first episode of psychosis. Features of this included evidence of thought disorder, auditory hallucinations, delusional thought content, thought withdrawal, and a significant decline from premorbid functioning. A risk assessment was completed, and it was felt that he did not present with risk towards self or others, and he was more perplexed by his current situation.

Joseph was accepted under the care of the early intervention services, with the aim of treating the acute psychotic symptoms, and provide support to Joseph and his family to reduce stigma associated with psychosis. Support included:

■ **Medical intervention** – Joseph was provided with pharmacological treatment for psychosis, aimed at symptom management, and minimising side effects. This was a collaborative approach, and Joseph was involved in the decision-making process. This approach supported Joseph's understanding of the use of medication, and helped to improve compliance with medication.

■ **Psychological support** – Initially, this was through psychoeducation around psychosis. As Joseph's mental state improved, he was keen for support in understanding and management of his anxiety symptoms. Joseph began cognitive behavioural therapy (CBT) with a therapist in the early intervention team.

■ **Social and vocational support** – This was aimed at promoting inclusion in the community environment and providing support with the recovery process. Joseph's care coordinator was able to work with college in providing Joseph with specific supports and opportunities within this setting.

■ **Family interventions** – Support was provided to Joseph and his family, with the aim of helping them understand what has happened and how they may work at finding practical solutions to day-to-day problems.

Joseph and his family engaged well with the early intervention service, and this helped to reduce the duration of untreated psychosis. Through this collaborative, multidisciplinary approach, his symptoms of psychosis were well controlled, and his overall level of functioning significantly improved.

Conclusion

It must be remembered that psychosis is a very rare condition. However, it can have a significant impact on the affected child and family. We would hope that this chapter will increase awareness of this important condition. Early recognition can enhance recovery and increased understanding can help CYP with this condition to be understood and supported in their communities.

References

American Psychiatric Association (2013) *Diagnostic and Statistical Manual of Mental Disorders* (5th edition). Washington, DC: APA.

Birchwood M, Connor C, Lester H, Patterson P, Freemantle N, Marshall M, Fowler D, Lewis S, Jones P, Amos T, Everard L and Singh SP (2013) Reducing duration of untreated psychosis: care pathways to early intervention in psychosis services. *British Journal of Psychiatry* **203** (1) 58–64.

Burd L and Kerbeshian J (1987) A North Dakota prevalence study of schizophrenia presenting in childhood. *Journal of the American Academy of Child & Adolescent Psychiatry* **26** (3) 347–350.

Department of Health (2000) *NHS Plan*. London: Department of Health.

Gillberg C (1984) Infantile autism and other childhood psychoses in a Swedish urban region. Epidemiological aspects. *Journal of Child Psychiatry and Psychology* **25** 35–43.

Gillberg C (2001) Epidemiology of early onset schizophrenia. In H. Remschmidt (ed) *Schizophrenia in Children and Adolescents*, pp43–59. Cambridge: Cambridge University Press.

Hellgren L, Gillberg C and Enerskog I (1987) Antecedents of adolescent psychoses: a population-based study of school health problems in children who develop psychosis in adolescence. *Journal of the American Academy of Child and Adolescent Psychiatry* **26** 351–355.

National Institute for Health and Care Excellence (2013a) *Psychosis and Schizophrenia in Children and Young People: Recognition and management* [online]. London: NICE. Available at: https://www.nice.org.uk/guidance/cg155 (accessed 26 June 2019).

National Institute for Health and Care Excellence (2013b) *Psychosis and schizophrenia in children and young people: recognition and management* (full guidelines) [online]. London: NICE. Available at: https://www.nice.org.uk/guidance/cg155/evidence/full-guideline-pdf-6785647416 (accessed 26 June 2019).

NHS England, the National Collaborating Centre for Mental Health and the National Institute for Health and Care Excellence (2016) *Implementing the Early Intervention in Psychosis Access and Waiting Time Standard: Guidance* [online]. London: NHS England/NCCMH/NICE. Available at: https://www.england.nhs.uk/mentalhealth/wp-content/uploads/sites/29/2016/04/eip-guidance.pdf (accessed 26 June 2019).

World Health Organization (1992) *The International Classification of Diseases-10 Classification of Mental and Behavioural Disorders*. Geneva: WHO.

World Health Organization (2018) *ICD-11 for Mortality and Morbidity Statistics* [online]. Geneva: WHO. Available at: https://icd.who.int/browse11/l-m/en (accessed 26 June 2019).

Zubin J and Spring B (1977) Vulnerability: a new view on schizophrenia. *Journal of Abnormal Psychology* **86** 103–126.

Chapter 17: Neurodevelopmental Conditions in Children and Young People

Rachel Elvins, Jonathan Green, Paul Abeles, and Louise Theodosiou

Key learning points

- Attention deficit hyperactivity disorder (ADHD) and autistic spectrum disorder (ASD) are developmental conditions arising early and enduring through development. Their developmental symptoms can be highly impairing in themselves and also increase vulnerability to other mental health problems.

- Depending on the breadth of definition used, ADHD affects between 1.6–8 % and ASD 1.2–1.8% of the population.

- Management of both conditions should be framed within an enduring development context; with a mixture of case management, specific treatment for the core developmental symptoms, and management of any co-morbidities.

- After diagnosis, both conditions benefit from family psychoeducation and support.

- Following this, the core developmental symptoms are most effectively treated with medication in the case of ADHD, and psychosocial social communication therapy in the case of ASD.

- Other mental health needs should be treated with the evidenced appropriate therapy adapted to each condition's neurodevelopmental profile.

Keywords

Autistic spectrum condition; attention deficit hyperactivity disorder; neurodevelopmental disorder; medication; social communication therapy

Introduction

ADHD and autism spectrum conditions (ASC) are conditions that arise early in childhood. While the nature of inheritance of these two developmental conditions is not fully understood, they are both known to have an inherited component. ADHD and ASC are not caused by parenting, they are conditions that reflect differences in the brain. Both conditions benefit from being recognised early. Early recognition enables families to support children and allows education systems to put in place the support that children and young people need.

Attention deficit hyperactivity disorder (ADHD)

There are three core symptoms of hyperkinetic disorder, also known as ADHD; restlessness, difficulties with impulse control and impaired concentration (World Health Organization, 1992). Children and young people (CYP) usually show evidence of ADHD in the first five years of life (World Health Organization, 1992) and will display these features in a range of settings:

- School, where educational performance can be impacted and CYP can struggle with behavioural expectations.

- Home, where the symptoms of ADHD can impact on family life.

- Social settings, which change with time and development.

The symptoms should be pervasive and, in many cases, these symptoms persist throughout a child's life. Broad criteria for ADHD traits have an estimated population prevalence of 4-8% in childhood (Faraone *et al*, 2003). The more narrowly defined 'hyperkinetic disorder' affects around 1.6-5% of 19-year-olds in the UK (NHS Digital, 2018) with higher rates in boys (2.6%) than girls (0.6%).

CYP with ADHD are more likely to:

- leave school early without qualifications (National Institute for Health and Care Excellence, 2018)

- come in contact with youth justice systems (Hughes *et al*, 2012)

- use drugs and alcohol (NICE, 2018)

- are possibly more susceptible to the negative consequences of digital gaming (Lam, 2014).

Adults with ADHD have increased difficulties with family relationships, employment and physical health (NICE, 2018). CYP with ADHD are more vulnerable to additional mental health needs; the symptoms and their impact on a child's performance and social interaction can adversely affect emotional wellbeing, with increased rates of depression and anxiety (NICE, 2018). NICE (2018) also notes that ADHD causes significant emotional and financial costs to families, children and the healthcare system both in terms of the impact on family systems and the cost of treatment.

What causes ADHD?

This neurodevelopmental condition is often associated with other neurodevelopmental difficulties (such as cerebral palsy, epilepsy, and co-ordination difficulties), and poorer reading ability (Sayal *et al*, 2018).. These findings support the conceptualisation that ADHD has an underlying biological basis. Clinical practice also suggests that environmental and family factors can exacerbate difficulties and impairment. In terms of possible causes, a large body of research indicates that the aetiology of ADHD is complex and likely to involve a variety of factors. Genetic studies have consistently found strong evidence of a genetic contribution and that ADHD is highly heritable (average heritability is around 0.8), and more likely to be found in closer biological relatives than more distant relatives. Neuroanatomical and neuropsychological studies demonstrate consistent group differences (between children who do and do not have ADHD) in terms of the volume of particular regions of the brain and performance on tests measuring specific functions, such as executive function, delay aversion and response inhibition. Other, more environmental risk factors may also play a role, perhaps interacting with a genetic vulnerability. These include maternal use of tobacco, alcohol, or other psychoactive substances during pregnancy, prematurity, birth complications, and head injury.

Farooq

Farooq is an 8 year old boy who has received a number of fixed term exclusions from school. He lives with his mother and younger sister. His mother has had to leave work to collect him on a number of occasions and is concerned about her job. His school reports that Farooq struggles to sit still, cannot concentrate and has been involved in a number of fights.

Assessment and diagnosis of ADHD

Although ADHD is now much more widely recognised and understood, many CYP with ADHD are not recognised. A lot of work has been done raising awareness of this important condition in education, youth justice and wider healthcare systems. NICE (2018) recommends that assessments for ADHD need to involve an understanding of the CYP's presentation in education, home and clinic settings and should be undertaken by clinicians with specialist experience, such as child adolescent psychiatrists or psychologists, nurses or paediatricians. The assessment should be comprehensive, involving the child, parent, and the child's school. When working with Farooq it would be important to understand the impact of his symptoms at home, school and in social settings.

The clinician will often make use of standardised screening tools e.g. the SNAP (Atkins *et al*, 1985) which would be completed by parent and teacher. This is often accompanied by the Qb test (Hall *et al*, 2017), an objective, computerised test of continuous performance. The Qb test compares the subject with many people of the same age and gender and provides information about attention, activity levels and impulsivity. While it is not diagnostic, it does provide a useful indication. These tools will be a useful adjunct to clinical assessment.

Diagnosis of ADHD has been based on the ICD-10 criteria; ICD-11 is now published (World Health Organization, 2018). It requires the presence of symptoms for at least six months.

Treatment of ADHD

There are helpful national guidelines for the treatment of ADHD (American Academy of Child and Adolescent Psychiatry, 2007; NICE, 2018). NICE (2018) advises the first line availability after diagnosis of ADHD psychoeducation and support for parents and children. For CYP with moderate to severe ADHD, medication is the evidenced treatment for symptom reduction (NICE, 2018). NICE advises that the first line medication to be considered is the stimulant methylphenidate; this is generally used in a long acting form. If methylphenidate does not prove effective, then there are second line medications that can be used, for example, the stimulant dexamphetamine, and the non-stimulants atomoxetine and guanfacine. Decisions about the choice of treatment should be made jointly with the child and the family and their views and preferences fully taken into account. Some families may not want medication. Before medication is started, clinicians will undertake a physical history, excluding a family history of heart disease. Children will have their pulse, blood pressure, height and weight checked. Children with ADHD have increased rates of other mental health needs. It is important to be mindful of this increased vulnerability.

For children who are under 5 years old with symptoms of ADHD, the first line treatment is an ADHD-focused group parent-training programme.

For CYP with moderate to severe ADHD who are over 5 years old, medication is the evidenced treatment for symptom reduction (NICE, 2018). Where children and young people continue to experience significant difficulties while on medication, it can be helpful to offer cognitive behavioural therapy alongside medication. However there is not enough evidence to support a parent training programme being offered to parents of CYP with ADHD. NICE advises that the first line medication to be considered is the stimulant methylphenidate; this is generally used in a long acting form.

Conclusions

ADHD is a common condition in childhood that is often associated with other mental health and developmental difficulties and can lead to adverse outcomes. Although recognition rates have increased in recent years, many children with ADHD remain undiagnosed. All professionals working with children are well placed to notice possible symptoms and to make further enquiries of parents and other professionals, such as teachers.

Autism spectrum disorder

Autism spectrum disorder (ASD) is a neurodevelopmental condition with a prevalence of between 1.2 and 2% of the population worldwide, depending on the definition used (Elsabbagh *et al*, 2012). It is a priority in the *NHS 10 Year Plan* (2019) and represents a significant public health challenge; combined health and societal costs of autism in the UK are estimated as £32 billion per annum, exceeding costs of stroke, heart disease and cancer combined (Buescher *et al*, 2014).

ASD is a spectrum with a variation in presentation, but common features are atypicalities in reciprocal social functioning in development, along with a pattern of restricted and repetitive behaviours (WHO, 2018). These are seen across contexts but may vary in expression with situation. These atypicalities emerge gradually during the first few years of life, beginning most probably from atypical brain development in utero. The condition is usually diagnosable from about 3 years old, although in some cases, later. Most cases are primarily genetic and familial in origin, with multiple genetic variants of small effect contributing to the heritability of about 80% (Sandin *et al*, 2017). ASD often runs in families with mild traits or the full condition being found in other family members. A minority of cases (about 10%) arise from known genetic condition or other brain injury (e.g. encephalitis, epilepsy), and some environmental exposures (foetal exposure to sodium valproate or alcohol; severe early social deprivation) are linked to ASD. As an enduring condition, once established, ASD is persistent in development and usually life-long. This fact is important in considering its 'treatment'.

Assessment and diagnosis

Diagnosis is based on careful consideration of the child's behavioural development; there are no blood or other biological tests. The key elements necessary for assessment are set out by NICE (2011). There needs to be a detailed family and developmental history, best collected in standardised form. Reports from parents and others must be balanced with direct observations and standardised assessments of the child's social and cognitive behaviour in clinic and school. Standardised diagnostic observational assessments such as ADOS are available. Multi-professional assessment should be the norm and diagnosis and assessment should not just be based on questionnaire measures. As well as categorical diagnosis, there should be functional assessment of degree of impairment in different areas, as well as the family and social context. Diagnosis should be as early as possible so that appropriate management and adjustment can begin.

Management and treatment

While there is an emerging intervention science base, many treatments currently offered to families within and beyond mainstream health services are not evidenced (Green & Garg, 2018). Research on management of other enduring health conditions suggests a priority should be placed on *patient /family self-management* of the condition (Taylor *et al*, 2014), coupled with accessible ongoing *key-working case management* (Archer *et al*, 2012), combined with timely *'Step-up' care to more specialist service* when necessary (Bower & Gilbody, 2005). Current evidence (Green & Garg, 2018) suggests how a developmental sequence of interventions can achieve these aims in a planned way (see Figure 17.1 , Green 2019).

Table 17.1: Support around diagnosis

Around diagnosis

Parents should be offered a brief *post-diagnostic support and psychoeducation group* to help adjust and orientate to their child's different development. These do not yet have evidence of effectiveness but are clinically intuitive.

The pre-school and early school age period following diagnosis

The best evidence (NICE, 2013; IAPT, 2016) is for an initial *'Social Communication Intervention'* delivered individually to parents to reduce child core ➔

---

autism symptom severity and optimise social adaptation. Currently, parent-mediated Preschool Autism Communication Therapy (PACT, http://research.bmh.manchester.ac.uk/pact/about/) has the best evidence for producing long-term reduction in autism symptom severity of his kind, which was sustained for six years after treatment end (Pickles *et al*, 2016; Figure 17.2). This has the additional spin-off benefit of increasing parental empowerment, resilience and the ability to self-manage the condition in their child going forward. No medication or other biological therapy has yet been shown to reduce autism symptoms.

Into the school years

Life for a child with autism can become stressful and they can present with mental health co-morbidities. The presenting problem can often be understood as the result of the autistic child being within a poorly adapted relational, educational or physical environment; autism-aware and responsive environments at home, in school and in society are a key for optimising health.

For established co-morbid conditions, NICE recommends the use of already-evidenced interventions for specific co-morbidities with appropriate adaptations – examples would be *ADHD* (stimulant medication management; family guidance), *anxiety* (adapted CBT and/or anxiolytics), *mood disorder* (adapted psychotherapy or SSRI) or *OCD* (adapted behavioural intervention, CBT, SSRI). Adaptations to psychological treatments have focused more on the visual presentation of material, using 'social stories' (Gray & Garrand, 1993), placing less emphasis on the specific aspects of the therapeutic relationship and more emphasis on evaluation of treatment outcomes (Abeles, 2014). For *concerning (or challenging) behaviours**, initial evaluation of other underlying causes is important since these behaviours are often an expression of anxiety, environmental distress, trauma, or physical pain in a child with poor capacity for communication – they must not just be treated symptomatically. Once other causes are excluded, ASD-adapted individual parent-training has good initial evidence for conduct disorder symptom reduction (Bearss *et al*, 2015) and in severe cases medication management with neuroleptics, such as aripriprazole.

(*The term 'concerning behaviours' is recommended – there is widespread (and often understandable) resistance from parents and others to 'disruptive/oppositional behavior' terminology, which they feel is stigmatising their parenting and channels families down CD/ODD 'parent-training' intervention pathways; an important dynamic behind the so-called 'pathological demand avoidance' concept.)

Transitions and adolescence

Ongoing clinical case-management can be the interface of multi-agency collaborative care between health, social care and education and responsive to difficulties – supporting family self-care and resilience (Taylor *et al*, 2014). It reflects a health system designed around ASD as an enduring condition within development, rather than a system reacting to crises. Its effectiveness is not yet empirically researched in ASD but it has clinical face-validity; it could be facilitated in the future by newer digital tracking technologies and online communication. ➔

Later, as part of individuation, many autistic children and adolescents will be able and wish to set their own treatment goals in collaboration with families and professionals; increasingly the intervention work will be with the adolescent themselves, at the service of their adjustment into adulthood and transition planning. There is little good evidence of effectiveness, but informed case management is intuitive.

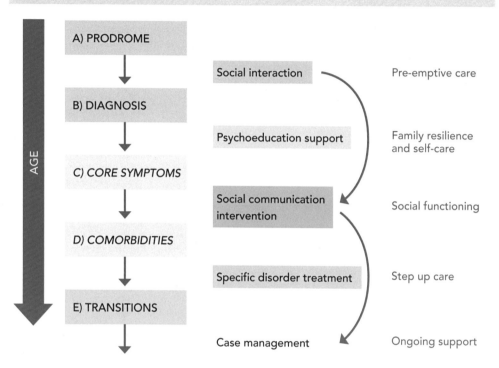

Figure 17.1: Sequential Intervention Model. Intervention column: strength of colour fill reflects strength of current supporting evidence. From Green J (2019) Editorial perspective: delivering autism intervention through development. *Journal of Child Psychology and Psychiatry*. Early online: doi:10.1111/jcpp.13110.

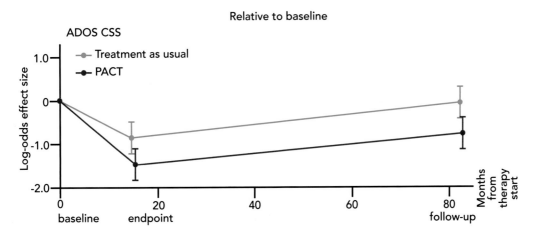

Figure 17.2: Long-term symptom effects of social communication intervention. From Pickles A, Le Couteur A, Leadbitter K, Salomone E, Cole-Fletcher R, Tobin H, Gammer I, Lowry J, Vamvakas G, Byford S, Aldred C, Slonims V, McConachie H, Howlin P, Parr J, Charman T and Green J (2016) Parent-mediated social communication therapy for young children with autism (PACT): longterm follow-up of a randomised controlled trial. *Lancet* **388** 2501–2509.

Conclusion

ASD is both prevalent and impairing with high health and societal costs (Green, 2019). Models of management for enduring conditions, combined with current evidence on autism intervention, supports an integrated developmental model of management of autism from diagnosis through early development. Post-diagnostic support, including education and support to adapt to diagnosis, is followed by a primary parent-mediated social communication intervention to optimise early social development, reduce symptom severity and increase family empowerment and resilience. Interventions with demonstrated long-term effects on development are ideal. Key working is introduced during this time within a local autism virtual expert team, coupled with a register database to underpin ongoing support. Later in development as needed, there is timely access to step-up care for emerging secondary problems. A flexible and creative approach to delivering psychological therapies improves engagement and management. Case management continues to support the family as needed through predictable transitions and unpredictable life events. Although not specifically tested for, the above model could in theory be applicable more widely for social communication problems in childhood – for instance, social (pragmatic) communication disorder (SCD).

References

Abeles P (2014) Modifying cognitive behaviour therapy for high functioning autism spectrum disorder. *Cutting Edge in Psychiatry in Practice* **4** 137–142.

American Academy of Child and Adolescent Psychiatry (2007) Practice parameter for the assessment and treatment of children and adolescents with attention deficit/hyperactivity disorder. *Journal of the American Academy of Child and Adolescent Psychiatry* **46** 894–921.

Archer J, Bower P, Gilbody S, Lovell K, Richards D, Gask L, Dickens C and Coventry P (2012) Collaborative care for depression and anxiety problems. *Cochrane Database of Systematic Reviews* **10**. Art. No.: CD006525. Available at: DOI: 10.1002/14651858.CD006525.pub2 (accessed 26 June 2019).

Atkins MS, Pelham WE and Licht MH (1985) A comparison of objective classroom measures and teacher ratings of Attention Deficit Disorder. *Journal of Abnormal Child Psychology* **13** (1) 155–67.

Bearss K, Johnson C, Smith T, Lecavalier L, Swiezy N, Aman M, McAdam DB, Butter E, Stillitano C, Minshawi N, Sukhodolsky DG, Mruzek DW, Turner K, Neal T, Hallett V, Mulick J, Green B, Handen B, Deng Y, Dziura J and Scahill L (2015) Effect of parent training vs parent education on behavioral problems in children with autism spectrum disorder: a randomized clinical trial. *Journal of American Medical Association* **313** (15) 1524–33. .

Bower P and Gilbody S (2005) Stepped care in psychological therapies: access, effectiveness and efficiency; narrative literature review. *British Journal of Psychiatry* **186** 11–17.

Buescher AVS, Cidav Z, Knapp M and Mandell DS (2014) Costs of autism spectrum disorders in the United Kingdom and the United States. *JAMA Pediatrics* **168** (8) 721–728.

Elsabbagh M, Divan G, Koh YJ, Kim YS, Kauchali S, Marcín C, Montiel-Nava C, Patel V, Paula CS, Wang C, Yasamy MT and Fombonne E (2012) Global prevalence of autism and other pervasive developmental disorders. *Autism Research* **5** (3) 160–179.

Faraone SV, Sergeant J, Gillberg C and Biederman J (2003) The worldwide prevalence of ADHD: is it an American condition? *World Psychiatry* **2** 104–113.

Gray CA and Garand JD (1993) Social stories: improving responses of students with autism with accurate social information. *Focus on Autistic Behavior* **8** (1) 1–10.

Green J (2019) Editorial perspective: delivering autism intervention through development. *Journal of Child Psychology and Psychiatry*. Early online: doi:10.1111/jcpp.13110.

Green J and Garg S (2018) Annual Research Review: The state of autism intervention science: process, target psychological and biological mechanisms and future prospects. *Journal of Child Psychology and Psychiatry* **59** (4) 424–443. Available at: doi:10.1111/jcpp.12892 (accessed 26 June 2019).

Hall CL, Valentine AZ, Walker GM, *et al* (2017) Study of user experience of an objective test (QbTest) to aid ADHD assessment and medication management: a multi-methods approach. *BMC Psychiatry* **17** (1) 66. Available at: doi:10.1186/s12888-017-1222-5 (accessed 26 June 2019).

Hughes N, Williams H, Chitsabesan P, Davies R and Mounce L (2012) *Nobody Made the Connection: The Prevalence of Learning Disability in young people who offend*. Available at: https://www.childrenscommissioner.gov.uk/publication/nobody-made-the-connection/ (accessed 26 June 2019).

IAPT (2016) *Postgraduate Certificate in Evidence-based Psychological approaches for Children & Young People – Learning Disability and Autism Pathway*. Greater Manchester Mental Health NHS Foundation Trust. Available at: https://www.gmmh.nhs.uk/cyp-postgraduate-certificate---learning-disability-autism-pathway/ (accessed 26 June 2019).

Lam LT (2014) Risk factors of Internet addiction and the health effect of internet addiction on adolescents: a systematic review of longitudinal and prospective studies. *Curr Psychiatry Rep* **16** (11) 508.

National Institute for Health and Care Excellence (2011) *Autism Diagnosis in Children and Young People: Recognition, referral and diagnosis of children and young people on the autism spectrum. Clinical guideline 128*. London: NICE. Available at: http://guidance.nice.org.uk/CG128 (accessed 26 June 2019).

National Institute for Health and Care Excellence (2018) Attention deficit hyperactivity disorder; the Nice guidelines on diagnosis and management of ADHD in children, young people and adults. London: NICE. Available at: https://www.nice.org.uk/guidance/ng87/evidence/full-guideline-pdf-4783651311 (accessed 26 June 2019).

NHS Digital (2018) *Mental Health of Children and Young People in England, 2017 Hyperactivity Disorders*. Available at: https://files.digital.nhs.uk/10/D0A0B8/MHCYP%202017%20Hyperactivity%20 Disorders.pdf (accessed 26 June 2019).

Pickles A, Le Couteur A, Leadbitter K, Salomone E, Cole-Fletcher R, Tobin H, Gammer I, Lowry J, Vamvakas G, Byford S, Aldred C, Slonims V, McConachie H, Howlin P, Parr J, Charman T and Green J (2016) Parent-mediated social communication therapy for young children with autism (PACT): long-term follow-up of a randomised controlled trial. *Lancet* **388** 2501–2509.

Sandin S, Lichtenstein P, Kuja-Halkola R, Hultman C, Larsson H and Reichenberg A (2017) The heritability of autism spectrum disorder. *JAMA* **318** (12) 1182–1184.

Sayal K, Prasad V, Daley D, Ford T and Coghill D (2018) ADHD in children and young people: prevalence, care pathways, and service provision. *Lancet Psychiatry* **5** (2) 175-186.

Taylor SJC, Pinnock H, Epiphaniou E, Pearce G, Parke HL, Schwappach A *et al* (2014) A rapid synthesis of the evidence on interventions supporting self-management for people with long-term conditions: PRISMS – Practical systematic review of self-management support for long-term conditions. *Health Service Delivery Res* **2** (53).

World Health Organization (1992) *The International Classification of Diseases-10 Classification of Mental and Behavioural Disorders*. GWHO.

World Health Organization (2018) *International Classification of Diseases for Mortality and Morbidity Statistics (11th Revision)*. Available at: https://icd.who.int/browse11/l-m/en (accessed 26 June 2019).

Chapter 18: Attitudes Matter – Working with Children and Young People Who Self-harm

Rick Bradley and Briony Spedding

Key learning points

- The last decade has seen an increase in the prevalence of emotional disorders and behaviours, such as self-harm.

- Triggers are specific to each individual but include school life and academic pressures, changing hormones, low self-esteem, relationship issues, body image and social media.

- Self-harm is something to be taken seriously and should not be viewed as 'attention seeking'.

- There are some simple strategies that can be used to help support young people who self-harm.

- A range of professionals can play an important role in prevention and early intervention – helping young people to build resilience and coping strategies might divert them from requiring specialist support in the future.

- Evidence-based interventions for mild to moderate mental health needs delivered by non-clinical practitioners can demonstrate outcomes comparable to those of specialist services.

Keywords

Self-harm; mental health; children; young people; interventions; coping strategies

Introduction

Many children and young people will experience an episode of self-harm. This chapter will support professionals to explore and understand their reactions towards young people who express thoughts of self-harm or present in crisis after an episode of self-harm. We will explain ways of assessing and managing risk and models of long-term therapy. Perhaps most importantly, we will look to equip the reader with some of the core tools and techniques that can help put someone at ease and enable to get them the right support.

(NOTE: It is important to emphasise the parameters by which we are categorising self-harm in this chapter. Whilst some broader definitions may include certain eating behaviours and harmful drug and alcohol use, we are focusing on intentional acts of self-injury or self-poisoning as defined by the NICE guidelines.)

Why we need to talk about self-harm

Many children and young people will experience an episode of self-harm. In 2018, comprehensive new NHS data was published about the mental health of children and young people in England (NHS Digital, 2018). The report was the first of its kind in over a decade, looking at the extent young people are in contact with various health, social and education services. While other mental health conditions have actually remained fairly stable, over the last decade there has been a distinct increase in the prevalence of emotional disorders and behaviours, such as self-harm.

Self-harming is not in itself a mental health diagnosis, rather a set of behaviours that may indicate someone is trying to manage difficult thoughts or feelings, to feel something or perhaps looking to gain a sense of control (Royal College of Psychiatrists, 2019). Actions might be a one-off or could persist for years, often away from the gaze of friends, partners and families (despite the inaccurate 'attention seeking' label).

Whilst the reasons behind self-harm are specific to each individual, there are regular themes that we see highlighted in our work: school life and academic pressures, changing hormones, low self-esteem, relationship issues, and worries about body image are triggers regularly cited by young people (Addaction, 2018). The overarching role of social media can exacerbate these elements, with today's adolescents getting little respite from lives which are increasingly lived online.

Self-harm is something to be taken seriously. Dismissing someone cutting or burning themselves as being attention-seeking minimises the clear risks that may motivate individuals to take such actions. It is worth remembering that of the roughly 6000 people who take their own lives each year in the UK, at least half will have a history of self-harm (NHS Digital, 2018), with around 25% having been treated in hospital for self-harm the previous year (NICE, 2019). Once a person has been hospitalised for self-harm, the likelihood that they will take their own life increases by 50-100 times (NICE, 2019).

Since 2011, the number of young people seeking medical attention for self-harm has risen in some groups by 68%. In spite of this, many young people who self-harm do not meet the threshold for specialist mental health services. A recent survey of 1000 GPs based across the UK revealed that 90% of respondents said mental health services for children and young people are inadequate, with 68% of GPs seeing more young patients self-harming within the preceding two years (Stem4, 2018).

We also know that those accessing medical attention are just the tip of the iceberg (Hawton *et al*, 2018) with many others hiding their behaviours due to embarrassment, fear and stigma (Addaction, 2018). It is clear that existing mental health services are overstretched; to properly address this, increased funding is essential, as is investment in prevention and early intervention. In addition to this, there is a vital role to be played by professionals sitting outside of traditional clinical settings (Bradley, 2018).

Increasing demands require staff in schools, youth services and other settings to be well-informed and there are some simple ways that vital help can be offered.

What to do and say (and what not to)

The second part of this heading is actually very important. People generally have the best of intentions around this topic but some interactions actually create more problems than they solve.

In schools, creating an environment where students will feel comfortable to talk with staff members is essential. Young people may not explicitly ask for help but providing a safe space in which they can talk to a trusted person is an important foundation. When these conditions are in place, people are more likely to share their worries and ask for support.

Focus groups from the 'Mind and Body' programme have highlighted that having the right people in the right roles is especially important. Students are frequently directed to speak with a designated member of staff (commonly a member of the leadership team) but that person may not be seen as approachable or someone they feel comfortable with. Allowing a range of support options is ideal to give young people more encouragement to get help.

Kelly

Kelly is a 15-year-old girl who has been struggling with her school work in recent weeks. She has specific learning needs in relation to reading and spelling. She has been noted to be more withdrawn as the pressure of her exams increases. Kelly has been wearing long sleeves as the weather gets warmer.

Many professionals do have concerns that if self-harm is spoken about, other young people will have ideas about copying such behaviours. There is little evidence that this is actually the case (Knightsmith, 2015). Whilst it is important to ensure no in-depth information on self-harm is circulated which may be triggering for people, it is vital that discussions about mental health are normalised, so that there are appropriate outlets for young people to seek support.

How self-harm disclosures are received by professionals can be pivotal, potentially influencing how that person will feel about getting support both at that time and in the future. It is important that we respond well and appropriately each time. This is not said to put extra pressure on such situations as there really are some simple ways to set people at ease. It is difficult to condense all the relevant skills and techniques but our top tips are as follows:

1. *Thank them.* This may be the first time they have talked about self-harm or their mental health with anyone before. Even if not, this is something very personal and it benefits the therapeutic relationship if this is recognised.

2. *Acknowledge their distress and that it may have been hard to talk.* Let them know that you have heard what they told you, that you have really listened to them. Avoid responses like 'don't worry' or 'everything will be fine' – those are not things we can control – but reassure them that you will help how you can. For example, in the case study above, Kelly may be concerned that she will be blamed or judged, she may believe that she will be put in hospital.

3. *Remain calm, don't be shocked and don't judge.* Sharing how they feel can be a relief for some but others might feel embarrassed or ashamed. Don't look shocked or say things like 'why do you do it?' – that's likely to make people question whether they should have said anything at all. Similarly, don't downplay what they are feeling or pretend to understand what they're going through if you do not. Listen and give them time and space to talk.

4. *Don't tell them simply to stop.* Of course we want to keep the person safe but again, this advice is unlikely to be helpful. If someone is self-harming, there will be a reason (even if they do not understand it fully themselves). Addressing feelings of low self-worth or emotional pain can be a long process, so indicating it's an easy choice shows a lack of empathy.

NOTE: Some people also hurt themselves as a way of managing thoughts around suicide. Whilst self-harm is not a positive coping strategy, it is important to be mindful that it might keep some people in a slightly safer mind space in the short-term. Any concerns around this should be directed to a mental health specialist.

5. *Be collaborative – how do we put support in place?* Try and give the young person as much ownership over next steps whenever possible. Sharing information can be a big thing and it is common for people to worry about losing control about what happens now. Work in partnership to explore this. Set up care plans and/or safety plans together. Give them a say in who is included in this and who is notified about it, as much as you can. Look at how you can break the triggers for their self-harm together. *For example, it would be important to explain to Kelly that there is help available and that there are alternative strategies that she can be supported to learn.*

NOTE: Safeguarding processes can dictate that information be shared against the young person's wishes whenever obvious risks are identified. Clearly setting out confidentiality and information sharing processes is essential when you start working with young people. Regular reminders ensure young people are clear on the boundaries of your work and help the escalation of disclosures feel less like their trust is being breached. We would also argue that, even if they protest, most young people know certain information will need to be shared. When they say something, it is usually for a reason, that reason being that they do want and need help.

Assessing and managing risk

One of the most important elements to remember when you receive a disclosure about self-harm is the need to assess and manage risk. In many situations, the person who receives an initial disclosure that someone has self-harmed may be a friend, a parent or a teacher and they may not feel equipped to deal with the situation. In a hospital setting, non mental-health trained medical and nursing staff can also feel ill-equipped or trained to assess or support someone who has harmed themselves. NICE recommends that all children and young people who have harmed themselves have an initial assessment which aims to help identify any immediate physical risk so that steps can be taken to reduce this risk. On a practical level this can be as simple as trying to find out if the person needs medical attention as a result of hurting themselves and if they have anything with them which they might be tempted to use to hurt themselves. If so, would they be willing to give this to someone else to reduce the chance of them using it – consider whether the person should see a school nurse, a practice nurse, a GP or go to a walk-in centre or whether they might need to go to A&E. As described previously in this chapter, if someone chooses to share information that they have harmed themselves, the reaction of the person being told can be central to how the person might feel about getting support so it's important that we respond well.

Treating someone with compassion, respect and dignity and supporting them to make a decision about what should happen next should not require specialist training. NICE recommends a comprehensive psychosocial assessment takes place with the aim of identifying factors which may have contributed to the person hurting themselves. This can include information about their home or family circumstances and their current psychological state, whilst seeking to identify any immediate triggers for their actions or reasons why they may be feeling low. If this is something you feel unable to do yourself, consider the other support options available for both you and the young person. Could the young person see their GP or practice nurse for advice or could you or someone else do this on their behalf? Some schools or colleges have counsellors, nurses or designated members of staff available to offer advice and support an assessment. Additionally, in some areas voluntary sector organisations can offer one-to-one or group sessions aimed at providing practical and emotional support. The 2017 green paper (DoH & DforE, 2017) identifies that evidence-based treatment for mild to moderate mental health needs demonstrate outcomes comparable with specialist services when delivered by trained non-clinical staff with access to appropriate supervision. Addaction's 'Mind and Body' programme (Joiner et al, 2017) provides one such example.

If you are a professional working with children and young people, find out – before you need to know – who in your organisation is available to offer support and advice. (Clinical supervision can be hugely important in ensuring appropriate steps are taken for the young person in question, helping to protect both them and the practitioner(s) involved.)

In terms of more formal assessment and management of risks there are a range of scales and tools used across mental health services, urgent care and emergency departments which try to assess and determine risk. However, there is no single standardised clinical tool used in practice and where they are used, evidence indicates their accuracy is limited and they should not be used in isolation to determine what treatment and support is offered (Carter et al, 2018;

Quinlivan *et al*, 2017; Steeg *et al*, 2018.) Working collaboratively with the young person enables a mutually agreed risk management plan to be formulated; this could include employing practical measures to reduce the risks to which they're exposed. It is worth emphasising that reducing someone's access to the means they may choose to harm themselves is a key factor in keeping someone safe from further self-harm or suicide (Hawton *et al*, 2012). Consider whether aspects of their home or family circumstances need to be addressed. Might they benefit from involvement from specialist mental health services? Any plan aimed at reducing risks to the young person should be agreed with them, shared with them (plus other relevant individuals involved in their care) and should include what they can do if they are thinking about hurting themselves as well as who they can contact in a crisis. We know that the number of young people seeking medical attention after self-harm has increased (Stem4, 2018) and it is estimated that around 10% of those who harm themselves will do so again (Hawton *et al*, 2012).

Self-harm can be a strong predictor of subsequent suicide; of the estimated 6000 people who take their own lives in the UK each year, at least half have a history of self-harm (Hawton *et al*, 2012; NHS Digital, 2018) so it is important that those in contact with children and young people work together to provide appropriate support. In terms of the case study, you would need to ensure that Kelly is not depressed and has no plans of suicide.

When specialist support is required

It is well established that the key to any successful therapeutic intervention is the relationship between the person and their therapist – being able to relate to someone, to show empathy and warmth are important factors (Lambert & Barley, 2001.) Even those not specifically trained in mental health assessment, care and treatment can still play a pivotal role in supporting people who self-harm. Important factors to consider when deciding an appropriate route to support someone is to think about how often someone has harmed themselves, how serious it was, how distressed they are and whether they think they will do so again. For those working with and supporting children and young people who self-harm, trying to understand the factors that contribute to someone wanting to self-harm can be the key to knowing what services might be the most appropriate to offer support (Hawton *et al*, 2012). If children and young people are experiencing difficulties in their home or family circumstances or difficulties in school it can be helpful for them to have a positive relationship with someone they know and trust and can open up to and talk about things.

Any intervention or therapy should be tailored to the assessed and identified needs of the young person and should include consideration of what the person themselves wants to achieve and what they want to engage with. Psychological therapies or interventions won't be successful if the person isn't ready or in a position to engage with them. Some therapies available in more formal settings and services include family therapy, mentalisation-based therapy, cognitive behavioural therapy, psychodynamic therapy and problem-solving support (NICE). These therapies are not available everywhere and when they are, can have long waiting lists. They may also not be suitable for some individuals.

For some young people, self-harm might be linked to the way they have learned to deal with distress; for others it could be related to their neurodevelopment. For some people it might be linked to an underlying mental illness. For those children and young people requiring more specialist assessment and intervention a referral to Child and Adolescent Mental Health Services (CAMHS) might be required.

CAMHS teams are usually multidisciplinary teams made up of nurses, psychiatrists, social workers, occupational therapists, psychologists and support staff. They are usually NHS run services that work with children and young people who are experiencing difficulties with their emotional or behavioural wellbeing. They can carry out specialist assessments, make diagnoses and provide a range of therapies and treatments for children and young people. They will often see children and young people one-to-one but also involves families in some of the work they do.

Where a young person is experiencing a specific mental illness such as depression, anxiety or psychosis and has used self-harm as a way of coping with difficult thoughts and feelings associated with an illness, psychological therapies might be helpful. If someone is so unwell that talking about things is too difficult for them – for example, someone experiencing serious depression or episode of psychosis – it may be that talking therapy is not suitable until such time as the person is in a position to be able to engage with it. It could be that following an assessment by a psychiatrist, medication might be prescribed to treat the underlying illness and this in turn might alleviate or reduce distressing symptoms, enabling a young person to reduce or stop self-harming. Not all children and young people who self-harm will be prescribed medication and any decision to prescribe medication to children or young people should be made by a specialist clinician. There may also be some physical health checks required and once prescribed, the medication should be reviewed by the psychiatrist in conjunction with the young person (Royal College of Psychiatrists, 2019).

Conclusion

Many children and young people will experience an episode of self-harm so it is important that discussions about mental health are normalized; children and young people should have the opportunity to talk about their fears and worries and be able to ask for help if they need it. We might not be able to prevent all young people from hurting themselves but the more accessible we can make support at an early stage, the less likely help will be needed later on.

Anyone working with children and young people can help to build positive relationships; mutual respect and trust provides an excellent foundation from which important conversations can take place. Within this, there is a vital role to be played by professionals sitting outside of traditional clinical settings (Bradley, 2018). It is not helpful to simply tell or encourage children and young people to stop harming themselves. Young people need to feel listened to and to be involved in decisions about what care or support they can be offered. If those supporting young people have training and support to facilitate this, and can recognise and manage their own emotional response to self-harm, they will be in a better position to safely help.

Helpful links

Twitter can be a great way of keeping up-to-date with relevant research, news and resources. Here are some of our favourite accounts which are well worth a follow:

@PookyH	@Andy_Bell_	@CYPMentalHealth
@IanA_Mac	@mirandarwolpert	@EBPUnit
@SelfHarmNotts	@sjblakemore	@CORCcentral
@MentalElf	@sisupportorguk	@SchoolMHealth
@DrAPitman	@_MindandBody	@CharlieWtrust
@AlysColeKing	@AFNCCF	@selfharmUK

There are also plenty of websites for professionals, young people and families, including helpful information and guidance, plus films, tutorials and other resources. These include:

time-to-change.org.uk	mentalhealth.org.uk
youngminds.org.uk	pookyknightsmith.com
minded.org.uk	nspcc.org.uk
cwmt.org.uk	themix.org.uk
selfharm.co.uk	nhs.uk/conditions/self-harm/
papyrus-uk.org	kooth.com

References and further reading

Addaction (2018) *Youth in Crisis? A survey of wellbeing and self harm among 13 to 17 years olds.* [online]. Available at: https://www.addaction.org.uk/sites/default/files/public/attachments/addaction_youth_in_crisis_spreads_4.pdf (accessed 26 June 2019).

Bradley R (2018) *Young People's Mental Health is Changing. We need new thinking. Addaction Voices* [online]. London: Addaction. Available at: https://medium.com/addaction-voices/young-peoples-mental-health-is-changing-we-must-react-1aa8332f8659 (accessed 26 June 2019).

Carter T, Walker GM, Aubeeluck A and Manning JC (2018) Assessment tools of immediate risk of self-harm and suicide in children and young people: a scoping review. *Journal of Child Health Care* **23** (2).

Department of Health (2015) *Future in Mind*. London: The Stationery Office.

Department of Health and Department for Education (2017) *Transforming Children and Young People's Mental Health Provision: A green paper*. London: DH/DfE.

Hawton K, Geulayov G, Casey D, McDonald KC, Foster P, Pritchard K, Wells C, Clements C, Kapur N, Ness J and Waters K (2018) Incidence of suicide, hospital-presenting non-fatal self-harm, and community-occurring non-fatal self-harm in adolescents in England (the iceberg model of self-harm): a retrospective study. *Lancet: Psychiatry* **5** (2) 167–174.

Hawton K and James A (2005) Suicide and deliberate self-harm in young people. *British Medical Journal* **330** 891–894.

Hawton K, Saunders KEA and O'Connor RC (2012) Self-harm and suicide in adolescents. *Lancet* **379** 2373–2382.

Joiner R, Roberts V, Russell C, Nice T, Bowles M, Bowes A and Howe E (2017) *Mind and Body Programme Impact Report 2017*. London: Addaction.

Knightsmith P (2015) *Self-Harm and Eating Disorders in Schools: A guide to whole school strategies and practical support*. London: Jessica Kingsley Publishers.

Knightsmith P (2016) *The Healthy Coping Colouring Book and Journal*. London: Jessica Kingsley Publishers.

Knightsmith P (2018) *Can I Tell You About Self-Harm?* London: Jessica Kingsley Publishers.

Lambert MJ and Barley DE (2001) Research summary on therapeutic relationship and psychotherapy outcome. *Psychotherapy: Theory, Research, Practice, Training* **38** (4) 357-361.

Morgan C, Webb RT, Carr MJ, Kontopantelis E, Green J, Chew-Graham CA, Kapur N and Ashcroft DM (2017) Incidence, clinical management, and mortality risk following self-harm among children and adolescents: cohort study in primary care. *British Medical Journal* **359** j4351.

National Institute for Health and Care Excellence (2013, reviewed 2019) *Self-harm: Quality standard.* London: NICE. Available at: https://www.nice.org.uk/guidance/QS34 (accessed 26 June 2019).

NHS Digital (2018) *Mental Health of Children and Young People in England, 2017* [online]. London: NHS Digital. Available at: https://digital.nhs.uk/data-and-information/publications/statistical/mental-health-of-children-and-young-people-in-england/2017/2017 (accessed 26 June 2019).

Public Health England (2015) *Promoting Children and Young People's Emotional Health and Wellbeing.* London: PHE.

Quinlivan L, Cooper J, Meehan D, Longson D, Potokar J, Hulme T, Marsden J, Brand F, Lange K, Riseborough E, Page L, Metcalfe C, Davies L, O'Connor R, Hawton K, Gunnell D and Kapur N (2017) Predictive accuracy of risk scales following self-harm: Multicentre, prospective cohort study. *British Journal of Psychiatry* **210** (6) 429–436.

Royal College of Psychiatrists (2019) *Self-harm in Young People: For Parents and Carers* [online]. Available at: https://www.rcpsych.ac.uk/mental-health/parents-and-young-people/information-for-parents-and-carers/self-harm-in-young-people-for-parents-and-carers (accessed 26 June 2019).

Steeg S, Quinlivan L, Nowland R, Carroll R, Casey D, Clements C, Cooper J, Davies L, Knipe D, Ness J, O'Connor RC, Hawton K, Gunnell D and Kapur N (2018) Accuracy of risk scales for predicting repeat self-harm and suicide: a multicentre, population-level cohort study using routine clinical data. *BMC Psychiatry* **18** 113. Available at: https://doi.org/10.1186/s12888-018-1693-z (accessed 26 June 2019).

Stem4 (2018) *99% of GPs Fear that Young Patients Will Come to Harm While on the Waiting List for Mental Health Services* [online]. Available at: https://stem4.org.uk/wp-content/uploads/2018/12/FINAL-PRESS-RELEASE-Stem4-GP-survey-CYP-MH-18-12-18-PL.pdf (accessed 26 June 2019).

Chapter 19: Eating Disorders in Children and Young People

Rachel Elvins, Jane Whittaker and Ruth Marshall

Key learning points

- Eating disorders are complex, serious difficulties that often occur in adolescence.

- Many young people can have eating difficulties without meeting criteria for a 'disorder'. These can still cause considerable distress and impairment in functioning.

- Physical health consequences of eating disorders usually need treatment from professionals with expertise in the area.

- Research on the early recognition and psychological treatment of young people with eating disorders needs further investment, but family based and cognitive therapies can be successful.

Keywords

Anorexia nervosa; bulimia nervosa; ARFID

Introduction

In this chapter we will explore the types of eating disorders and how common they are, what can contribute to the development of an eating disorder and evidence-based approaches to treatment. Short case studies with questions, and key learning points will be highlighted. The aim is to give readers a basic understanding of how eating disorders can affect young people and how to recognise young people who may be at risk.

A short history and definitions of eating disorders

The first descriptions of anorexia nervosa in the Western world date from the 12th and 13th centuries, most famously Saint Catherine of Siena, who denied herself food as part of a spiritual denial of self (Bell, 1985). By the sixteenth century, ascetics were considered witches or heretics, and burned at the stake.

There are several clinical descriptions of 'wasting disease' in the 17th-19th century, including Richard Morton's *Treatise of Consumptions* in 1689, which described two case studies in older adolescents (one male, one female) and posited that anorexia nervosa could be caused by 'sadness and anxious cares'. Neither patient had initially sought help for their illness.

A Parisian physician, Marce, described the underlying psychological difficulties and behaviours in anorexia in 1862, including continuing refusal of food, despite evidence of the patient being underweight. Shortly after, Gull (1874) presented a complete medical description and coined the term 'anorexia nervosa' to distinguish the condition from the term 'hysteria', resulting in anorexia being considered a psychological condition.

In 1973, Hilde Bruch published a book with a number of case studies and proposed that self-starvation in anorexia nervosa represents a struggle for autonomy, competence, control and self-respect. As the condition reached public awareness in the 1970s, recognition of cases increased. The first clinical paper on bulimia nervosa was published in 1979 (Russell), where it was described as a variant of anorexia, but with other physically dangerous behaviours such as binge eating and purging. Sufferers were described as being more likely to have co-occurring depressive symptoms. Since then, various subtypes and variants of the two best described eating disorders have been defined in internationally recognised diagnostic handbooks such DSM-5 (APA, 2013).

Anorexia nervosa

Anorexia nervosa (AN) is characterised by restriction of dietary intake resulting in deliberate weight loss, a fear of weight gain and a distortion of body image (Garfinkel *et al*, 1996). There can be secondary endocrine and metabolic changes and disturbances of bodily function. In addition excessive exercise, induced vomiting and purging can be observed as well as the use of appetite suppressants and diuretics. It is serious psychiatric illness with amongst the highest mortality (death) rates of any mental health condition in adolescence and up to 18% in long term studies (Arcelus *et al*, 2011). In older adolescents, the mortality risk is higher than for other serious chronic diseases such as asthma or Type 1 diabetes (Hoang *et al*, 2014).

The incidence of AN is relatively stable (around 0.3%), with a lifetime prevalence of 2-4% in females (Smink *et al*, 2014). Peak age at diagnosis is 15-19 years with 24% having an age of onset between the ages of 10-14 years (Micali *et al*, 2013). It most frequently occurs in adolescent girls but can occur in males, with a ratio of about 9:1. It is frequently associated with other mental health difficulties including depression, anxiety, ocd, self-harm and suicidality.

Bulimia nervosa

Bulimia nervosa is characterised by recurrent episodes of over eating (bingeing), frequently followed by vomiting or purging (including the use of laxatives and diuretics). There is a preoccupation with body shape and weight (APA, 2013), although young people with bulimia can be underweight, normal weight or overweight. Repeated vomiting or purging can result in disturbances of kidney and heart function and other physical complications. Shame and secrecy often inhibit disclosure of symptoms and seeking treatment. There is often, but not always, a history of an earlier episode of anorexia nervosa and there can be overlap of symptoms between the two conditions. Prevalence estimates vary with between 0.1-2% of young females meeting strictly applied criteria (Merikangas *et al*, 2010). Some young people with bulimia also present with other impulsive behaviours such as substance misuse, and self-harm.

Binge eating disorder (BED)

BED is characterised by recurrent episodes of unusually large amounts of food intake without compensatory behaviours to get rid of the food that has been consumed, and it is associated with subjective experience of feeling of loss of control and marked distress. There is usually an association with eating more quickly, feeling uncomfortably full, eating when not hungry, distress and feelings of disgust and guilt afterwards (APA, 2013). To fulfil the diagnosis these episodes must occur at least once a week for three months. An increased prevalence of ED symptoms among youths aged 14-16 years has been evidenced, with two peaks of onset of BED, the first immediately after puberty, at a mean age of 14 years (Smink *et al*, 2014) and the second in late adolescence (19-24 years), between 18 and 20 years (Stice, 2013).

Other specified feeding or eating disorders (OFSED)

This category, new to DSM-5, replaces some others in earlier diagnostic manuals. OFSED is used for feeding and eating problems that cause distress and impairment but do not meet the diagnostic criteria for other defined conditions (APA, 2013)

Avoidant restrictive food intake disorder (ARFID)

ARFID is diagnosed when there is weight loss or persistent low weight when food is available (APA, 2013). Unlike anorexia or bulimia there is no presence of disturbed thinking regarding weight and body shape/size and no desire to lose weight, there is no underlying physical cause, but psychosocial functioning is impaired. Children and young people with ARFID tend to be younger than those with either AN or BN, are more likely to be male, often have a longer duration of illness and a greater likelihood of comorbid medical and/or psychiatric symptoms (Fisher *et al*, 2014).

Risk factors and maintaining factors in eating disorders

The causes of eating disorders are complex and there is evidence for multiple risk and maintenance factors. Integrative theories that combine biological, psychological and social risk factors have been proposed (Munro *et al*, 2016).

Eating disorders appear to be more common in industrialised societies where there is an abundance of food and obesity is also more common (Fairburn & Harrison, 2003) such as the United States, Canada, Europe, Australia, New Zealand, and South Africa. It's postulated therefore that being thin in these cultures, especially for women, is considered both physically attractive and also to indicate rarer and therefore desired personality attributes, for example the ability to exercise restraint in the face of temptation. Lack of food and/or economic depression is inversely correlated with anorexia nervosa onset (Palazzoli, 1985; Dell'Osso *et al*, 2016).

Rates of eating disorders are increasing in Asia, especially in Japan and China, where women are more rapidly exposed to Western influenced cultural change (Smink *et al*, 2012). African American women are more likely to develop bulimia and more likely to purge. Pressure to achieve particular body shapes in order to excel at certain activities may also be relevant, for example, female athletes involved in running, gymnastics, or ballet and male body builders or wrestlers are at increased risk of disordered eating (Miller & Pumariega, 2001).

Eating disorders are often found to 'run in families' – female relatives of those with anorexia have 11 times more chance of developing anorexia than the general population, and female relatives of bulimics have four times more chance of developing bulimia (Schimdt, 2005). There is considerable evidence that neurotransmitter mechanisms are disturbed in anorexia (dopamine, serotonin and noradrenaline) and brain imaging studies have shown changes in the prefrontal cortex of young people with anorexia (Munro *et al*, 2016). General risk factors for an eating disorder are aversive life events and childhood anxiety, particularly social anxiety. However, young people with anorexia are also more likely to have obsessive-compulsive personality traits, be perfectionistic and display high levels of exercise in childhood (Crane, 2007). Specific risk factors for bulimia are childhood obesity, dieting behaviour in adolescence and family factors such as parental drug and alcohol use and parental mental illness (Jacobi *et al,* 2004).

Treasure and Schimdt (2013) proposed a model of predisposing and perpetuating factors in anorexia - a genetic predisposition to obsessionality and anxiety, leading to difficulties in coping and an anxious cognitive style, which in combination with a stressor e.g. being bullied around weight, or a stressful event, results in rigid dieting behaviour. A vicious circle is set up where poor brain nutrition leads to an increase in preoccupation with dieting/shape/weight and an increase in rigid, ritualised behaviour around food, leading to poorer brain nutrition and so on. They also described a risk that parents and other family members may have a similar cognitive style or similar personality traits, which may impact on the young person's ability to recover.

There is evidence to support a stage model of illness in restricting eating disorders, with neurobiological progression and concomitant poorer outcome the longer the illness continues, particularly in eating disorders which result in prolonged low weight (Schmidt *et al*, 2016). Symptoms such as excessive exercise and food restriction appear to become self-perpetuating, or habitual, as the course of the disease continues, suggesting that changes in brain function progress with increasing illness duration (O'Hara *et al*, 2015).

Treatment for eating disorders

The key interventions for children and young people at low weight, or with physical complications caused by their eating disorder, are safe nutritional restoration allowing for body recovery, working with families and providing individual talking treatments.

The cornerstone of nutritional recovery is supporting the young person towards a healthy enough diet that supports graded, not rapid, weight gain and reduces medically risky behaviours like vomiting, purging and misuse of insulin if they are diabetic. Wherever and however nutritional recovery is started people supporting the young person need to be aware of re-feeding syndrome, meaning that the body is reacting to the sudden arrival of healthy of nutrition. This condition requires careful medical monitoring and sometimes supplemental salts to ensure body metabolism remains stable. Equally important is underfeeding syndrome, meaning that by lack of knowledge or by the young person bargaining, adults provide an inadequate diet that means that weight loss and all its consequences persist. The key intervention is a balanced diet ideally prescribed by a professional who has expertise. A key component of family work is helping carers or parents to be confident in managing this meal plan (Junior Marsipan Group, 2012).

Research on different treatment approaches suggests that specialist eating disorder outpatient care (rather than a generic mental health team), supported by brief (medical) inpatient management for correction of acute physical complications is the preferred approach for children and adolescents with anorexia nervosa (Gowers et al, 2010). This is reflected in existing guidelines, which suggest that outpatient treatments should be offered to the majority, with inpatient treatment offered in rare cases (NICE, 2016). Further research is needed to establish which patients (if any) might respond to inpatient psychiatric treatment when unresponsive to outpatient care, the positive and negative components of inpatient settings, and the optimum length of stay. Family-based therapy has superior outcomes compared to individual psychological treatments in adolescent anorexia nervosa (Zipfel et al, 2016) and is the recommended treatment in the UK alongside careful nutritional support and physical health monitoring (NICE, 2016). However, family work appears more successful for patients with a short duration of illness (Couturier et al, 2013). Evidence for the efficacy of pharmacological (medication) treatments is weak in AN, with low acceptability and tolerability (Brockmeyer et al, 2017) although medical treatments may be helpful in individuals with co-occurring depression and anxiety. Treatment often succeeds in restoring weight but individuals are at an exceedingly high risk for early relapse (up to 50%) (Khalsa et al, 2017) and approximately 20% of patients develop a severe, enduring form of illness (Steinhausen, 2002).

A high dose of the antidepressant fluoxetine (60 mg/day) reduces core bulimic symptoms of binge eating and purging and associated psychological features of the eating disorder in the short term in adults. Few studies have been done with adolescents, but there is some emerging evidence for this treatment approach (Hail & Le Grange, 2018). An early study by Schmidt et al (2007) suggested that a stepped approach beginning with guided self-care may be sufficient for some, whereas other adolescents will ultimately require a more intensive level of treatment. Recent trials of family-based therapy for bulimia nervosa (FBT-BN) indicate that it is more effective in promoting abstinence from binge eating and purging than individual CBT in adolescents in the short term (Le Grange *et al*, 2015) although psychotherapy or CBT in an extended format may also be helpful (Stefini *et al*, 2017).

To date, little research has examined the effectiveness of either psychological or medical treatments for patients diagnosed with avoidant/restrictive food intake disorder (ARFID), and there is little evidence to guide clinicians treating children and adolescents with this condition. Young people are often treated pragmatically using a combination of medical monitoring, family therapy, medication, and cognitive behavioural therapy (Spettigue *et al*, 2018).

Laura

Laura is a 14-year-old who became vegetarian one year ago after being taught in school about healthy eating. She was slightly overweight at that time and became very worried about her weight and shape, particularly the size of her thighs. Subsequently she has cut other food groups from her diet and now eats very little. She has lost weight and her BMI is now under 16. She is academically bright, pushes herself to achieve the best grades and belongs to a dancing school where she attends five sessions each week as well as playing for various school sports teams. Laura hides how little she is eating from her family, for example telling them that she has had tea with a friend.

What risk factors are present in Laura's case that predisposes her to anorexia nervosa?

What treatment might help?

Chantelle

Chantelle is a 17-year-old girl with a BMI in the normal range. She doesn't eat regular meals as she would like to be thinner. She often however finds herself eating at night when her family are in bed, as she can't control her cravings for crisps and chocolate after a day of not eating very much. Her mum has found food packets hidden under her bed and thinks she has heard Chantelle being sick in the toilet at night and doing squats in her room once or twice, but Chantelle denies this.

What diagnosis do you think applies to Chantelle?

References and further reading

American Psychiatric Association (2013) *Diagnostic and Statistical Manual of Mental Disorders* (5th ed). Washington, DC: APA.

Arcelus J, Mitchell AJ, Wales J and Nielsen S (2011) Mortality rates in patients with anorexia nervosa and other eating disorders. A meta-analysis of 36 studies. *Archives of General Psychiatry* **68** (7) 724–31.

Bell RM (1985) *Holy Anorexia*. Chicago: University of Chicago Press.

Bell RM and Weinstein D (1982) *Saints and Society: The Two Worlds of Western Christendom, 1000–1700*. Chicago: University of Chicago Press.

Brockmeyer T, Freiderich HC and Schmidt U (2017) Advances in the treatment of anorexia nervosa: a review of established and emerging interventions. *Psychological Medicine* **48** 1–37.

Bruch H (1973) *Eating Disorders: Obesity, Anorexia Nervosa, and the Person Within*. New York: Basic Books.

Couturier J, Kimber M and Szatmari P (2013) Efficacy of family based treatment for adolescents with eating disorders: a systematic review and meta analysis. *International Journal of Eating Disorders* **46** 3–11.

Crane AM, Roberts ME, Treasure J (2007) Are obsessive-compulsive personality traits associated with a poor outcome in anorexia nervosa? A systematic review of randomized controlled trials and naturalistic outcome studies. *International Journal of Eating Disorders* **40** (7) 581-588.

Dell'Osso L, Abelli M, Carpita B, Pini S, Castellini G, Carmassi C and Ricca V (2016) Historical evolution of the concept of anorexia nervosa and relationships with orthorexia nervosa, autism, and obsessive–compulsive spectrum. *Neuropsychiatric Disease and Treatment* **12** 1651–60.

Druce M and Bloom S (2006) The regulation of appetite. *Archive of the Disabled Child* **91** 183–187.

Fairburn CG and Harrison PJ (2003) Eating disorders. *Lancet* **361** 407–416.

Fisher M, Rosen D, Ornstein R, Mammel K, Katzman D, Rome E, Callahan T, Malizio J, Kearney S and Walsh T (2014) Characteristics of avoidant/restrictive food intake disorder in children and adolescents: a "new disorder" in DSM-5. *Journal of Adolescent Health* **55** (1) 49–52.

Garfinkel P, Lin E, Goering P and Spegg C (1996) Should amenorrhoea be necessary for the diagnosis of anorexia nervosa?: evidence from a Canadian community sample **168** (4) 500–6.

Gowers SG, Clark AF, Roberts C, Byford S, Barrett B, Griffiths A, Edwards V, Bryan C, Smethurst N, Rowlands L and Roots P (2010) A randomised controlled multicentre trial of treatments for adolescent anorexia nervosa including assessment of cost-effectiveness and patient acceptability - the TOuCAN trial. *Health Technology Assessments* **14** (15) 1–98.

Gull WW (1874) Anorexia nervosa. *Trans Clin Soc Lond* **7** 22–28.

Hail L and Le Grange D (2018) Bulimia nervosa in adolescents: prevalence and treatment challenges. *Adolescent Health, Medicine and Therapeutics* **9** 11–16.

Hans W Hoek (2016) Review of the worldwide epidemiology of eating disorders. *Current Opinion* **29** (6).

Hoang U, Goldacre, M and James A (2014)Mortality following hospital discharge with a diagnosis of eating disorder: national record linkage study, England, 2001-09. *The International Journal of Eating Disorders* **47** 507-15.

Jacobi, C, Hayward, C, De Zwaan M, Kraemer, HC and Agras W (2004) Coming to terms with risk factors for eating disorders: application of risk terminology and suggestions for a general taxonomy. *Psychological Bulletin* **130** 19-65.

Junior Marsipan Group (2012) *Junior MARSIPAN: Management of Really Sick Patients under 18 with Anorexia Nervosa*. London: Royal College of Psychiatrists.

Khalsa S, Portnoff L, McCurdy-McKinnon D and Feusner J (2017) What happens after treatment? A systematic review of relapse, remission, and recovery in anorexia nervosa. *Journal of Eating Disorders* **5** (20).

Le Grange D, Lock J, Agras W, Bryson S and Booil J (2015) Randomized clinical trial of family-based treatment and cognitive-behavioral therapy for adolescent bulimia nervosa. *Journal of the American Academy of Child and Adolescent Psychiatry* **54** (11) 886–894.

Merikangas KR, He JP, Brody D, Fisher PW, Bourdon K and Koretz DS (2010) Prevalence and treatment of mental disorders among US children in the 2001–2004 NHANES. *Pediatrics* **125** (1) 75–81.

Micali, N Hagberg KW, Petersen, I Treasure, JL (2013) The incidence of eating disorders in the UK 2000-2009: findings from the General Practice Research Database *BMJ Open* **3**.

Miller MN and Pumariega AJ (2001) Culture and eating disorders: a historical and cross-cultural review. *Psychiatry* **64** (2) 93–110.

Morton R (1694) *Phthisiologia – or a Treatise on Consumptions*. London: Smith & Walford at the Prince's Arms in St Paul's Churchyard.

Munro C, Randell L and Lawrie SM (2016) An integrative bio-psycho-social theory of anorexia nervosa. *Clinical Psychology and Psychotherapy* **24** (1) 1–21.

NICE (2017) *Eating Disorders: recognition and treatment* [online]. Available at: https://www.nice.org.uk/guidance/ng69 (accessed 29 October 2019).

O'Hara CB, Schmidt U and Campbell IC (2015) A reward centred model of anorexia nervosa: a focussed narrative review of neurological and psychophysiological literature. *Neuroscience and Biobehaviour Review* **52** 131–52.

Palazzoli MS (1985) Anorexia nervosa: a syndrome of the affluent society. *J Strat Syst Ther* **22** 199–205.

Russell G (1979) Bulimia nervosa: an ominous variant of anorexia nervosa. *Psychological Medicine* **9** (3) 429–48.

Schmidt U (2005) Epidemiology and aetiology of eating disorders. *Psychiatry* **4** 5–9.

Schmidt U, Brown A, McClelland J, Glennon D and Mountford VA (2016) Will a comprehensive, person centred, team based early intervention approach to first episode illness improve outcomes in eating disorders? *International Journal of Eating Disorders* **49** 374-377.

Schmidt U, Lee S, Beecham J, Perkins S, Treasure J, Yi I, Winn S, Robinson P, Murphy R, Keville S, Johnson-Sabine E, Jenkins M, Frost S, Dodge L, Berelowitz M and Eisler I. (2007) A randomized controlled trial of family therapy and cognitive behavior therapy guided self-care for adolescents with bulimia nervosa and related disorders. *American Journal of Psychiatry* **164** (4) 591–598.

Schwartz MW, Woods SC, Porte D Jr, Seeley RJ and Baskin DG (2000) Central nervous system control of food intake. *Nature* **404** 661–71.

Shapiro J, Berkman N, Brownley K, Sedway J, Lohr K and Bulik C (2007) Bulimia nervosa treatment: a systematic review of randomized controlled trials. *International Journal of Eating Disorders* **40** 321–336.

Smink F, van Hoeken D and Hoek (2012) Epidemiology of eating disorders: incidence, prevalence and mortality rates. *Current Psychiatry Reports* **14** (4) 406–414.

Smink FR, van Hoeken D, Oldehinkel AJ and Hoek HW (2014) Prevalence and severity of DSM-5 eating disorders in a community cohort of adolescents. *International Journal of Eating Disorders* **47** (6) 610–619.

Spettigue W, Norris M, Santos A and Obeid N (2018) Treatment of children and adolescents with avoidant/restrictive food intake disorder: a case series examining the feasibility of family therapy and adjunctive treatments. *Journal of Eating Disorders* **6** (20).

Steinhausen HC (2002) The outcome of anorexia nervosa in the 20th century. *American Journal of Psychiatry* **159** 1284–93.

Stefini A, Salzer S, Reich G, Hildegard H, Winkelmann K, Bents H, Rutz U, Frost U, von Boetticher A, Ruhl U, Specht N and Kronmüller K-T (2017) Cognitive-behavioral and psychodynamic therapy in female adolescents with bulimia nervosa: a randomized controlled trial. *Journal of American Academic Child Adolescent Psychiatry* **56** (4) 329–335.

Stice E, Marti CN and Rohde P (2013) Prevalence, incidence, impairment, and course of the proposed DSM-5 eating disorder diagnoses in an 8-year prospective community study of young women. *Journanl of Abnormal Psychology* **122** (2) 445–457.

Treasure J and Schmidt U (2013) The cognitive-interpersonal maintenance model of anorexia nervosa revisited: a summary of the evidence for cognitive, socio-emotional and interpersonal predisposing and perpetuating factors. *Journal of Eating Disorders* **1** (13).

Zipfel S, Giel KE, Bulik CM, Hay P and Schmidt U (2016) Anorexia nervosa: aetiology, assessment and treatment. *Lancet Psychiatry* **2** 1099–1111.

Chapter 20: Drugs and Mental Health

Louise Theodosiou and Sangeeta Ambegaokar

Key learning points
- Many young people experiment with substances, most commonly tobacco, alcohol and cannabis.

- Some adolescents may be more vulnerable to developing problematic relationships with substances.

- When offering support to young people who are struggling with substance use, it is important to undertake a full assessment of wellbeing and developmental needs, family circumstances, educational pressures and social circumstances.

Keywords
Substance misuse; mental health needs; social factors

Introduction

Substance use is common among adolescents and rates are higher among young people who are 'looked after children', have additional wellbeing and developmental health needs and are in contact with the criminal justice system. This chapter will describe the different substances that young people may be using and discuss strategies for assessing and treating substance use in children and young people. Vulnerability factors which can increase drug use will be explored. The chapter will also address models of treatment and outcomes.

What does drug use mean?

Any substance which causes a physiological effect when it is introduced into the body is a drug; this chapter addresses drugs which can change a young person's state of mind or emotions. Many drugs are taken every day and they can range from caffeine in coffee through to drugs such as cannabis. There are different types of drugs, for example:

- common legal drugs e.g. cigarettes and alcohol

- common illegal drugs e.g. cannabis

- new substances which are developed all the time, often called 'novel psychoactive substances' or 'legal highs'

- sometimes, children may take prescribed drugs e.g. drugs for anxiety that are not prescribed to them.

The National Institute on Drug Abuse (2018) has a list of common drugs of abuse.

Drugs and the law

Some drugs can be legally used by adults, such as alcohol or nicotine, but are not legally available to children. Ages at which these drugs may become legal can vary from country to country. Other drugs are almost universally illegal e.g. heroin or cocaine. There are three main statutes regulating the use and availability of drugs in the UK – the Medicines Act (1968), the Misuse Of Drugs Act (1971) and the Psychoactive Substance Act (2016). The Medicines Act governs the manufacture and supply of medicine, for example, dividing them into ones that can be bought and those which need to be prescribed. The Misuse Of Drugs Act controls both medicinal drugs and those which have no current medicinal use and includes drugs such as heroin, cocaine and cannabis. These drugs are termed 'controlled drugs' and are divided into three classes – A, B and C – with Class A drugs treated by the law as the most dangerous. Offences under the act include possession, supply and production of drugs. The UK Psychoactive Substances Bill (2016) was brought in to address innovations in drug manufacture and bans production and trading but not solely possession of all current and future novel psychoactive substances.

Drugs and safety

Drugs which are legalised and bought from licensed retailers are manufactured to set standards, however some can still damage health simply by their use, such as cigarettes. Other drugs are manufactured to be safe to consume within recommended limits, e.g. alcohol, but can damage health if they are used to excess. Drugs such as cocaine which are bought through illegal routes can themselves be damaging to the body e.g. by raising blood pressure, but may also contain other unregulated substances which can damage health.

In addition to the direct damaging effect drugs may have on the body, they can also alter a person's mental state. In the short term this can alter a person's ability to make decisions which may lead to increased accidents, injuries and illness. Some drugs can make a person feel good in the short term, but then bad the next day. Over time such drugs can lead to effects on mental health such as low mood or feelings of paranoia. Some people may find a drug makes them feel bad from the moment that it starts affecting them.

Rates of drug and alcohol use

The association between youth and substance use is iconically illustrated in every medium of communication and echoed in the literature. Equally present is the dynamic nature of this problem; illegal drugs are by their very nature hidden and changing while alcohol and nicotine are proffered in a profusion of innovatively marketed methods. The United Nations Office on Drugs and Crime notes that the range of drug markets is expanding as never before.

NHS Digital notes that a survey of UK pupils in 2016 identified that:

- 24% had ever taken drugs, while
- 18% had taken drugs in the past year, and
- 10% in the last month
- the prevalence of drug use increased with age; at 15 years old 37% of pupils had taken drugs while at 11 years 11% had tried drugs at least once
- the most common drug was cannabis with 8% having used in the last year
- 4% had used volatile substances (glue, gas, aerosols or solvents) in the last year
- 3% had used a Class A drug (heroin, cocaine (including crack), methadone, ecstasy, LSD, and magic mushrooms).

This was the first survey to measure novel psychoactive substance use, with 4% having used nitrous oxide in the last year and 2% other substances.

The European School Survey Project on Alcohol and other Drugs (2015) gathered information from 35 European countries and identified that:

- 23% of students had smoked
- 47% had tried alcohol
- 3% had tried cannabis before the age of 13.

The National Institute on Drug Abuse (2017) notes that tobacco use has fallen in the United States, while alcohol use has dropped, at least 62% of high school students had tried alcohol before the end of school. Vaping was the commonest way of consuming tobacco, but was also noted to be a way of inhaling cannabis.

Definitions of addiction

The International Classification of Diseases Version 10 was produced by the World Health Organization (1992). The category of 'Mental and behavioural disorders due to psychoactive substance use' describes the different relationships with substances from 'acute intoxication' through to dependence and withdrawal. Dependence is defined as:

a. *'a strong desire or sense of compulsion to take the substance;*

b. *difficulties in controlling substance-taking behaviour;*

c. *a physical 'withdrawal state when substance use has ceased or been reduced';*

d. *evidence of tolerance;*

e. *progressive neglect of alternative pleasures or interests;*

f. *persisting with substance use despite clear evidence of overtly harmful consequences'.*

The *International Classification of Diseases Version 11* is available in beta form and once again maintains a central focus on 'dependence' (Saunders, 2017). The Psychiatric American Association (2013) have produced the 5th edition of the *Diagnostic and Statistical Manual of Mental Disorders*. The criteria differ in terms of concepts in relation to abuse and dependence. The number of young people in the UK reporting primary use of a drug associated with dependence e.g. heroin is very small at less than 1%.

Children and young people who may be more vulnerable to using substances Green *et al* (2004) found that 11-16 year olds with emotional and conduct disorders were more likely than their peers to drink, smoke and take drugs. Frisher *et al* (2007) identified that higher adolescent drug use was associated with lower self-esteem and reduced parental supervision and higher rates of drug use by peers. The Center for Behavioural Health Statistics and Quality (2013) noted that substance use which started before adulthood was far more likely to lead to later drug dependence. National Institute for Health and Care Excellence (NICE, 2018) identified that children with ADHD had higher rates of substance use in later adolescence. NICE (2005) notes that there is no clear systematic research identifying the relationship between substance misuse and depression in young people. There is, however, evidence to suggest that teenage boys who are smoking have a higher risk of both substance misuse and psychopathology which includes depression (Boys *et al*, 2003; Meltzer *et al*, 2003).

Children who are looked after by social care rather than living with their parents, those with mental health problems and not in education, employment and training (NEETs) have higher rates of substance use (NICE, 2017). Finally, a study from Africa (Paikoff, 1997) reported that parental support can reduce adolescent risk-taking as well as levels of alcohol and substance use and mental health needs.

Treatment

Universal prevention in the form of drug education should be offered to all young people (Royal College of Psychiatrists, 2012). The valuable role of schools in supporting the wellbeing and health needs of pupils is increasingly recognised, and education should be supported to deliver information to children. More research is needed to identify who would benefit best from more targeted interventions or multi-agency interventions (Royal College of Psychiatrists, 2012). Professionals should ensure that children and their families are at the centre of the decisions about their treatment. It is also important to ensure that treatment for any other health needs, for example, ADHD, depression and anxiety is addressed.

There is also evidence for family work in the form of multi-dimensional family therapy (MDFT). This is a family-based outpatient treatment for adolescents with behaviour difficulties who are using drugs. In MDFT, young people receive therapy sessions with their family and wider social systems using a systemic model. MDFT has been found to be effective in the US (Liddle *et al*, 2008) and Europe (Phan *et al*, 2011).

Multi-systemic therapy (MST) involves a multi-modal intervention targeted at the young people and their families, schools and peers. Evaluation studies of MST in different countries have been promising (Hengeller *et al*, 2009; Ogden *et al*, 2007) and it has proved effective for adolescents who have substance misuse disorders (Hengeller *et al*, 2009). Criticisms of MST include the high level of therapeutic expertise required and the cost of implementation. While MST is unsuitable as a universal intervention for all offenders, it may be cost-effective for those who are at risk of more serious long-term antisocial behaviour (NICE, 2009).

How we can support young people who are using substances?

Substance use can be an emotive topic for people, in terms of the impact of intoxication, addiction and the complex intersection of drugs and the legal system. A comprehensive assessment should be undertaken to explore the reasons why children and young people are using drugs. This will need to identify all of the possible precipitants and vulnerability factors.

A formulation can be developed with the young person that involves parents, carers and professionals who can support the young person to access the help that they need.

- Help the young person address wellbeing needs such as low mood and anxiety.

- Unpick underlying developmental difficulties such as learning needs, attention and social communication problems. It is important that these are carefully assessed and that current difficulties are not automatically attributed to drug use.

- Explore environmental factors such as home pressures, academic problems and peer dynamics.

- Once a formulation has been developed, the team around the young person can work with the young person to start to address their needs. Other chapters in this book explain how to work with conditions such as depression and ADHD. It is important to ensure that all of the young person's needs are explored.

Long-term outcome

While many young people may experiment with drugs with no discernible impact on their adult lives, some types of adolescent drug use may become associated with poorer adult outcomes. Public Health England (2017) noted that 92% of children who later entered specialist drug treatment reported starting to use drugs before age 15, while 60% reported polydrug use. In Australia, Kelly *et al* (2015) found that polydrug use is associated with non-completion of schooling. Kokkevi *et al* (2014) analysed data from the European School Survey Project on Alcohol and Other Drugs and noted that poly-drug use by children was associated with risky sexual behaviour and trouble with the police. Boys' use was also associated with increased rates of aggressive behaviour and girls' use increased interpersonal difficulties. Finally, Lee *et al* (2011) examined trajectories into adulthood and noted that use of cannabis reduced as people entered their 20s while rates of alcohol use and abuse rose.

Jenna

Jenna is a 16-year-old girl who lives with her mother. She is not in contact with her father. Jenna has long standing difficulties with anxiety, has recently started college and is struggling with the changed social environment. Jenna has been spending time with a girl who smokes cannabis, and started smoking before lessons. Jenna was noted to be intoxicated at the start of the college day. This was raised with Jenna and she became tearful and acknowledged that her anxiety was getting worse. Jenna is keen to maintain her college placement but she identifies that she is struggling.

Which aspects of Jenna's health needs would you treat first?

Joe

Joe is a 15-year-old boy. He was with his mother when she died of a heart attack a year before. Joe had behavioural difficulties before his mother's death and their relationship was challenging. Joe is using cannabis and Xanax on a daily basis and this is impacting on his physical health. He struggles to talk to mental health staff, but is keen to undertake grief related work.

References and further reading

Andersson B, Hibell B, Beck F, Choquet M, Kokkevi A, Fotiou A, Molinaro S, Nociar A, Sieroslawski J and Trapencieris M (2007) *Alcohol and Drug Use Among European 17–18-year-old Students Data from the ESPAD Project* [online]. Available at: http://www.espad.org/sites/espad.org/files/17_18_Year_Old_Students_Full_Report.pdf (accessed 6 July 2019).

American Psychiatric Association (2013) *Diagnostic and Statistical Manual of Mental Disorders* (5th edition). Washington, DC: APA.

Boys A, Farrell M, Taylor C and Marsden J (2003) Psychiatric morbidity and substance use in young people aged 13–15 years: results from the Child and Adolescent Survey of Mental Health. *British Journal of Psychiatry* **182** 509–517.

Center for Behavioural Health Statistics and Quality (2013) *Results from the 2012 National Survey on Drug Use and Health: Summary of national findings (HHS Publication No. SMA 13-4795, NSDUH Series H-46)* [online]. Rockville, MD: Substance Abuse and Mental Health Services Administration. Available at: https://www.samhsa.gov/data/sites/default/files/NSDUHresults2012/NSDUHresults2012.pdf (accessed 7 July 2019).

European Monitoring Centre for Drugs and Drug Addiction (2009) *Polydrug Use: Patterns and Responses* [online]. Available at: http://www.emcdda.europa.eu/attachements.cfm/att_93217_EN_EMCDDA_SI09_polydrug%20use.pdf (accessed 7 July 2019).

European School Survey Project on Alcohol and other Drugs (2015) *ESPAD Report 2015: Results from the European school survey project on alcohol and other drugs* [online]. The ESPAD Group. Available at: http://www.espad.org/sites/espad.org/files/ESPAD_report_2015.pdf (accessed 7 July 2019).

Frisher M, Crome I, Macleod J, Bloor R and Hickman M (2007) Home Office Online Report 05/07 *Predictive Factors for Illicit Drug Use Among Young People: A literature review* [online]. Available at: http://dera.ioe.ac.uk/6903/1/rdsolr0507.pdf (accessed 7 July 2019).

Green H, McGinnity A, Meltzer H, Ford T and Goodman R (2004) *Mental health of children and young people in Great Britain* [online]. Available at: http://content.digital.nhs.uk/catalogue/PUB06116/ment-heal-chil-youn-peop-gb-2004-rep2. pdf (accessed 7 July 2019).

Hengeller S, Scoenwald S, Borduin C, Rowland M and Cunningham P (2009) *Multi-systemic Therapy for Antisocial Behaviour in Children and Adolescents* (2nd Edition). New York: Guildford Press.

Kelly A, Evans-Whipp T, Smith R, Chan G, Toumbourou J, Patton G, Hemphill S, Hall W and Catalano R (2015) A longitudinal study of the association of adolescent polydrug use, alcohol use and high school non-completion. *Addiction* **110** (4) 627–35.

Kokkevi A, Kanavou E, Richardson C, Fotiou A, Papadopoulou S, Monshouwer K, Matias J and Olszewski D (2014) Polydrug use by European adolescents in the context of other problem behaviours. *Nordic Studies on Alcohol and Drugs* **31** (4) 323–342.

Lee CY, Winters KC and Wall MM (2010) Trajectories of substance use disorders in youth: identifying and predicting group memberships. *Journal of Child and Adolescent Substance Abuse* **19** (2) 135–157.

Liddle H, Dakota G, Turner R, Henderson C and Greenbaum P (2008) Treating adolescent drug abuse: a randomised trial comparing multi-dimensional family therapy and cognitive behavioural therapy. *Addiction* **103** 1660–1670.

McCabe S, West B, Teter C, Cranford J, Ross-Durow P and Boyd C (2012) Adolescent nonmedical users of prescription opioids: brief screening and substance use disorders. *Addictive Behaviors* **37** (5) 651–656. Available at: http://doi.org/10.1016/j.addbeh.2012.01.021 (accessed 7 July 2019).

Meltzer H, Gatward R, Goodman R *et al* (2003) Mental health of children and adolescents in Great Britain. *International Review of Psychiatry* **15** 185–187.

Molina B, Howard A, Swanson J, Stehli A, Mitchell J, Kennedy T, Epstein J, Arnold L, Hechtman L, Vitiello B and Hoza B (2018) Substance use through adolescence into early adulthood after childhood-diagnosed ADHD: findings from the MTA longitudinal study. *Journal of Child Psychology and Psychiatry* **59** (6) 692–702.

National Institute for Health and Care Excellence (2005) *Depression in Children and Young People Identification and Management in Primary, Community and Secondary Care. (National Clinical Practice Guideline Number 28)* [online]. Available at: https://www.nice.org.uk/guidance/cg28/evidence/full-guideline-pdf-193488883 updated to https://www.nice.org.uk/guidance/ng134 (accessed 7 July 2019).

National Institute for Health and Care Excellence (2014) *Interventions to Reduce Substance Misuse Among Vulnerable Young People* Evidence Update April 2014. London: NIHCE.

National Institute for Health and Care Excellence (2017) *Drug Misuse Prevention: Targeted Interventions* [online]. Available at: https://www.nice.org.uk/guidance/ng64/resources/drug-misuse-prevention-targeted-interventions-pdf-1837573761733 (accessed 7 July 2019).

National Institute for Health and Care Excellence (2018) *Attention Deficit Hyperactivity Disorder: Diagnosis and Management of ADHD in Children, Young People and Adults (National Clinical Practice Guideline Number 72)* [online]. Available at: https://www.nice.org.uk/guidance/ng87/evidence/full-guideline-pdf-4783651311 (accessed 7 July 2019).

National Institute on Drug Abuse (2017) *Monitoring the Future* [online]. Available at: https://www.drugabuse.gov/related-topics/trends-statistics/monitoring-future (accessed 7 July 2019).

National Institute on Drug Abuse (2018) *Commonly Abused Drugs Charts* [online]. Available at: https://www.drugabuse.gov/drugs-abuse/commonly-abused-drugs-charts (accessed 7 July 2019).

NHS Digital (2017) *Statistics on Drugs Misuse England, 2017* [online]. Available at: http://webarchive.nationalarchives.gov.uk/20180328135520/http://digital.nhs.uk/catalogue/PUB23442 (accessed 7 July 2019). London: NHS Digital.

NHS England (2015) *Future in Mind* [online]. Available at: https://www.gov.uk/government/uploads/system/uploads/attachment_data/file/414024/Childrens_Mental_Health.pdf (accessed 7 July 2019). London: NHSCB.

NHS England (2015) *Commissioning for Quality and Innovation (CQUIN) Guidance for 2017–2019* [online]. Publications Gateway Reference. Available at: https://www.england.nhs.uk/wp-content/uploads/2016/03/cquin-guidance-16-17-v3.pdf (accessed 7 July 2019).

Ogden T, Hagen K and Anderson O (2007) Sustainability of the effectiveness of a programme of multisystemic treatment (MST) across participant groups in the second year of operation. *Journal of Children's Services* **2** 4–14.

Paikoff R (1997) Applying developmental psychology to an AIDS prevention model for urban African American youth. *Journal of Negro Education* **65** 44–59.

Phan O, Henderson C, Angelidis T, Weil P, Van Toorn M, Rigton R, Soria C and Rigter H (2011) European youth centre sites serve different populations of adults with cannabis use disorder. Baseline and referral data from the INCANT trial. *BMC Psychiatry* **11** (110).

Public Health England (2017) *Young People's Statistics from the National Drug Treatment Monitoring System (NDTMS) 1 April 2015 to 31 March 2016* [online]. Available at: http://www.nta.nhs.uk/uploads/young-peoples-statistics-from-the-ndtms-1-april-2015-to-31-march-2016.pdf (accessed 7 July 2019).

Royal College of Psychiatrists (2012) *Practice Standards for Young People with Substance Misuse Problems* [online]. Available at: https://assets.publishing.service.gov.uk/government/uploads/system/uploads/attachment_data/file/664945/Young-people-statistics-report-from-the-national-drug-treatment-monitoring-system-2016-2017.pdf (accessed 7 July 2019).

Saunders JB (2017) Substance use and addictive disorders in DSM-5 and ICD 10 and the draft ICD 11. *Current Opinion Psychiatry* **30** (4) 227–237.

Helpful resources

- DrugWise: Promoting evidence-based information on drugs alcohol and tobacco https://www.drugwise.org.uk/factsheets-and-infographics/ (accessed 7 July 2019).

- Frank: https://www.talktofrank.com/support-near-you (accessed 7 July 2019).

- The Royal College of Psychiatrists Mental Health and Growing Up factsheet: https://www.rcpsych.ac.uk/mental-health/parents-and-young-people

- Royal College of Psychiatrists: Drugs and Alcohol: Information for young people factsheet: https://www.rcpsych.ac.uk/healthinformation/parentsandyoungpeople/youngpeople/drugsandalcohol.aspx (accessed 7 July 2019).

Websites

The European School Survey Project on Alcohol and other Drugs (2015) http://www.espad.org/ (accessed 7 July 2019)

United Nations Office on Drugs and Crime (2018) *Drugs and Age: Drugs and associated issues among young people and older people* [online]. Available at: https://www.unodc.org/wdr2018/prelaunch/WDR18_Booklet_4_YOUTH.pdf (accessed 7 July 2019).

World Health Organization (1992) *The ICD-10 Classification of Mental and Behavioural Disorders: Clinical descriptions and diagnostic guidelines*. Geneva: World Health Organization.

World Health Organization (2018) *ICD-11 for Mortality and Morbidity Statistics* [online]. Available at: https://icd.who.int/browse11/l-m/en (accessed 7 July 2019).

World Health Organization (2017) *Management of Substance Abuse* [online]. Available at: http://www.who.int/substance_abuse/facts/cannabis/en/ (accessed 7 July 2019).

Public Health England (2018) *Young People's Statistics from the National Drug Treatment Monitoring System (1 April 2017 to 31 March 2018 Public Health England)* [online]. Available at: https://assets.publishing.service.gov.uk/government/uploads/system/uploads/attachment_data/file/762446/YPStatisticsFromNDTMS2017to2018.pdf (accessed 7 July 2019).

Chapter 21: Impact of Social Media and Digital Technology on Children and Young People

Louise Theodosiou and Sarah Stansfeld (with thanks to Andy Bell, Henrietta Bowden-Jones and Fin Webb)

Key learning points

- Digital technology has changed significantly in the past decade. Many families now have access to portable devices that can be used to connect with others by text, verbally or video link, watch television, surf the net and play games.

- Digital technology provides wonderful opportunities for children and young people to interact with others, learn and play.

- Children and young people need to be supported to develop healthy relationships with technology, balancing the use of devices with other activities, such as face-to-face contact, exercise, school work and sleep in order to be able to maintain good mental health and wellbeing.

- Some children and young people may be more vulnerable to being negatively affected by technology.

Keywords

Digital technology; vulnerable children and young people; opportunities for learning and play

Introduction

It is acknowledged that the environment that we live in impacts on our health and wellbeing. The rapid advance in technological development has brought changes to the way we spend our time and interact with others and it is not yet clear how this will impact on young people's mental health and wellbeing.

Is this a new phenomenon?

One of the challenges of parenting and working with children is balancing boundary setting with the provision of opportunities for growth and development. What must be remembered is that technology is not innately damaging to a child. Parents have been worried about the effect of how children spend their leisure time for hundreds of years. Arnim Polster (1993) noted that children's reading in 1780s Germany was viewed with 'anxiety, if not outright alarm'. Similar concerns were expressed about the arrival of other communication technologies (including television, computer games and video) and their impact of CYP's safety, wellbeing and behaviour during the twentieth century.

Like words, technology is now a part of human existence and this chapter seeks to explore the challenges of supporting CYP to interact safely with digital technology.

Why is it so hard to stop using technology?

Technology has been explicitly designed with great investment with the intention of maximising the time which people spend using it (Fogg, 2003). Phones and games consoles have become smaller and, crucially, portable so that it is very difficult to escape being online. Software features such as rewards, e.g. 'likes' on social media, or collecting items on games keep you engaged and notifications draw you back in. Content is designed to be exciting and to stimulate the senses with auditory, visual and tactile feedback, adrenaline-soaked battle scenes and intricate puzzles. Continually updating feeds and 24-hour news give the message that you are missing out if you do not check in again. With all of these hooks it is understandable that young people and adults find technology so compelling and the capacity for time spent on technology to increase exponentially should not be underestimated.

Given the barriers to being able to put the device down and do something else which are an intrinsic part of the technology itself, it is not surprising that data shows increasing use of technology by CYP year on year. A key aspect of executive function (control of one's behaviour) is the ability to delay gratifying rewards. This skill is developing during adolescence but can be harder to acquire for children with developmental conditions such as attention deficit hyperactivity disorder (ADHD) (Wang *et al*, 2017). This includes the capacity to put down an immediately rewarding activity – such as playing on a games console, in favour of an activity which has a deferred reward, such as completing a homework assignment.

It is possible to change settings to disable notifications or use programs to set time limits for use of games or other compelling content e.g. social media apps. Addressing the persuasive aspects of technology is essential when considering how to regulate people's use of technology, particularly in young people who may be especially susceptible to them. It may be in the future that there is regulation of these aspects of technology to help make it easier for people to manage their use.

How does use of technology impact on CYP mental health?

It is well known that a response to anxiety is to avoid the anxiety-provoking situation. Technology such us gaming and going online provides a powerful distraction and escape. Young people may be spending long periods of time on technology if they are feeling distressed as a way of coping. This may be related to environmental factors such as bullying, school pressure, conflictual relationships or underlying mental health problems such as anxiety or depression. This can bring short term relief from distress, however, if the cause of the distress is not addressed time spent on technology, avoiding the situation may actually exacerbate the underlying problem.

There is a risk that content which CYP can access online could have a direct impact on their mental health and wellbeing.

Young people with neurodevelopmental differences such as learning difficulties or ADHD may find it more difficult than their peers to stop using technology e.g. gaming in favour of less immediately rewarding tasks. They may need their carers to help them, or technological solutions such as software which time limits access to the technology to help with setting boundaries around use in order to achieve a healthy balance.

Young people with pre-existing emotional, self-esteem or mental health problems may be more vulnerable to experiencing distress when exposed to distressing images or content online.

Young people who engage in risky behaviours offline are more likely to engage in risky behaviours online.

Potential risks of the internet and digital gaming

Unhelpful comparisons

The Centre for Mental Health (2018) notes that CYP who are constantly made aware of the lives of other people may experience a negative impact on their mental health if they make comparisons about their own lives. Both individual accounts and research studies have suggested that negative image and self-esteem can be linked to feeling inferior to other people on social media. Image-manipulation techniques and photo sharing on platforms such as Instagram and Snapchat (Education Policy Institute, 2017) have brought into focus the concept of the 'idealised' body image with CYP reporting a negative impact on their self-esteem when they spend a lot of time looking at such images. A connection is suggested between negative self-image, body surveillance and online media use in children from their pre-teenage years (RSPH, 2017; Tiggeman & Slater, 2013).

Jealousy

'Facebook envy' has emerged in the public consciousness and the literature. A link has been suggested between people who can see what others within their social circle are doing on social media sites and feeling excluded from activities that they would not have otherwise known about. 'Fear of missing out' (FOMO) has been described by Przybylski et al (2013) as 'a pervasive apprehension that others might be having rewarding experiences from which one is absent'. The experience of FOMO increases with the intensity of social media use. It has been connected to the experience of anxiety, distress and feelings of inadequacy which can then be exacerbated by further social media use (RSPH, 2017; Przybylski et al, 2013).

Online and offline relationships

When social media activity is substituted for other interaction, the risk of loneliness can be increased (Nowland et al, 2018). Furthermore, Casale and Fioravanti (2015) suggest that CYP who use social media for self-presentation have higher levels of social anxiety. Anxious CYP may be drawn towards interaction online with the opportunity to experiment with more confident presentations of themselves without finding that they are more able to engage socially offline, and with their feelings of loneliness intensified. The suggestion has been made (Turkle, 2011) that the 'always on' nature of the virtual world can impair the capacity for self-reflection capabilities and damage mental wellbeing.

Safeguarding

CYP can potentially access dangerous online advice and information. The Centre for Mental Health (2018) notes that there are examples of sites which may trivialise mental health needs with suicide and self-harm used as punchlines in attempts at dark humour (e.g. 'memes'). The Government Green Paper raises concerns about 'pornography affecting children online', 'commercial content and advertising targeted at children and adults', 'fake news', 'exposure to hate content', cyberbullying, trolling, sexting, providing personal information online and 'catfishing' (HM Government, 2017). This is echoed by the Office of the Chief Medical Officer paper (2019).

Cyberbullying

It is of note that research suggests that many CYP who are cyberbullied are also bullied offline (Schneider *et al*, 2012). Ofcom (2017) identified that around 1 in 8 CYP report being bullied online. Daine *et al* (2013) suggest a strong association between cyberbullying and mental health problems, specifically relating to suicide and self-harm. An association between cyberbullying and eating disorders has also been identified (Marco *et al*, 2018; Ditch the Label, 2018).

Opportunity cost of using technology

There is a small amount of evidence to suggest that high levels of screen time can be linked to a loss of sleep and poorer quality sleep (Stiglic & Viner, 2018). There is also evidence to suggest that increased screen time can be linked to reduced exercise (American Academy of Child and Adolescent Psychiatry, 2015) and impaired academic performance (Jacobsen & Forste, 2011).

Potential positives of the internet and digital gaming

The internet can be a wonderful space for CYP to explore, the limitless settings of age appropriate online games can create a cost-free playground for CYP to build cities, interact with peers and express their creativity. Peers can educate one another about their mental health needs leading to reduction in stigma and a space for questions. CYP can play electronic games with friends that they have met offline, while gender and physical ability can exert less influence in virtual worlds. CYP who perceive their offline relationships to be stronger use online media tools to message and text (Education Policy Institute, 2017). Furthermore, some young people have been identified as developing more positive social relationships offline and experiencing a reduction in loneliness through online use (Nowland *et al*, 2018).

The internet hosts good quality educational sites and there is evidence that accessing such sites can enhance academic performance (Kim *et al*, 2017). CYP can access information about physical health and wellbeing needs with the potential to obtain facts about mental health or learn where they can potentially access online or face-to-face help. Delays in seeking help for mental health needs are known to potentially cause problems to get worse. A survey suggests that 78% of CYP who contact Childline now do so online (Education Policy Institute, 2017). Furthermore, CYP with anxiety and depression who struggle to access face-to-face care, could potentially benefit from online platforms to support them (Thom *et al*, 2018; Ebert *et al*, 2015). The RSPH *Status of Mind* report identifies that social media platforms can enhance mental health awareness, while also promoting self-expression and facilitating campaigns. YouTube has scored very positively in measures of self-expression and identity, awareness and also community building (Royal Society for Public Health, 2017). Finally, an online survey has suggested that CYP would like to be able to disclose bullying in an online setting (Scott *et al*, 2016).

Health implications of internet use

Technology use has been linked to weight gain (Stiglic & Viner, 2018) and impaired sleep (Carter *et al*, 2016). Many of the studies are cross-sectional rather than longitudinal studies thus we cannot fully identify what the connection is between technology use and the health of CYP. However, it is of note that internet use has been linked to increased self-harm (Marchant *et al*, 2017), depression (Stiglic & Viner, 2018), and has impacted on self-image (Holland & Tiggeman, 2016). What must be emphasised is that some CYP may be more vulnerable than others (NHS Digital, 2018). Furthermore, the impact of the content of digital technology needs to be understood (HM Government, 2017).

Taking action to improve wellbeing and reduce risk

There is consistent feedback that more research needs to be done to understand the potential risks of technology for CYP. The Centre for Mental Health (2018) notes that there are significant risks, but it is unclear whether some young people are affected more than others, what might mitigate those risks and what benefits might also be brought about. Stakeholders in mental health policy such as the Department of Health and Social Care, Department for Education, think tanks and charities must work in conjunction with CYP, the social media industry and regulators in order to establish facts and causal inferences, and to take effective action accordingly. Coordination and communication efforts between relevant groups and organisations should produce a shared mental health promotion and prevention strategy for social media which addresses their negative impacts, whilst making use of their positive potential and not restricting users' freedom to engage in online communities. Policy ideas may include increased signposting efforts as well as the use of 'nudge' policies and behavioural economics.

Leroy

Leroy was 15 years old and had completed a course of cognitive behavioural therapy through a voluntary sector organisation when he attended CAMHS. He had low mood, difficulty sleeping, low self-esteem and anxiety, particularly around attending school. This had impacted on his school attendance for two years; he had not been able to attend for over six months. Leroy had experienced bullying in early high school.

Leroy set high expectations for himself academically with intense fears of failure. The more school he missed, the more certain he was that he would not achieve what he felt he must. He had friends in school but worried how they would perceive his school attendance and difficulties with anxiety, thus he avoided meeting with them outside of school. He was critical of himself and conveyed a deep sense of shame about his difficulties viewing himself as a failure.

Leroy described panic symptoms which would be bad on Sunday night or the evening before he planned to try to attend school. This would make it difficult to get to sleep. In the morning it would be difficult for his mother to wake him and he would be angry at being woken and would argue with his mother who would try to encourage him to get ready and go to school. The morning was a fraught time for the family as both parents needed to get to work and take his younger sister to school.

Leroy described deciding that he could not attend school that day usually giving the reason that he was too tired and would be unable to manage. Once his parents had left, he would spend the day at home playing on his games console. Leroy expressed his relief at escaping into the immersive world of narrative driven computer game play. Where he was able to leave behind his own identity and enjoy the experience of being a hero or adventurer. This provided both short-term relief from his anxiety but was also highly rewarding and reinforced the pattern of missing school. Rather than face his fears and learn that he could manage he escaped into a virtual world. The longer he avoided school, the greater his anxiety about attending. This would lead to feelings of shame that he had not achieved what he felt he should have which reinforced his anxiety and low self-esteem. The gaming was not the →

cause of his problems but the pattern of using his games console did exacerbate his anxiety. Leroy perceived the games console as one of the only positive things in his life and would become very angry when his parents tried to restrict use.

Leroy was engaged to understand how his gaming was affecting his anxiety, although from his perspective it helped him to feel more relaxed. He was able to recognise that he would emerge from episodes of game playing to find that his problems were still waiting. Leroy was understandably opposed to giving up his games console, however he did agree to changing when he used it. We agreed that his parents would restrict access to his console during the day, but he could play in the evenings outside school hours, even when not attending school. Console time was used as a reward for undertaking small activities which challenged his anxiety such as going to the shop.

Leroy's parents had found it difficult to enforce boundaries when Leroy did not see a problem with his gaming. However, with his understanding and agreement, changes were made. These were accompanied with treatment of his anxiety and depression and Leroy's functioning slowly improved. He was able to gradually access a specialist provision for young people who could not access mainstream school, and a work experience placement. He returned to his local rugby team and reported that his anxiety, depression and sleep had improved.

Conclusion

Technology is an important part of young people's lives. When young people have underlying difficulties or vulnerabilities, the content of what they are viewing or the pattern of use can relieve or exacerbate their distress. The context of a young person's life must form part of the lens when considering the impact of technology on mental health and wellbeing; their sense of self, social and family relationships and educational functioning. Technology use should not be perceived as innately negative.

References

American Academy of Child and Adolescent Psychiatry (2015) *Screen Time and Children* [online]. Available at: https://www.aacap.org/AACAP/Families_and_Youth/Facts_for_Families/FFF-Guide/Children-And-Watching-TV-054.aspx (accessed 30 June 2019).

Carter B, Rees P, Hale L, Bhattacharjee D and Paradkar MS (2016) Association between portable screen-based media device access or use and sleep outcomes: a systematic review and meta-analysis. *JAMA Pediatrics* **170** (12) 1202–1208.

Casale S and Fioravanti G (2015) Satisfying needs through social networking sites: A pathway towards problematic internet use for socially anxious people? *Addictive Behaviours Reports* 1 34–39. Available at: https://doi.org/10.1016/j.abrep.2015.03.008 (accessed 30 June 2019).

Centre for Mental Health (2018) *Briefing 53: Social Media, Young People and Mental Health* [online]. Available at: https://www.centreformentalhealth.org.uk/publications/social-media-young-people-and-mental-health (accessed 30 June 2019).

Daine K, Hawton K, Singaravelu V, Stewart A, Simkin S and Montgomery P (2013) The power of the web: a systematic review of studies of the influence of the internet on self-harm and suicide in young people. *PLoS ONE 8(10): e77555* [online]. Available at: https://doi.org/10.1371/journal.pone.0077555 (accessed 30 June 2019).

Ditch the Label (2018) *Cyberbullying Statistics: What They Tell Us – Ditch the Label* [online] Available at: https://www.ditchthelabel.org/cyber-bullying-statistics-what-they-tell-us/ (accessed 30 June 2019).

Ebert DD, Zarski AC, Christensen H, Stikkelbroek Y, Cuijpers P, Berking M and Riper H (2015) Internet and computer-based cognitive behavioral therapy for anxiety and depression in youth: a meta-analysis of randomized controlled outcome trials. *PLoS One* **10** (3).

Education Policy Institute (2017) *Social Media and Children's Mental Health* [online]. Available at: https://epi.org.uk/publications-and-research/social-media-childrens-mental-health-review-evidence/ (accessed 30 June 2019).

Fogg, BJ (2003) *Persuasive Technology: Using computers to change what we think and do (A volume in interactive technologies)*. London: Morgan Kauffmann.

HM Government (2017) *Internet Safety Strategy – Green Paper*. London: The Stationery Office. Available at: https://assets.publishing.service.gov.uk/government/uploads/system/uploads/attachment_data/file/650949/Internet_Safety_Strategy_green_paper.pdf (accessed 30 June 2019).

Holland G and Tiggemann M (2016) A systematic review of the impact of the use of social networking sites on body image and disordered eating outcomes. *Body Image* **17** 100–10.

Jacobsen W and Forste R (2011) The wired generation: academic and social outcomes of electronic media use among university students. *Cyberpsychology Behaviour and Social Networking* **14** (5) 275–280.

Kim S, Kim M, Park B, Kim J and Choi H (2017) The associations between internet use time and school performance among Korean adolescents differ according to the purpose of internet use. *PLoS One* **12** (4) e0174878.

Marchant A, Hawton K, Stewart A, Montgomery P, Singaravelu V, Lloyd K, Purdy N, Daine, K and John A (2017) A systematic review of the relationship between internet use, self-harm and suicidal behaviour in young people: The good, the bad and the unknown. *PLoS One* **12** (8) e0181722.

Marco JH and Tormo-Irun MP (2018) Cyber victimization is associated with eating disorder psychopathology in adolescents. *Frontiers in Psychology* **9** 987.

NHS Digital (2018) *Mental Health of Children and Young People in England, 2017 Behaviours, lifestyles and identities* [online]. Available at: https://files.digital.nhs.uk/C9/999365/MHCYP%20 2017%20Behaviours%20Lifestyles%20Identities.pdf (accessed 30 June 2019).

Nowland R, Necka EA and Cacioppo JT (2018) Loneliness and social internet use: pathways to reconnection in a digital world? *Perspectives in Psychological Science* **13** (1) 70–87.

Ofcom (2017) *Children and Parents: Media use and attitudes report 2017* [online]. Available at: https://www.ofcom.org.uk/__data/assets/pdf_file/0020/108182/children-parents-media-use-attitudes-2017.pdf (accessed 30 June 2019).

Office of the Chief Medical Officer (2019) *Chief Medical Officers' commentary on 'Screen-based activities and children and young people's mental health and psychosocial wellbeing: a systematic map of reviews'* [online]. Available at: https://assets.publishing.service.gov.uk/government/uploads/system/uploads/attachment_data/file/777026/UK_CMO_commentary_on_screentime_and_social_media_map_of_reviews.pdf (accessed 30 June 2019).

Polster A (1993) On the use and abuse of teading: Karl Philipp Moritz and the dialectic of pedagogy in late-enlightenment Germany. In W Daniel Wilson and C Holub Robert (eds) *Impure Reason: Dialectic of Enlightenment in Germany*, pp465–84. Detroit, MI: Wayne State University Press.

Przybylski AK, Murayama K, DeHaan CR and Gladwell V (2013) Motivational, emotional, and behavioral correlates of fear of missing out. *Computers in Human Behavior* **29** (4) 1841–1848.

Royal Society for Public Health (2017) #*Status of Mind – Social Media and Young People's Mental Health and Wellbeing* [online]. Available at: https://www.rsph.org.uk/uploads/assets/uploaded/d125b27c-0b62-41c5-a2c0155a8887cd01.pdf (accessed 7 July 2019). London: RSPH.

Schneider SK, O'Donnell L, Stueve A and Coulter RW (2012) Cyberbullying, school bullying, and psychological distress: a regional census of high school students. *American Journal of Public Health* **102** (1) 171–7.

Scott E, Dale J, Russell R and Wolke D (2016) Young people who are being bullied – do they want general practice support? *BMC Family Practice* **17** (1).

Stiglic N and Viner R (2018) Effects of screentime on the health and wellbeing of children and adolescents: a systematic review of reviews. *BMJ Open* **8** e023191.

Thom RP, Bickham DS and Rich M (2018) Internet use, depression and anxiety in a healthy adolescent population: prospective cohort study. *JMIR Mental Health* **22** 5(2) e44.

Tiggemann M and Slater A (2013) NetGirls: The internet, Facebook, and body image concern in adolescent girls. *International Journal of Eating Disorders* **46** (6) 630–633.

Turkle T (2011) The tethered self: technology reinvents intimacy and solitude. *Continuing Higher Education Review* **75** 28–31.

Wang B, Yao N, Zhou X, Liu J and Lv Z (2017) The association between attention deficit/hyperactivity disorder and internet addiction: a systematic review and meta-analysis *BMC Psychiatry* **17** (1) 260.

Chapter 22: Working with Young People to Prevent Suicide

Roshelle Ramkisson and Louise Theodosiou

Key learning points

- Identifying cumulative risk of a vulnerable child with recent stress e.g. children and young people (CYP) with mental health needs.

- Targeted suicide prevention interventions include support for CYP bereaved by suicide.

- CYP living with additional pressures e.g. looked after children, families experiencing difficulties with money or housing.

- Mental health support for children and young people with exam stress/ academic pressure.

- Identifying CYP who may need additional support, such as children exploring their gender or sexual identity.

- Promotion of online safety and sensitive media reporting.

Keywords
Suicide prevention; children and young people; surveillance; awareness; multi-sectorial, locally-driven initiatives

Introduction

When a life ends through suicide, there is a long-lasting impact on loved ones and the wider community. Those contemplating suicide may struggle to seek help due to societal and cultural factors as well as shame and stigma associated with suicide. Children and young people are a priority for intervention and support. There is a particular concern about the rates of suicide globally in the age group between the ages of 15-25 years. However, rates and vulnerabilities vary and individualised local action plans are needed.

Suicide prevention is a priority

Suicide is a public health concern and globally is the second leading cause of death in 15-25-year olds (WHO, 2018). There are variations in rates due to different monitoring systems and in the UK suicide is the leading cause of death in 10-19-year-olds. It is suspected the actual rates are higher and the under reporting is due to legal, cultural, society and surveillance factors. NHS Digital (2018) found that 52% of 17-19-year-olds in a national UK prevalence study who had mental health needs reported having attempted suicide or self-harmed. In the same study, it was identified that 25.5% of 11-16-year-olds with mental needs had self-harmed or attempted suicide. There are differences between developed and developing countries and this supports the need for locally driven action plans supported by national government initiatives.

Any prevention strategy requires accurate data, and needs to identify specific clusters to target. In the UK, between 2003 and 2013, an average of 428 people aged under 25 died by suicide in England per year; of those 137 were aged under 20, and 60 were aged under 18 (PHE, 2016). The National Suicide Prevention Strategy was refreshed in 2016/2017. The renewed plan emphasises the need to effectively target people at increased risk of suicide, for example people in contact with the criminal justice system. Public Health England has identified 95% of local authorities are either working towards developing a suicide prevention plan or have one in place.

Previous acts of self-harm and the disclosure of suicidal thoughts are early indicators for community, families and professionals to respond to. According to the National Confidential Inquiry into Suicide and Homicide by People with Mental Illness Suicide by Children and Young People in England, over half of the young people who die by suicide have a history of self-harm (Manchester University, 2016; 2017). However, a Lancet UK based cohort study by Geulayov *et al* (2018) reported that a majority of those who self-harm do not die by suicide.

In 12-14 year-olds (Geulayov *et al*, 2018):

- For every boy who died by suicide, 109 attended hospital following self-harm and 3067 reported self-harm in the community.
- For every girl who died by suicide, 1255 attended hospital for self-harm and 21,995 reported self-harm in the community.

In 15-17 year-olds (Geulayov *et al*, 2018):

- For every boy who died by suicide, 120 boys presented to hospital with self-harm and 838 self-harmed in the community.

- For every girl who died by suicide, 919 girls presented to hospital for self-harm and 6406 self-harmed in the community.

Suicide is more common in males though females are more likely to present to services. The most common methods of suicide in 15-17 year-olds is death by hanging or asphyxiation (Geulayov *et al*, 2018; Kutcher, 2018).

Vulnerable groups are at higher risk and these include:

- looked after children

- lesbian, gay, bisexual and transgender (LGBT) young people

- CYP experiencing mental illness or with additional mental health needs

- CYP whose parents have attempted or completed suicide

- CYP who are using drugs and alcohol

- those experiencing childhood trauma or abuse

- isolated individuals with economic hardships and limited social support (NCISH, 2017; Samaritans, 2017).

Of those CYP who died by suicide in England, on average 28% were bereaved, 22% bullied and 15% abused or neglected with a quarter having used the internet in a relevant way and a quarter facing academic pressures. Of concern is that approximately 73% did not express recent suicidal ideation (NCISH, 2017). Finally, there is increasing recognition (HM Government, 2019) of the need for CYP to be kept safe online. The Government response to the Internet Safety Strategy (HM Government, 2018) notes the need for mechanisms to report concerning content relating to suicide as well as online sources of support for CYP who are experiencing thoughts of suicide.

Suicide prevention strategies

Suicide is a preventable cause of death and is the result of biological, genetic, psychological and social interactions with far reaching effects on bereaved family, friends and the community at large. The *Comprehensive Mental Health Action Plan* delivered by World Health Organization member states have set a global target to reduce the suicide rates in countries by 2020. The suicide rate is one of the agreed United Nations Sustainable Development goals for 2030 (WHO, 2018). The international concern and call for action have been recognised nationally in the UK.

Within the UK, key national bodies have worked to commission documents to support locally-delivered initiatives with the aim of reducing the suicide rate in the general population and providing better support for those bereaved by suicide. There are policy documents, guidance and directives from the National Institute of Health and Care Excellence (NICE, 2004; 2011; 2018), the Royal College of Psychiatrists (2010) and Public Health England (2016). Further to this, the *Zero Suicide Policy* (NHS England, 2016) and the appointment of a Minister for Suicide Prevention in England adds weight to the national agenda of prevention and reduction of suicide rates (Fearnley, 2016). The Suicide Prevention National Transformation Programme has arisen from a national commitment to reduce deaths by suicide by 10%, by 2020/21 (Royal College of Psychiatrists, 2019). NHS England commissioned the National Collaborating Centre for Mental Health to work in partnership with *National Confidential Inquiry into Suicide and Safety in Mental Health (NCISH)* with eight Sustainability and Transformation Partnerships to improve quality and safety, and support local plans to reduce suicide.

There are six areas for action identified by Public Health England:

1. Reduce the risk of suicide groups deemed to be at higher risk.
2. Improve mental health in specific groups.
3. Reduce access to the means of suicide.
4. Provide better information and support for those bereaved by suicide.
5. Support media sensitivity with regards to suicide and suicidal behaviour.
6. Support research data collection and monitoring.

A multidimensional local approach that identifies and responds to suicide clusters, preventing suicide in public places and supporting people bereaved by suicide, reaching out to marginalised isolated members of society who are deemed to be at greater risk is called for. The focus is to address the pain of those who feel that suicide is the only option.

Addressing the health inequalities of CYP is a key strand of suicide prevention. This highlights the need for collaborative multi-agency working; involvement of the local authority in suicide prevention through support with housing, responding to childhood abuse and addressing employment needs. Multidimensional working with health, the local authority, education, the youth and adult justice system, the voluntary sector and the wider community enables holistic care. This can then start to address the complexity of cumulative risk and move towards preventing death by suicide.

The development of robust multidimensional networks will enhance the wellbeing and resilience of all CYP. However, it is also important to address the vulnerabilities and risks of individual CYP. These will include working to meet the physical and/or mental health needs (including suicidal ideation and self-harm behaviours) of CYP. Supporting challenged family systems especially where there is parental mental illness and suicidal behaviours and addressing exposure to abuse and neglect.

Negative peer interactions as a result of bullying, suicide-related internet use, social isolation and withdrawal, exam pressures and academic decline are risk factors associated with suicide in children and young people. Early identification of patterns of cumulative risk is necessary and cannot be stressed enough. Exposure to early life adversities, such as neglect or abuse, increases the vulnerability of CYP. A further recent stress, such as school pressures or impact of a physical health condition, can act as a final straw. Public health campaigns and school-based awareness programmes, interagency working and close follow up of high-risk groups is required to reach out and connect to children and young people in preventing suicide.

Table 22.1: Terms used to describe thoughts and acts of harming oneself

Suicidality, is a broad term referring to both thoughts and acts of inflicting harm to one self or ending one's life.
Thoughts of self-harm relates to having urges, contemplating or thinking about hurting oneself and is non-suicidal.
Self-harm are acts of hurting oneself with a purpose of either numbing emotional pain, regulating one's emotions or to feel physical pain without fatal intent.
Suicidal ideations are thoughts, preoccupations or feelings of wanting to end one's life. These thoughts are broader and general, often closely related to expressions of hopelessness.
Suicidal planning is the specific thoughts about an attempt to end one's life which may include details regarding method(s), access, final wishes to say goodbye, organising one's affairs and avoid being disturbed or found.
Suicidal act is a purposeful attempt to end one's life with fatal intent.

The primary prevention strategies involve wider community awareness campaigns, universal support for disadvantaged and high-risk groups. Secondary prevention strategies focus on screening, early identification of needs (particularly mental health) with swift multi-agency risk management. Reaching out through the internet, support numbers, e.g. the Samaritans, and education-based approaches all form part of the prevention strategies. There should be appropriate follow up of individuals and support by frontline agencies that address the various factors following a comprehensive psychosocial assessment.

Case examples of local suicide prevention action plan: Mersey Zero Suicide Prevention Campaign

One of the champion campaigns recognised by NHS England is NO MORE Suicide, which is a zero suicide strategy for Cheshire and Merseyside. The initial campaign ran between 2015 and 2017 and focused on four outcomes:

1. Safer suicide community.
2. Suicide safer care.
3. Support after suicide.
4. Integrated Suicide Prevention Network that consists of four components: strategic board; operational task groups; local suicide prevention groups; and a stakeholder network.

The board membership optimises multi-agency working with a range of professionals with relevant expertise and seniority (NO MORE Suicide, 2017). The campaign has identified four task areas to focus on to accentuate the work and ensure sustainability. These are:

■ leadership
■ prevention
■ safer care
■ support after suicide and intelligence.

It is of note that one of the priority areas identified in the 2017 update was CYP.

The Cheshire and Merseyside Joint Audit Report 2017 revealed 13% of the 248 deaths with a recorded conclusion were under 25 years in 2015, a total of 17 CYP were aged between 10-19 years and 16 aged between 20-25 years. The focus on CYP addressing bullying, promoting wellbeing by building resilience and developing coping skills through the education and community involvement was incorporated in the strategic action plan. The campaign to eliminate suicide across the age range in the Cheshire and Merseyside region encompasses the national directives and is an example of a locally delivered action plan to be added to the global challenge in suicide prevention (www.no-more.co.uk).

Conclusion

Suicide prevention in children and young people, particularly in later teen years requires local action plans to address individual, family, peer, education, technological and societal factors. Collaboration and a shared role amongst risk management teams from various agencies and the public is needed. The complex interaction of factors results in greater cumulative risk. National guidance, toolkits and guidance require local sign up of partnerships with stakeholders and community engagement to be effective.

Suicide is a preventable condition and this prevention should surely be a priority for all professionals working with children and young people. To quote Professor Appleby (University of Manchester, 2017):

'Suicide is the leading cause of death in young people in England and Wales. Although there is no single cause, bereavement was an important theme in many of the deaths we examined. Some of the young people had experienced the suicide of someone close to them – it's tragic that the trauma of suicide may lead young people to take their own lives.'

References

Fearnley D (2016) *The Zero Suicide Policy Challenges* [online]. NHS England. Available at: https://www.england.nhs.uk/blog/david-fearnley/ (accessed 30 June 2019).

Geulayov G, Casey D, McDonald KC, Foster P, Pritchard K, Wells C, Clements C, Kapur N, Ness J, Waters K and Hawton K (2018) Incidence of suicide, hospital-presenting non-fatal self-harm, and community-occurring non-fatal self-harm in adolescents in England (the iceberg model of self-harm): a retrospective study. *Lancet Psychiatry* **5** (2) 167-174.

HM Government (2018) *Government response to the Internet Safety Strategy Green Paper* [online]. Available at: https://assets.publishing.service.gov.uk/government/uploads/system/uploads/attachment_data/file/708873/Government_Response_to_the_Internet_Safety_Strategy_Green_Paper_-_Final.pdf (accessed 30 June 2019).

HM Government (2019) *Preventing Suicide in England: Fourth progress report of the cross-government outcomes strategy to save lives* [online]. Available at: https://assets.publishing.service.gov.uk/government/uploads/system/uploads/attachment_data/file/772184/national-suicide-prevention-strategy-4th-progress-report.pdf (accessed 30 June 2019).

Kutcher S (2018) Suicide risk management. *BMJ Best Practice* [online]. Available at: https://bestpractice.bmj.com/topics/en-gb/1016 (accessed 30 June 2019).

Manchester University (2016) *National Confidential Inquiry into Suicide and Homicide by People with Mental Illness Annual Report and 20 Year Review* [online]. Available at: http://documents.manchester.ac.uk/display.aspx?DocID=37580 (accessed 30 June 2019).

Manchester University (2017) *National Confidential Inquiry into Suicide and Homicide by People with Mental Illness Annual Report 2017* [online]. Available at: http://documents.manchester.ac.uk/display.aspx?DocID=37560 (accessed 30 June 2019).

National Institute of Health and Care Excellence (2004) *Self-harm in Over 8s: Short-term management and prevention of recurrence (Clinical Guidelines CG16)* [online]. Available at: https://www.nice.org.uk/guidance/cg16 (accessed 30 June 2019).

National Institute of Health and Care Excellence (2011) *Self-harm in Over 8s: Long-term management Clinical guideline [CG133]* [online]. Available at: https://www.nice.org.uk/guidance/cg133 (accessed 30 June 2019).

National Institute of Health and Care Excellence (2018) *Preventing Suicide in Community and Custodial Settings [NG105]* [online]. Available at: https://www.nice.org.uk/guidance/ng105 (accessed 30 June 2019).

NHS Digital (2018) *Mental Health of Children and Young People in England, 2017 Summary of key findings* [online]. Available at: https://files.digital.nhs.uk/C9/999365/MHCYP%202017%20 Behaviours%20Lifestyles%20Identities.pdf (accessed 30 June 2019).

No More Suicide (2017) *A Zero Suicide Strategy for Cheshire & Merseyside 2015–2020* [online]. Available at: http://www.no-more.co.uk/files/no-more-strategy-2017.pdf (accessed 30 June 2019).

Public Health England (2016) *Local Suicide Prevention Planning (Publications gateway number: 2016392)*. London: PHE.

Royal College of Psychiatrists (2010) *Self-harm, Suicide and Risk: A summary (Position Statement) PS3/2010* [online]. Available at: https://www.rcpsych.ac.uk/pdf/PS03-2010x.pdf (accessed 30 June 2019).

Royal College of Psychiatrists (2019) *Suicide Prevention National Transformation Programme* [online]. Available at: https://www.rcpsych.ac.uk/improving-care/nccmh/national-suicide-prevention-programme (accessed 30 June 2019).

Samaritans (2017) *Inequality and Suicide* [online]. Available at: https://www.samaritans.org/about-samaritans/research-policy/inequality-suicide/ (accessed 30 June 2019).

University of Manchester/Healthcare Quality Improvement Partnership (2016) *Suicide by Children and Young People in England* [online]. Available at: https://www.hqip.org.uk/wp-content/uploads/2018/02/8iQSvI.pdf (accessed 30 June 2019).

University of Manchester (2017) *Suicide in Children and Young People Linked to Bereavement, New Report Finds* [online]. Available at: https://www.manchester.ac.uk/discover/news/suicide-in-children-and-young-people-linked-to-bereavement-new-report-finds/ (accessed 30 June 2019).

World Health Organization (2013) *Comprehensive Mental Health Action Plan 2013–2020* [online]. Available at: https://www.who.int/mental_health/action_plan_2013/en/ (accessed 30 June 2019)

World Health Organization (2018) *Preventing Suicide: A community engagement toolkit*. Geneva: WHO. Available at: https://apps.who.int/iris/bitstream/handle/10665/272860/9789241513791-eng.pdf (accessed 30 June 2019).

Chapter 23: Links Between a Child's Physical Health and Mental Health

Josephine Neale and Lee Hudson

Key learning points

- Recognise organic conditions presenting with psychiatric symptoms and mental health problems presenting with physical health symptoms.

- Understand the importance of the interaction of mind and body.

- Implement understanding of links between a child's physical and mental health to provide holistic care.

Keywords

Mental health; holistic care; parity of esteem

Introduction

Mind and body are often regarded as separate entities, although in reality there can be no such clear division. Common sayings give clue to the co-existence of the mind-body link in everyday life: 'butterflies in the stomach' represent anxiety, the lost love felt as 'heartache' and carrying 'the weight of the world' with a burdensome emotional problem. It is well established that poor physical health increases the risk of mental health problems and vice versa. Moreover, the association between mental wellbeing and physical wellbeing can have a substantial impact on children's quality of life if either is affected. Sadly, mental health and physical health do not have equal status in both healthcare and wider society and so we must continue to strive for closer integration. In this chapter we will outline key examples of where physical health and mental health overlap and the importance of developing a healthcare service in which all needs of children and young people can be well supported.

Physical health of children and young people with mental health problems

Recent statistics show that three quarters of children with mental health issues (i.e. those that cause significant distress or impairment of functioning) had a co-existing physical or developmental problem (for example, migraine or obesity), and 26% had a limiting long-term illness (defined as a condition lasting 12 months or more, which reduced the child's ability to carry out day-to-day activities), compared to only 4% of children without a mental health condition (NHS Digital, 2018). This association means that children and young people with mental health problems need to be monitored closely for physical health problems and treated in a setting where they have equally good access to care for both their mental and physical health. Risky health behaviours were also seen more commonly in 11 to 16 year olds with mental health condition than those without, including higher rates of tobacco, alcohol and illicit drug use (NHS Digital, 2018).

Many presentations arising from a disturbance in mental health will directly result in physical health problems. Short-term low levels of anxiety or emotional stress on a short-term basis may be expressed as headaches or abdominal pain, a concept known as 'somatisation', when psychological symptoms manifest as physical problems. There can be more severe physical health effects, for example as a result of deliberate self-harm (cutting, burning, self-poisoning, etc), anorexia nervosa (in which significant weight loss can lead to heart problems, nerve damage, osteoporosis and loss of periods in girls) and conversion disorder (a rare condition in which psychological distress is experienced as physical symptoms such as paralysis or blindness, with no associated physical cause).

For those with chronic stress (arising from psychological distress, social adversity or long-term conflict or trauma, either alone or in conjunction with a mental health problem), there are a number of established adverse effects on physical health. Stress experienced over a prolonged period of time causes circulating cortisol levels to rise, suppressed immune function, slow wound healing, increased risk of diabetes and raised blood pressure. These consequences predispose the child to long-term physical health problems and raised cardiovascular risk as adults.

There are a number of barriers for children with mental health problems accessing appropriate care for physical problems. The first of these barriers can be a consequence of experienced or perceived stigma, or what is sometimes called 'diagnostic overshadowing'. This is when physical symptoms may be attributed to the mental health problem, resulting in inadequate diagnosis or treatment. This concept is most evident in children with learning disabilities, who are more likely to experience both mental and physical health problems than other children, but there has been a tendency for problems to be inappropriately attributed to the learning disability itself (e.g. a change in behaviour could be a symptom of infection but may be dismissed as part of their learning disability). Secondly, young people with mental health problems may be less effective at expressing their needs and therefore less likely to receive appropriate help. Thirdly, children with mental health problems are often managed in settings where staff may be less experienced in the screening and management of physical health problems.

Medication for mental health problems

Medications for mental health conditions have a well-established evidence base and, alongside psychological therapies, can have a significant positive impact on the course of a child's recovery. While the benefits are clear and medications are recommended in various health conditions, medications prescribed for mental health problems can have as many side effects as those prescribed for physical health problems.

Antidepressants such as fluoxetine have been shown to be effective in children with moderate to severe depression, obsessive compulsive disorder (OCD) and bulimia nervosa. Physical health risks associated with fluoxetine include headaches, nausea, vomiting, diarrhoea, constipation and a rare complication called 'serotonin syndrome', which causes fever, shaking, sweating and confusion, and if untreated can lead to seizures and death. However, it is important to note that the benefits of fluoxetine in depression have been clinically proven to outweigh the risks (NICE, 2017).

Antipsychotic medications (those used to treat conditions which include psychotic experiences, such as schizophrenia, bipolar affective disorder and mania) have previously held a poor reputation for physical health risks and the older, 'first-generation' medications were much more likely than today's newer drugs to cause extrapyramidal symptoms (unusual movements such as shaking, stiffness and slow movements) and drowsiness. Side effects that remain important to monitor with newer antipsychotics such as olanzapine or risperidone include weight gain, metabolic effects (such as insulin resistance and increased blood glucose levels, increasing the risk of type 2 diabetes mellitus) and a rise in the hormone prolactin (which can lead to abnormal secretion of milk from nipples in both girls and boys, lack of periods in girls and erectile dysfunction in boys) (Correll, 2011).

Despite these potential effects, treatment of a first psychotic episode in a young person has been proven to be more effective when delivered in conjunction with antipsychotic medication (NICE, 2016).

There are rare circumstances in which antipsychotics can cause serious harm to physical health and, in most cases, benefits outweigh any potential risk. Neuroleptic malignant syndrome, a potentially fatal response to antipsychotics of muscle stiffness, fever, sweating, increased heart rate and fluctuating changes in blood pressure, may require medical intensive care. Clozapine, an antipsychotic drug used only in the treatment of schizophrenia when other medications have failed, carries an additional risk of depletion of white blood cells, blood clots and heart problems, all of which can be fatal. For this reason, clozapine requires additional blood monitoring to other antipsychotics.

Methylphenidate (commonly known as Ritalin®) helps reduce hyperactivity and impulsive behaviour in attention deficit hyperactivity disorder (ADHD), but requires careful monitoring of blood pressure (which can increase with this medication) and growth (both weight and height can be affected).

Many medications used for mental health problems are unlicensed for use in those under the age of 18. This does not make them dangerous *per se*, and many have good evidence for use in adults following clinical trials proving that they are both safe and effective. However, facilitating clinical trials of medicines in children can be difficult and so these medicines are used 'unlicensed' or 'off-label', enabling doctors to have more choice over which medication to use, but without full knowledge of all possible side effects in this age group.

Mental health of CYP with physical health problems

It is well established that chronic physical illness in children and young people is associated a significantly increased rate of mental illness compared to those without physical illness (Hysing *et al*, 2007; Pinquart & Shen, 2011). This is especially true of epilepsy: one study found 61% of a sample of children with epilepsy had a psychiatric diagnosis (Katon *et al*, 2006). Recent national data tells us that epilepsy is up to five times more common in children with a mental health condition than in those without (NHS Digital, 2018). Type 1 diabetes mellitus is strongly associated with depressive symptoms in children and adolescents, nearly double the rate seen in the general population (Hood *et al*, 2006). In addition to the anxiety of developing a long-term physical health problem and the burden of managing symptoms or medications, those who are physically unwell and/or attending hospital on a regular basis may miss out on key academic and social opportunities, placing them at risk of emotional disorders.

Certain medications used to treat physical health problems can lead to psychiatric side effects, even in the absence of any pre-existing mental health conditions. These effects are more likely to occur when multiple medications are prescribed, high doses are used or if the young person has impairment of the liver or kidneys, as this may affect their ability to eliminate the drug from the body. Steroids are used in treatment of a variety of physical health conditions, ranging from asthma to cancer, and in some children can precipitate depression, psychosis (including delusional beliefs, hallucinations and paranoia) or severe behavioural disturbance (Drozdowicz & Bostwick, 2014). This is usually managed either by withdrawal of the steroid, where possible, or with the administration of antipsychotic medications and, as already discussed, these come with their own physical health risks. Depression, suicidal thinking and suicide attempts have been reported in those taking isotretinoin for severe acne, which by nature is more common in young people. Anti-epileptic medications, anaesthetic agents and pain relief drugs have all been associated with adverse effects on mental health; any child prescribed a medication which acts on the central nervous system should be monitored carefully for behavioural changes, mood disturbance or symptoms of psychosis. It is also important to remember that effects may also become apparent after the withdrawal of medications as well as at initiation.

Delirium is a common state seen in children and young people with physical health problems and describes a fluctuating consciousness level with confusion and disorientation, sometimes with hallucinations, resulting from a range of conditions including severe physical illness, surgery, pain, head injury and changes in medication. A number of physical health conditions, such as brain infection or inflammation, some cancers, multiple sclerosis and systemic lupus erythematosus can also present with symptoms of mental illness, and may be easily mistaken for mental illnesses, delaying accurate diagnosis and treatment of the underlying cause.

It is crucial that clinicians working in physical health settings have access to psychological services to support the needs of children and young people, although barriers to this may include the way services are set up and developed, finance streams and commissioning, lack of training and lack of adequate supervision (particularly with regard to screening for mental health conditions).

Clinical practice and training

Outside of primary care, many services are not set up for provision of physical and mental healthcare simultaneously. Most psychiatric hospitals are located on separate sites from general hospitals; when they are run by different organisations there can be logistical and financial barriers to clinicians working together in the best way to support patients. Gradually, we are seeing more integration of care, with a holistic approach being possible in places where physical health, mental health and socioeconomic factors can all be considered together, for example, psychiatric services being provided in primary care and paediatric clinicians delivering expertise as part of psychiatric teams. Good practice has been demonstrated by the recent expansion of Community Eating Disorder Services for Children and Young People (CEDS-CYP), for which it is recommended that both consultant psychiatric and consultant paediatric involvement is necessary to provide a safe and effective service (National Collaborating Centre for Mental Health, 2015).

We continue to train the future generations of doctors and nurses in silos, producing experts in either physical or mental health but gradually we are seeing more crossover in skills between these two domains. This is reflected in some of the learning objectives of the curriculum for trainees in Child and Adolescent Psychiatry (RCPysch, 2018):

- Consider the possibility of physical illness in a child or young person seen by them and include this in their differential diagnosis.

- Keep up-to-date with the effects, interactions and side-effects of prescribed psychotropic medication or medication prescribed in paediatrics with possible psychiatric side-effects.

- Recognise the need for a more expert paediatric or general medical opinion.

The Royal College of Psychiatrists has also been proactive in educating those in its Faculty of Child and Adolescent Psychiatry, publishing a report outlining what child and adolescent psychiatrists need to know and do regarding the physical health of young people, a collaboration between psychiatrists, paediatricians and a general practitioner (RCPsych, 2014).

All paediatricians are expected to have knowledge and skills in mental health and furthermore there has been a recent introduction of subspecialty training for paediatricians who want to work in mental health. For those following this subspecialty, the Royal College of Paediatrics and Child Health's curriculum (RCPCH, 2018) ensures achievement of the following learning objectives:

- Demonstrates a thorough knowledge and application of theoretical frameworks in mental health.

- Demonstrates expertise in the diagnosis and management of children with mental and psychological difficulties.

- Takes a leading role in advocacy for children with mental health difficulties and promotes parity of esteem.

What needs to happen to bring about necessary changes in policy and practice?

The development of the Rapid Assessment, Interface and Discharge (RAID) integrated model has been shown to improves access to psychiatric assessment and reduce the cost of health service provision in an acute hospital (Tadros *et al*, 2013). This has been applied to adults and older people but services for children and young people are still in the emerging phase.

Progress has been made over recent years, with increasing recognition of the term 'parity of esteem' between mental and physical health, suggesting that mental healthcare needs to be equally as good as physical healthcare. The NHS *Five Year Forward View* (2014) introduced Sustainability and Transformation Partnerships and Integrated Care Systems to deliver care from mental health services, physical health services and social care in a collaborative way (NHS England, 2014). Service level agreements need to be in place between paediatric, psychiatric and primary care settings to ensure this becomes a reality. The *NHS Long-Term Plan* (NHS, 2019) offers to continue support by increasing funding for children and young people's mental health.

Education is essential: early education in schools will help children and young people develop the language to discuss their mental and physical health needs, and make headway in breaking down the stigma against mental health that is still seen in wider society.

We need to continue to develop the evidence-base on how best to improve the available support of mental health of children and young people with chronic physical illnesses (Bennett *et al*, 2015), and we need to promote training opportunities for learning between mental and physical health professionals, which will also have an impact on the stigma existing within healthcare systems.

Sarah

At the age of 14, Sarah gradually reduced the amount she was eating, believing she was overweight. Her weight was in normal range for her height and age, but when Sarah looked in the mirror she felt fat. She focused on her calorie intake, avoided fatty foods and intentionally lost weight. She had previously been healthy but as Sarah lost more weight and reduced her food intake even further, she became dizzy, easily fatigued and weak. Despite becoming seriously underweight, Sarah still believed she was overweight and fainted several times.

Sarah was diagnosed with anorexia nervosa and admitted to an inpatient psychiatric unit for treatment, undergoing a full assessment of her mental and physical health. She was supported by:

- mental health nurses to express her feelings
- a psychiatrist to think about treatment options for her condition
- a family therapist to support Sarah and her parents
- a paediatrician to monitor her acute physical health risk and consider the long-term impact of being underweight on her growth and bones
- a dietitian to provide education on a balanced diet.

Sarah gradually gained weight and was discharged after eight weeks on the ward, continuing long-term follow up and treatment. Had Sarah not been supported by a team keeping both physical and mental health in mind, she could have suffered serious adverse consequences of anorexia nervosa, of which there are potentially many. Anorexia nervosa is the mental health condition with the highest death rate and treatment requires a true multidisciplinary approach.

James

James was a 16-year-old boy whose mother brought him to A&E after he became paranoid, confused and started acting differently. He had been unwell a few days before that, with a headache and a slight temperature. When James was assessed, he did not know where he was or what time of year it was, becoming suspicious of the clinicians who assessed him. He appeared to see things in the room that they could not and was unable to remember events of the previous few days. James was previously well and had no history of contact with mental health services and no physical health problems. The only relevant family history was his mother's brother had paranoid schizophrenia. ➔

James was admitted to an inpatient psychiatric unit and treated for first-episode psychosis. He was treated with antipsychotic medication, but his condition did not improve. Routine blood tests, heart tracing, urine screen for illicit substances and a brain scan showed no obvious abnormalities, yet James continued to display psychotic symptoms and over the next week developed aggressive behaviour, leading to physical restraint. His antipsychotic dose was increased with little response. He remained confused and disorientated. Three weeks later, and after consultation with neurological colleagues with further investigations, James was diagnosed with autoimmune encephalitis (inflammation of the brain caused by an abnormal immune response). Treatment with steroids and antibody therapy resulted in a slow but steady recovery. After three months in the psychiatric unit he was discharged and made a full recovery.

Medical conditions that present with psychiatric symptoms should be recognised by those working in children's mental health. Even when there is a positive family history of mental illness, all possible organic causes of a new onset psychiatric presentation should be considered. Early exclusion of organic causes can lead to a more rapid diagnosis and treatment of the cause.

References

Bennett S, Shafran R, Coughtrey A, Walker S and Heyman I (2015) Psychological interventions for mental health disorders in children with chronic physical illness: a systematic review. *Archives of the Disabled Child* **100** 308–16.

Correll CU (2011) Addressing adverse effects of antipsychotic treatment in young patients with schizophrenia. *Journal of Clinical Psychiatry* **72** e01.

Drozdowicz LB and Bostwick JM (2014) Psychiatric adverse effects of pediatric corticosteroid use. *Mayo Clin Proc* **89** 817–34.

Hood KK, Huestis S, Maher A, Butler D, Volkening L and Laffel LM (2006) Depressive symptoms in children and adolescents with Type 1 diabetes: association with diabetes-specific characteristics. *Diabetes Care* **29** 1389–91.

Hysing M, Elgen I, Gillberg C, Lie SA and Lundervold AJ (2007) Chronic physical illness and mental health in children. Results from a large-scale population study. *Journal of Child Psychology and Psychiatry* **48** 785–92.

Katon WJ, Richardson L, Russo J, Lozano P and McCauley E (2006) Quality health care for youth with asthma and cormorbid anxiety and depression. *Medical Care* **44** 1064–72.

National Collaborating Centre for Mental Health (2015) *Access and Waiting Time Standard for Children and Young People with an Eating Disorder (Commissioning guide version 1.0)*. London: NCCMH. Available at: https://www.england.nhs.uk/wp-content/uploads/2015/07/cyp-eating-disorders-access-waiting-time-standard-comm-guid.pdf (accessed 30 June 2019).

NHS (2019) *The NHS Long Term Plan* [online]. Available at: https://www.longtermplan.nhs.uk/publication/nhs-long-term-plan/ (accessed 1 July 2019).

NHS England (2014) *NHS Five Year Forward View*. London: NHS England. Available at: https://www. england.nhs.uk/wp-content/uploads/2014/10/5yfv-web.pdf (accessed 30 June 2019).

NHS Digital (2018) *Mental Health of Children and Young People in England, 2017* [online]. Available at: https://digital.nhs.uk/data-and-information/publications/statistical/mental-health-of-children-and-young-people-in-england/2017/2017 (accessed 30 June 2019).

NICE (2016) *Psychosis and Schizophrenia in Children and Young People: Recognition and management (Clinical guidelines CG155)*. London: NICE. Available at: https://www.nice.org.uk/guidance/cg155 (accessed 30 June 2019).

NICE (2017) *Depression in Children and Young People: Identification and management in primary, community and secondary care.* (National Clinical Practice Guideline Number 28) [online]. Available at: https://www.nice.org.uk/guidance/cg28 (accessed 30 June 2019).

Pinquart M and Shen Y (2011) Behavior problems in children and adolescents with chronic physical illness: a meta-analysis. *Journal of Pediatric Psychology* **36** 1003–16.

RCPCH (Royal College of Paediatrics and Child Health) (2018) *RCPCH Progress Curriculum* [online]. Available at: https://www.rcpch.ac.uk/resources/child-mental-health-sub-specialty (accessed 1 July 2019).

RCPSYCH (Royal College of Psychiatrists) (2014) *When to See a Child and Adolescent Psychiatrist (CR195)* [online]. Available: https://www.rcpsych.ac.uk/docs/default-source/members/faculties/child-and-adolescent-psychiatry/frcap02.pdf?sfvrsn=4a41559_2 (accessed 1 July 2019).

RCPSYCH (Royal College of Psychiatrists) (2018) *A Competency Based Curriculum for Specialist Training in Psychiatry* [online]. Available at: https://www.gmc-uk.org/-/media/documents/dc10704-app-child-and-adolescent-psychiatry-curriculum-74802808.pdf (accessed 1 July 2019).

Tadros G, Salama RA, Kingston P, Mustafa N, Johnson E, Pannell R and Hashmi M (2013) Impact of an integrated rapid response psychiatric liaison team on quality improvement and cost savings: the Birmingham RAID model. *The Psychiatrist* **37** 4–10.

Chapter 24: Mind Out! LGBT Children, Young People and Mental Health

Simon Blake and Louise Theodosiou

Key learning points
- Understand the unique mental health challenges for LGBT children and young people (CYP).
- Understand the experience of discrimination for LGBT CYP.
- Develop practical tools to open up conversation and support LGBT children and young people effectively.
- Develop a commitment to greater learning and inquiry.

Keywords
LGBT; discrimination; support

Introduction

We want this chapter to help everybody to learn more about gender and sexual identity to help support LGBT children and young people (CYP) to be their best selves. By the end of the chapter we hope readers will have gained more knowledge, and crucially to have a heightened sense of inquiry about LGBT issues, to have developed some more empathy with the realities and experiences of LGBT people and to understand the fear often experienced daily. Most of all we want you to be advocates for LGBT CYP.

As adults we all share responsibility for making all CYP feel cared for and valued. We want LGBT CYP to know they are as valid and important as their cisgender and heterosexual peers. Currently, there is clear evidence that despite some progress, there are still too many CYP who are bullied and hurt because their gender and sexual identities do not fit the perceived norms. This is particularly true for gender queer CYP.

We are writing this chapter at a particular moment in time with an increasingly hostile environment against trans communities. Whilst there has been a lot of progress for lesbian, gay and bisexual people over the last 20 years, there is less understanding and acceptance of trans, gender fluid and non-binary CYP. Much of the prejudice and fear gay and lesbian CYP faced in the 1980s is now being experienced by trans, gender fluid and non-children and young people.

Why is intersectionality important?

Crenshaw (1989) addressed the intersection of 'race and sex' and noted that for black women, racism and sexism could be simultaneously amplified and yet not acknowledged by systems of power. Kapilashrami and Hankivsky (2018) note that intersectionality provides a lens through which to view the impact of experiences such as racism, misogyny and ableism on individuals. Through this perspective we can be mindful of the specific needs of LGBT CYP living in poverty or managing mental health needs. Individual experience is key and simple categories can be unhelpful, and must not drive our responses.

We want to provide opportunities for the reader to think about LGBT issues from the perspective of the CYP, to have empathy with their realities and to develop practical tools for opening up conversations.

Setting the context

Within the lifetime of some LGBT adults, homosexuality was classed as a mental illness (World Health Organization, 1978). In the same decade, just 50 years ago, the Stonewall Riots initiated the gay rights movement in the United States (1969). Thirty years ago, Stonewall (www.stonewall.org.uk) was established as a gay rights organisation in Great Britain (1989).

It is against this backdrop that we have seen a strong programme of legislative change in the UK which includes equalising the age of consent, civil partnerships, equal marriage, LGBT people being able to serve in the forces and homosexuality no longer being perceived as a mental illness (World Health Organization, 1992). Under the Equalities Act (2010) which consolidated legislation to prevent discrimination, gender, sex and sexual orientation are protected characteristics.

There has been significant progress in legislation but that hasn't reached every household, every playground, health professional or community and culturally, there is still a long way to go.

It is easy to make sweeping statements such as 'things have improved at a faster rate for lesbian and gay children and young people than for those who identify as bi, trans and non-binary', but the reality is that religion, ethnicity, family background, class, disability and a range of other factors all interplay and impact on the confidence, self-esteem, wellbeing and experience LGBT CYP have.

What does the research tell us?

Stonewall and YouGov's LGBT in *Britain Health Report* (2018) presents a concerning picture of an adult LGBT community experiencing disproportionate levels of mental health issues (Table 24.1). The same report notes that LGBT people report discrimination and harassment, including rejection, from one's friends and family and being subjected to hate crimes.

Table 24.1: Key facts about LGBT people

52% of LGBT people experience depression	79% of non-binary people experience anxiety
61% of LGBT people experience anxiety	71% of trans people experience anxiety
12% of LGBT people experience an eating disorder	24% of non-binary people experience an eating disorder
	19% of trans people experience an eating disorder
48% of LGBT people report deliberately harming themselves	41% of non-binary people report deliberately harming themselves
	35% of trans people report deliberately harming themselves
13% LGBT people aged 18-24 report attempting to take their own life	46% of trans people report thinking about killing themselves
	31% of lesbian, gay and bi people have thought about killing themselves
16% of LGBT people report drinking alcohol almost every day	→

13% of LGBT people aged 18-24 took drugs at least once a month	
19% of LGBT people aren't out to any healthcare professional when seeking care	40% of bi men and 29% of bi women aren't out to any healthcare professional when seeking care
14% of LGBT people have avoided treatment for fear of discrimination on the grounds of their sexual or gender identity	

Higher rates of mental health needs can also be seen in the recent NHS Digital (2018) survey of the mental health needs of CYP. While the number of lesbian, gay and bisexual CYP who participated was small, it is important to note that 1 in 3 CYP in this cohort experienced a mental health condition as opposed to 1 of 8 CYP who identified as heterosexual.

Building a shared language

Words can be a source of pride or a hate crime. The key to respectfully describing and understanding people is to understand the terms that they may use to describe themselves:

- **LGBT** – Lesbian, Gay, Bisexual and Transgender, a collective description for gender and sexual diversity.

- **Lesbian** – person who identifies as female and is attracted to people with female gender identities.

- **Gay** – person who identifies as male and is attracted to people with male gender identities.

- **Bi** – person who is attracted to people with male and also female gender identities.

- **Homosexual** – person who is attracted to people of the same gender identity as themselves.

- **Heterosexual** – person who is attracted to people of the opposite gender identity to themselves.

- **Pansexual** – person who is attracted to people on the full spectrum of gender identities.

- **Transgender (abbreviated to trans)** – person whose gender identity is not the same as their sex assigned at birth.

- **Gender fluid** – person who does not perceive their gender in binary terms. Often uses they/their pronouns.

- **Gender queer** – person whose gender identity does not lie within the parameters of masculine and feminine.

- **Non-binary** – person who does not perceive their gender in binary terms – often uses they/their pronouns.

- **Binary** – person who perceives their gender as female or male – uses she/her or he/him pronouns.

- **Cisgender** – person whose gender identity corresponds with their gender identified at birth.

- **Intersectionality** – theoretical model for understanding how gender identity intersects and interacts with other social factors such as race and ethnicity.

Think about the pronouns that you use: one way to convey an understanding of this important concept is to introduce yourself and include the pronouns that you use 'Hello, my name is Louise and I use she/her pronouns'.

How do LGBT people experience prejudice?

Whilst overall attitudes are changing and there is more representation of LGBT people in public life and on TV, CYP learn about and experience prejudice from a very early age, often before they have developed an awareness of their sexual and gender identity. Prejudice is transmitted both directly through what is said, indirectly through assumptions and stereotypes and, importantly, through what is not said or seen.

CYP may hear direct prejudice such as 'bi people want the best of both worlds, trans women are not real women, gay people and trans people are sexual predators' – they hear this at home, at school in the playground or alarmingly in the classroom, in the community and in the media. Indirect prejudice is less overt. It is concealed in the fabric of society expressions such as 'that is so gay' or assuming that a person is either straight or gay. As gay authors well beyond our teenage years, people still assume we have heterosexual partners. After decades of being 'officially out', with friends and family knowing, we still have to 'come out' regularly.

The media – news outlets, social media and entertainment platforms continue to demonstrate homophobia, biphobia and transphobia. This is combined with the relative invisibility of LGBT people in education except perhaps the odd mention in Relationships and Sex Education. Lesbians, bi and trans people experience amplified invisibility, as do those whose identity intersects with other liberation groups such as those who are black, Muslim and/or disabled. There is evidence that LGBT CYP experience emotional and physical bullying in the playground (Stonewall, 2017), in their communities and, sometimes, in their families.

This provides the backdrop against which LGBT CYP talk to you. It is not enough therefore to assume they know you believe them, that you value them and their identity, we have to be proactive. We have to reach out and tell them that we reject prejudice and hate and that we will do all we can to support them. Below are some pointers on ways you can do that well, and how to avoid inadvertently reinforcing the prejudice they have experienced.

Top tips for excellent conversations

Do

1. *DO work hard at being an ally* – remember that LGBT CYP are constantly disclosing their identities which can be lonely and tiring. Do everything you can to ensure LGBT people know they can trust you – a rainbow pin badge, a Stonewall poster in your office – anything that helps young people feel safe. Your role as an advocate is invaluable. Model the values of acceptance and understanding through what you say and how you say it: be sure to use the correct use of language and a positive tone with parents, carers, other professionals and peers.

2. *DO accept you are human, will have prejudices and then reflect on them* – we are as intersectional and diverse as the children and young people we work with. If you are struggling to accept or understand an LGBT identity think about why that might be. If possible, make use of safe and confidential supervision. If you don't have supervision, ask yourself how else you can get the support and opportunity to face into your biases.

3. *DO educate yourself/get trained (see the end of the chapter for websites and organisations)* – of course it is okay to ask questions, but children and young people will be grateful if you understand their identity and share your understanding with the team around them. If you can do your own research this can be very valuable.

4. *DO think about individuals not categories: throw unhelpful categories out of the window* — gender and sexuality are only one aspect of a person's intersecting

identity, listen to each child and young people and understand their experience and reality.

5. *DO make asking about and using the right pronouns an everyday thing* – we are so conditioned to see the world in him and hers, and it is embedded most strongly in our pronouns. We can make the world a better place for everybody by simply asking what pronouns they use. You will probably have to explain what pronouns are to some people and that is ok. To a young person who wants to define their own pronouns being asked will be music to their ears. It is okay to acknowledge that you might make mistakes if you have been working with a child or young person for a long time, but apologise when you make mistakes and keep trying.

6. *DO cheerlead children and young people and make sure you validate their feelings and experiences even and perhaps especially when you don't fully understand them* – we all celebrate our identity and what makes us unique, channel your knowledge of yourself and celebrate the identities of others.

7. *DO identify role models* – do your research and make a note of positive LGBT role models. Think about the individual young person and look for examples that would resonate for them, perhaps local figures, or people in sport, the media or politics. Many high profile LGBT role models have talked about the prejudice they have experienced, or some of their struggles – find ways to connect to their whole story, not just the glittery bit.

8. *DO find LGBT friendly and positive experiences for CYP* e.g. film festivals, local youth groups, novels and graphic novels.

Don't...

1. *DON'T assume the gender or sexual identity of any CYP* – expression is a complex process for everyone, reflect on assumptions that you may have about the ways that LGBT people present and then keep an open mind and develop good practice that you use with all CYP.

2. *DON'T make cis and heteronormative assumptions which cause CYP to feel 'othered'* – asking about relationships is a sensitive process and must be undertaken thoughtfully but without awkwardness. Think about your language and remember that may be creating a much-needed safe space.

3. *DON'T describe their identity as a phase* – yes, gender and sexual identities can develop and change, but to imply that an LGBT identity is transient is an invalidating and potentially alienating attitude. Make it clear that you respect the identity that has been disclosed and remember how hard this may have been for the CYP.

4. *DON'T confuse gender and sexual identities* – remember they are separate poles of identity and use the list of terms stated previously. Think about your own gender and sexuality; the way that you are treated as a result of those two dimensions is separate, although related.

5. *DON'T talk over their experiences* – if a young person is disclosing deeply personal aspects of their identity, make the space to listen.

6. *DON'T think that children and young people have been influenced by peer groups or the media* – LGBT people existed long before the internet and television.

7. *DON'T misgender children or young people* – once you know the pronouns people use, take a moment to ensure you will be getting them right, gently challenge misgendering from other people and check that letters and notes are correct.

8. *DON'T dehumanise and stereotype LGBT children and young people* – LGBT identities are diverse and changing, forget your assumptions and remember that these are valid lifestyle choices that can require courage to articulate.

Jamil

Jamil is a 15-year-old female who has been working with mental health services after a number of episodes of self-harm. She lives with her father who has mental health needs, and there have been previous safeguarding concerns. Jamil works well with her social worker and has recently disclosed that she identifies as gay. She is concerned that her father and supportive grandmother will struggle with this information. Jamil enjoys reading an online graphic novel which is updated regularly. Through the discussion board she has formed a relationship with a peer who identifies as female and reports that she is 16. Jamil communicates with this young person on a daily basis and finds this relationship very important. Jamil enjoys school and would like to study film at university. She has a small group of friends and has recently disclosed her sexuality to two members of her peer group. One reacted well; however, one has been very negative and has told two other young people who are now using unkind language when they see her. Jamil has been able to tell her social worker that she feels low in mood and isolated.

Things I would tell a young LGBTQ+ person

'There is a whole community of people ready to welcome you with open arms – the tricky part might be finding them. A lot of LGBTQ+ spaces are aimed at adults (e.g. bars and pubs), but an increasing number of groups and places accessible to people of all ages are becoming popular.

Social media has allowed people to connect with folks across the world who have similar experience. Whilst caution should always be exercised online, I know myself that social media is an incredibly powerful tool which, when used well, can transform the life of an isolated LGBTQ+ person.

The media around LGBTQ+ folks thrives on tragedy and it is hard not to feel hopeless in the face of a narrative that seems to have determined that you will be miserable. I wrongly used to think being gay was a death sentence, that it would never be possible to be happy, because I had never seen that as an option. It was only when I realised that there are LGBTQ+ people going about their content and ordinary lives every day that I realised that I could be that too, that being gay was not synonymous with a sad, hard existence.

However much it might feel as though no one has ever experienced what you are going through now, there have been people like you fighting the same battles throughout time. The history of our community is rarely found in textbooks, but LGBTQ+ people have struggled, fought and triumphed for a very long time. Whatever you are feeling, you are not alone.'
Ellen Jones

References

Crenshaw K (1989) *Demarginalizing the Intersection of Race and Sex: A Black Feminist Critique of Antidiscrimination Doctrine, Feminist Theory and Antiracist Politics.* Chicago: The University of Chicago Legal Forum. Available at: https://chicagounbound.uchicago.edu/uclf/vol1989/iss1/8/ (accessed 1 July 2019).

Kapilashrami A and Hankivsky O (2018) Intersectionality and why it matters to global health. *Lancet* **391** (10140) 2589–2591.

NHS Digital (2018) *Mental Health of Children and Young People in England, 2017 Behaviours, lifestyles and identities.* London: NHS Digital. Available at: https://files.digital.nhs.uk/C9/999365/MHCYP%202017%20Behaviours%20Lifestyles%20Identities.pdf (accessed 1 July 2019).

Stonewall (2017) *School Report* [online]. Available at: https://www.stonewall.org.uk/school-report-2017 (accessed 1 July 2019).

Stonewall (2018) *LGBT in Britain – Health* [online]. Available at: https://www.stonewall.org.uk/lgbt-britain-health (accessed 1 July 2019).

World Health Organization (1978) *International Classification of Diseases Version 9.* Geneva: WHO.

World Health Organization (1992) *International Classification of Diseases-10 Classification of Mental and Behavioural Disorders.* Geneva: WHO.

Other relevant titles from Pavilion

Postnatal Depression and Maternal Mental Health:
A handbook for front-line caregivers working with
women with perinatal mental health difficulties

By Sue Gellhorn

Postnatal Depression and Maternal Mental Health: A handbook for frontline caregivers working with women with perinatal mental health difficulties is an accessible handbook that is intended to support midwives, health visitors, community workers and frontline healthcare providers in their detection and assessment of postnatal depression and maternal mental health.

Midwives, health visitors, community workers and frontline healthcare providers for pregnant women, and mothers and babies in the first postnatal year, require better information on the kinds of help that women need, and resources they can use to support discussions about difficult and complex feelings.

It will provide readers with a good understanding of postnatal depression and the range of perinatal mental health difficulties they may come across in universal services for mental illness in pregnant and postnatal women. The handbook will support them in their detection and assessment of these difficulties in the women on their caseload.

Available from: https://www.pavpub.com/mental-health/depression/postnatal-depression-and-maternal-mental-health

Multi-agency Safeguarding (2nd Edition): A handbook for protecting children and vulnerable adults

By Nigel Boulton and Russell Wate QPM

Any practitioner who begins work in the difficult and unique professional arena of public protection feels that they are entering a different world, made up of its own unique processes and guidelines and which, on many occasions, appears to have a language of its own.

This long-awaited second edition of our best-selling book has been fully updated by its expert editors, Dr Russell Wate QPM and Nigel Boulton, both former police officers and current specialist consultants in safeguarding. It has been considerably expanded to include new legislation and guidance (including full compliance with Working Together 2018), as well as to tackle contemporary issues that are of much concern to workers in today's safeguarding arena, including:

- Lived experience of children
- Gangs and county lines
- Unaccompanied minors
- Private fostering
- Modern slavery
- Edge of care and transitioning
- Young carers
- GDPR
- Safeguarding in non-statutory settings
- Harmful cultural practices

The book is a vital aid to all those working in the field of child and adult services. It provides a valuable overview of the major and very different areas of public protection practice. It aims to translate the processes, guidelines and language to enable them to have a workable understanding of the varied areas of practice that may impact their own working lives.

Available from: https://www.pavpub.com/children-and-families/multi-agency-safeguarding-2nd-edition

Mental Health Needs of Children and Young People with Intellectual Disabilities (2nd edition)

By Jane McCarthy and Sarah H Bernard

Mental Health Needs of Children and Young People with Intellectual Disabilities (2nd edition) focuses on the care and support of those with moderate and severe learning disabilities (intellectual disabilities). In addition to bringing the content fully up to date, the editors, both longstanding experts in this field, have commissioned the most experienced contributors to address new topics such as gender issues and mental health in education. The importance of developing evidence-based practice is a key theme of the book, acknowledging its key role in helping professionals and practitioners to be able to provide high-quality personalised care for children and young people with intellectual disabilities who have mental health needs.

This handbook provides health and social care professionals with a sound knowledge base for shaping and enhancing their practice, along with the skills and confidence to improve the outcomes for these young people. Each chapter includes short case illustrations, examples of good practice, reflections on current practice, key learning points, references and key websites for further exploration.

Available to preorder from: https://www.pavpub.com/mental-health/mental-health-young-people-intellectual-disabilities

The Family Model Handbook: An integrated approach to supporting mentally ill parents and their children

By Adrian Falkov

The Family Model was a core component of the Crossing Bridges programme, and its aim was to aid a greater understanding of the complex interplay between mental ill health in parents, the development and mental health of their children, and the relationships within family units affected by mental ill health.

The model has proved extremely durable, and in this handbook the Family Model has been extensively revised and refined in the light of developments in the field over the last 10 years. Many features have been retained whilst enhancements have been added to ensure contemporary relevance in an ever-growing field. This enhanced Family Model provides the conceptual framework to support clinical approaches to family focused practice.

Additional principles have been added, including a service dimension to ensure that service provision is explicitly incorporated into thinking and practice, and a culture and community component to ensure that broader factors influencing individuals and impacting on family life are also addressed.

The Family Model: An integrated approach to supporting mentally ill parents and their children comes with a fully interactive CD-ROM to aid a greater understanding of the Family Model and to explain in a visually engaging way the principles of this approach to working with families affected by mental ill health.

Available from: https://www.pavpub.com/mental-health/children-mental-health/the-family-model-handbook

Parental Mental Health and Child Welfare Work (Volume 2)

By Dr Marie Diggins

Parental Mental Health and Child Welfare Work Volume 2 is the second volume in a series that explores the mental health of parents and its impact on child welfare. It acts as a yearly update on key research, policy developments and practice innovations, both in the UK and around the world.

This publication is a unique opportunity to explore and share ideas about 'success' and what 'leads to success' from the different perspective of parents, children and the professionals who work with them. Much like its predecessor, it draws together a range of experts in the field – researchers, policy makers, practitioners and service users – to identify both the opportunities and challenges, as well as to explore what works in which contexts, for whom and why.

Available from: https://www.pavpub.com/children-and-families/mental-health-children-and-families/parental-mental-health-and-child-welfare-work-volume-2